The Evil of Banality

The Evil of Banality

On the Life and Death Importance of Thinking

Elizabeth K. Minnich

ROWMAN & LITTLEFIELD
Lanham • Boulder • New York • London

Published by Rowman & Littlefield
A wholly owned subsidiary of The Rowman & Littlefield Publishing Group, Inc.
4501 Forbes Boulevard, Suite 200, Lanham, Maryland 20706
www.rowman.com

Unit A, Whitacre Mews, 26-34 Stannary Street, London SE11 4AB

British Library Cataloguing in Publication Information Available

Library of Congress Cataloging-in-Publication Data

Names: Minnich, Elizabeth Kamarck, author.
Title: The evil of banality : on the life and death importance of thinking /
    Elizabeth K. Minnich.
Description: Lanham : Rowman & Littlefield Publishers, 2016. | Includes
    bibliographical references and index.
Identifiers: LCCN 2016044739 (print) | LCCN 2016045274 (ebook) |
ISBN 9781442275959 (cloth : alk. paper) | ISBN 9781442276307 (pbk. : alk. paper) |
ISBN 9781442275973 (Electronic)
Subjects: LCSH: Banality (Philosophy) | Ethics. | Thought and thinking.
Classification: LCC B808.7 .M56 2016 (print) | LCC B808.7 (ebook) |
    DDC 170—dc23
LC record available at https://lccn.loc.gov/2016044739

♾™ The paper used in this publication meets the minimum requirements of American
National Standard for Information Sciences—Permanence of Paper for Printed Library
Materials, ANSI/NISO Z39.48-1992.

Printed in the United States of America

To Si Kahn, Nancy Barnes, Marguerite Kiely, my *sine qua non* friends for so long and through it all

Contents

Acknowledgments

In 2011, following an earlier talk I gave at California State University, Sacramento, sponsored by the faculty union (thank you, Christina Bellon), I was invited to give a keynote presentation for the 3rd International Conference on Genocide, also at CSUS. Spending time afterwards with the Rwandan Delegation, and with students (including several from Rwanda), was extraordinarily important. In response to some audience requests for this book, I promised to complete it. It took a while, but here it is.

It was particularly timely encouragement to be invited to contribute "The evil of banality/Arendt revisited" to the Special Issue of the fine journal, *Arts and Humanities in Higher Education*, vol. 13 (1–2), 2014: "Humanities and the Liberal University: Calls to Action and Exemplary Essays" (http://ahh. sagepub.com/content/13/1-2.toc). (Thank you, Jan Parker.)

The Second National Public Philosophy Network Conference, at which I gave the keynote in 2015 and subsequently received, among many illuminating responses, a one-liner that helped me trust that the book was ready to make its own case. (Thank you, Ann Cahill, and, for PPN, Sharon Meagher, Noelle McAfee.)

For a memorable discussion, I am grateful to the Committee on Social Theory at the University of Kentucky, Lexington, for co-sponsoring my talk, "The Banality of Evil"/The Evil of Banality: Arendt, Genocide, Education" in 2011 (thank you, Marion Rust).

For reading my work when it mattered most, I am not only deeply indebted to Nancy Barnes and Si Kahn, but also to Stephen Schulman, Sara Evans, Bat-Ami Bar On, and to Martha Crunkleton, Gayle Greene, Margaret Blanchard, Maureen Ryan, Paul Nagle. Bill Gay has also provided discussion and his astute questions more than once. So has my fine editor at Rowman & Littlefield, Chris Utter.

I most warmly also thank Stephanie Lerner Lapidus and Dan Lerner, for their part in the generous support and sustaining belief in my work by Gerda Lerner.

Introduction

What Were They Thinking?

Is our ability to judge, to tell right from wrong, beautiful from ugly, dependent upon our faculty of thought? Do the inability to think and a disastrous failure of what we commonly call conscience coincide? . . . An answer, if at all, can come only from the thinking experience, the performance itself, which means that we have to trace experiences rather than doctrines. Hannah Arendt.

In an interview, a man who worked as a killer of Tutsis thinks back to a particular day during the three months of the Rwandan genocide. He remembers one of his many victims: "Me, I knew this old man by name, but I had heard nothing unpleasant about him. That evening I told my wife everything. She knew only routine details about him, we did not discuss it, and I went to sleep."[1]

> *The killing was a job, not a vendetta; it was nothing personal; working hours pretty well contained it. The killers could sleep well, and, next day, continue their work.*

Holding in mind the searing history of such massive, violative harms done to all of humanity—these are crimes against humanity but experienced always individual by individual, as suffering is, and dying—I have for many years been asking myself, *How could they do it?* What was going on in the minds of those whose job it was to kill, to colonize, to exploit and oppress in Africa, America, under the Third Reich, in Armenia, Bosnia, Rwanda, Kosovo; in fields, factories, camps, homes—too many times and places, and still today? What were they thinking when they faced their victims, among them acquaintances, friends, unthreatening strangers, children, workers they saw every day? How can people actually, close in, choose and act as they must do to enslave, exploit unto death, rape as an act of war and genocide, traffic in children? It is a very old, searingly new question to which there are many responses.

I have not found most responses adequate both to the intensity and to the extent of the moral significance of the question, a question which carries within it its apparent obverse: how could some remain, do, be good when all around them others failed? Encountering the good with profound relief, I have again been asking: What were they thinking in those moments when their actions could have joined them to the harm-doing of others and they chose differently? This book is my report, or more aptly, my reflections from and on my effort to comprehend. It will take a winding path, circling in toward and back out around instances and thoughts that seem to me most difficult, and central, and illuminating.

Two of the most basic conclusions to which I have come are these:

No great harm to many people could ever be perpetrated if distorted systems had to rely on moral monsters to do it, nor would great good affecting many people happen if we had to depend on saints.

But great harm is done. I fear that this is also the case:

People who are not thinking are capable of anything.

A man who was in charge of and actively participated in some of the most bru- tal acts of apartheid South Africa, Eugene de Kock, later said, "[T]he dirtiest war you can ever get is the one fought in the shadows. And I was there in the middle of it. There are no rules except to win. There are no lines drawn to mark where you cannot cross. So you can go very low—I mean very low—and still it doesn't hit you. It's not like you stop and think. No. Your goal is to get it done."[2]

I have learned that when systems are turned bad, when the extraordinary becomes ordinary, it does not take a Hitler, an Idi Amin, a Jeffrey Dahmer, a Charles Manson, or any other unusual sort to become a perpetrator. It just takes a practiced conventionality, a clichéd conscience, emotional conformity, sus- ceptibility to small scale bribery by salary, loot, status, a sense of isolation and distrust of the reliability of others that works against taking a differing public stand. It just takes, that is, much of what in better times keeps a society and its economy provided with reliable and ambitious workers, status-anxious con- sumers, polite neighbors, agreeable team players, citizens who make no waves. It just takes, in short, an ability to go along thoughtlessly—by which I mean without paying attention, reflecting, questioning—to play the game as career- ists everywhere do, hoping to win if, by unquestioned rules, one plays it well.

Startling as it may be, we now know, for example, that Charles Manson,[3] leader of a small cult in California in the late nineteen sixties, taught himself how to recruit and keep the followers who later murdered seven people at his direction by reading one of the best-selling self-help/success books, Dale Carnegie's *How to Win Friends And Influence People* (1936). Carnegie's still-followed advice covers "self-improvement, salesmanship, corporate training, public speaking, and interpersonal skills."[4]

In *Becoming Eichmann: Rethinking the Life, Crimes, and Trial of a 'Desk Murderer,'* David Cesarani draws on decades of scholarship and recent research to help us understand Adolf Eichmann, the Nazi "engineer of The Final Solution," a man who has been described as deeply disturbed; an anti-Semitic monster; someone who was just following orders, being obedient to authority; a colorless bureaucrat. Cesarani tells us, in a passage that touches on several key issues, that, "Much as we may want Eichmann to be a psychotic individual and so unlike us, he was not. . . . Adolf Eichmann was a normal person who had what was for his time a normal upbringing and education. He had an active social life, girlfriends, and, later, a wife and family. He was, according to several who knew him, conventionally bourgeois."[5] He did not start out with virulent hatred of Jews, and only gradually, as the Nazis emerged from being misfits into real power and his career became involved with them, did he take up the already available, classic anti-Semitic view that there was a Jewish conspiracy to run the world. Even then, it took a while for Eichmann to lose all connection with the humanity of the people he first 'helped' to emigrate, and only later sent to their deaths in massive numbers. Cesarani observes that "the language and thinking of warfare merged with racial eugenics,"[6] and together blocked Eichmann's thinking about what he was doing except—and this matters greatly—in enclosed terms. He could and did think about warfare and eugenics, but also, and crucially, he thought about these as they enabled and gave meaning to his career. Eichmann rose in power and rank when, given this work to do, he "bent to his fresh task with all the managerial skills at his disposal. The deportation of humans to their death was treated with the same problem-solving skills, can-do, corporate mentality as arranging shipments of gasoline to petrol stations [an earlier job of Eichmann's]." Cesarani concludes, "Eichmann was not insane, nor was he a robotic receiver of orders. He was educated to genocide and chose to put what he learned into operation."[7]

Pumla Gobodo-Madikizla, a clinical psychologist originally from a township in South Africa who grew up knowing too well the violence against her own people, did the interview with de Kock cited above. As she talked to "Prime Evil," the name by which he was widely called then—a romanticizing name that marked de Kock's crimes off even from other apartheid perpetrators'—she realized that she "was more afraid of confronting" "a human being capable of feeling, crying, and knowing pain," a complexly human de Kock, than she was afraid of continuing to experience him as the dehumanized figure of "Prime Evil."[8] She had then to deal with "something I was probably not prepared for—that good and evil exist in our lives, and that evil, like good, is always a possibility. And that was what frightened me."[9] This is more striking because this psychologist is not saying that there is good even in some bad people, or that good people are capable of doing bad things. We all know that; even if untested, we know it from our own lives. What she encountered, as through the inquiry that drives this book will we, was something actually quite different: a "thin line" not between good and bad, but between good and evil. There is also, as we shall see, a startlingly close connection between what we usually call conventionality, banality, clichés, insider jargon and our ability to move even quite quickly from being conventionally good people to perpetrators of extensive evils.

THINKING CLOSE-IN

These are challenging things to think about carefully, to approach closely, or ought to be. As Dr. Gobodo-Madikizla discovered, the closer in we move, the harder it is to hold onto ways we have had of thinking about evildoers and, as it turns out, those who are remarkably good as well. I believe that close in is the only way we can think if we want to get past explanations and interpretations that have not reached us on levels that bring about real change. Many fine people I know would follow just that observation with a call to engage not just our minds, but our feelings, to find ways not only to instruct but to make people really care. I agree that we need to care more, but I am afraid that I do not trust feelings more than minds. I will say more about this later; for now, I simply want you to know that my focus really is on the questions, *What and how were they thinking, how and when were they not thinking*—the actual doers of great harm, the actual doers of great good, each always as individuals, to individuals, close-in, however massive the final numbers, of which we must also but differently take account.

WHY DO I WRITE?

Some years ago I was invited to discuss a paper of mine titled "Why Not Lie?"[10] with a group of prisoners at a men's medium security facility who were studying humanities with a professor from the local university at which I had been invited to speak. The men had been particularly taken with a paper of mine that the professor had included in their course reader and wanted to meet me. I was introduced; there was a moment of silence; I asked if they had anything they wanted to ask or say to me about what they had read. A large man at the end of the table around which we were gathered leaned back, cocked his head to one side, and said, *"Why did you write it?"* "What do you want to know?" I responded: "Help me, so I can answer what you're really asking, not just what I think you might want to know." *"What was your ulterior motive?"* "Oh," I said; "Well, I can assure you that it wasn't money, and it wasn't fame, and it wasn't power. Would those count as 'ulterior motives'?" *"Yes, I guess so."* "May I ask you another question?" *"Yes."* "Why does it matter to you whether I had an ulterior motive, and what it is?" *"Because I read your paper, and I'm taking it in, and for all I know, you might be toxic."* "Me, not the paper?" *"Yes, of course. Smart people can slip things by you, and you might never know it, but it can do harm to you."* To my mind, this man, who had become acutely aware that he had "gone wrong" in his life and was now being careful to think about what he took in, was the kind of serious reader anyone ought to want, and to honor: being fully attentive matters greatly (another thought to be explored further as we go).

I believe, then, that if we are going to think together through this book, which it is true that I, personally, have been motivated to write, I should tell you a bit about the long journey that led me to such conclusions and the need to write it as I have, as an ongoing inquiry through and about experiences. I have been looking for illumination, for meanings, more than, in any scientific sense, truth.

There are, of course, personal stories as well as philosophical and moral inclinations that inform any choice to undertake the journey of a long-term inquiry, and perhaps particularly so an inquiry that, I promise you I do know, most people would far rather avoid. I have wanted to stop, but simply could not. Among other reasons of which I am aware, there has always also been this: I cannot know how I would act if tested more severely than I have been, nor do I have reason to assume I would act well, or well enough. I profoundly wish that I did know, but I do not. My questions about others are never only about "them," as if I were morally safe, which also means there are no answers that are cut to fit all sizes, serve for all occasions.

MORE PERSONALLY

Like many children, I was early outraged by unfairness, but I confess that when I confronted it beyond the playground, in the adult world, what really gripped me and has led to my work of years now was realizing that I just could not understand it. That is a confession, I think: it turns out that, as much as injustice troubles me, what activates me most is a need to understand.

I was completely baffled by the two kinds of racial prejudice of which I first became aware, white/black racism and anti-Semitism. I encountered both where my family lived, outside of Washington, DC, when, in the 1950s—before the great justice movements of the late 1960s and 1970s had taken off, but as they were indeed in preparation—my parents decided we needed to find a new house. It came up, one day, that we were not looking in some neighborhoods because the people who lived there would not sell either to black people or to Jews. We were evidently neither, but my parents said they did not want prejudiced people as neighbors. More, they did not think such restrictions were acceptable in any way. That made sense to me. I was young, as I have said, and "That's not *fair!*" had some real passion behind it. What did not make sense was why anyone had anything against people of color and/or Jews. I cannot be sure that, had my seriously puzzled "Why?" been answered differently than it was, I would have resisted indoctrination. Maybe, maybe not. But I was fortunate—my parents made it clear that I was entirely right to be so confounded. It was a kind of (what my older self will now call) moral, political idiocy on the part of the excluders that was the real issue. Nothing whatsoever wrong with the recipients of that idiocy: about this, my parents were entirely clear. Racism, white against black, Christian against Jews, and its other ugly and ludicrous formulations, was and is and always shall be the failure of the racists. That does not, of course, mean that others do not suffer the problem of the racists. As long as the racists are also those in power, whole systems are deformed and the most vulnerable take the brunt of viral prejudice, clear unto dying from it when yet again common failings contribute to the rise and setting in of uncommonly rotten systems on a grand scale.

When my family was looking for a house in those years, what people restricting sales were doing was illegal. It was, however, still widely practiced. Signs I saw as we drove around read, for example, "Sensibly restricted." My first conscious hearing of "racist" and "prejudice" was coupled then not only with "unfair" but with "unjust," even when such practices were both common and legal. My mother later went to work for fair housing, going door to door to find out which of our neighbors—all white, I then realized, unless they were "foreign" and so, by prevailing white notions, okay—would sell to black people wanting to move from central DC to a Maryland suburb such as ours. I often went with my mother. The experience did nothing to help me comprehend what was going on with those who, usually politely but not always, quickly and firmly closed their door not only against us. I learned early on that usually polite, good citizens in nice houses in neighborhoods populated by professionals with extensive libraries could be part of great wrongs, that few of them indeed would take even small steps to act rightly. Still, some did; that, too, I learned.

Slowly through those years, as the fifties finally ended and the sixties stirred in the wind, I began to realize that, unspoken as it was, my family carried within it the effects of experiencing the massive harms and horrors that followed the Russian Revolution, born in such hope, and of the Third Reich, conceived in bloody nationalism and its scientized racisms, as well as in the ancient imperial and religious strife and poverty of the Old World. My beloved grandfather and his brothers had fled Russia after the revolution.

They were prominent intellectuals and liberals, both unsafe things to be in revolutionary times. My great-grandfather represented the Jews in the Duma, a short-lived parliament set up after the Czar was removed that did not survive the turmoil from which the Soviet order emerged. Working for justice through the law was a family tradition, aligning them, among others, with the idealistic reformer as well as the great writer, Leo Tolstoy. Part of the family fled to Germany, from where it then became necessary to move again. Although I cannot remember when or how, I found out that my grandfather and his brothers had twin sisters who had returned from France to Germany. They disappeared; if anyone knew what happened to them, I never heard it. When I first heard of the Nazi doctors' experiments on twins, my heart stopped. I still know nothing more.

There was almost no talk of those times, traumas, and losses, at least when the children were around. Perhaps you noticed that earlier I said my family was "evidently" neither black nor Jewish. I knew my grandfather, whose name was Emmanuel Goldenweiser, was Jewish, but I also knew that my grandmother, Pearl Ann Allen from Luray, Virginia, was not, and that they raised their children with no religion or old-country traditions. My father's family was Polish Catholic, immigrants determined to become American and leave all the old bloody wars and poverty behind. What I heard, or experienced in the silences and non-affiliations, was that my people came to America to escape the horrors and to work very hard not only to enjoy but, realists as they were, to build a better world. My originally Russian-Jewish maternal grandfather and my Polish no-longer-Catholic father studied economics and went to work against the causes of poverty; my mother went from fair housing to broader citizen work for democracy. One great uncle became an international lawyer who worked with refugees and immigrants, seeking and gaining reparations from Germany. Another great uncle was a noted, if controversial, anthropologist and Progressive. Radical as he was, he nonetheless spoke out early about changes that enabled the rise of Stalin.

Trying to understand in order to try to fix the world—just that: to work at it, not to believe in Grand Solutions—is nothing unusual. It was until recently simply central to my family's culture as it has been to so many. For my part, I have worked as an educator on the college and university level for more than a few decades. When I look back on that work and consider its relation to all that I have explored in trying to understand *how people can do such things, both good and evil*, I find that I have come to believe that education—given the unhappy record of other social, economic, and political institutions, most assuredly including religious ones—is at the very least a crucial strand of the weave of efforts we are morally required to explore if we are ever to make *Never again* anything other than a tragically failed cry of the heart. To ask,

What were they thinking? Were they thinking? seems to me evidently to lead to questions about how they, and we, and the future in its generations have been and will be educated.

HANNAH ARENDT, "THE BANALITY OF EVIL"

Passing over a great deal: in the late 1960s I returned from a Fulbright Fellowship to teach and to study classic Indian dance (*Bharat Natyam*) in Gujarat, India, and shortly thereafter started graduate work at the University of California, Berkeley. Those were stormy, fascinating, irregular times. I studied political science and theory, a fine accompaniment to all that was going on outside of class, but I left Berkeley just short of a year later, exhausted in part by the transition to California from my year in India and travels through the East. I drove to New York City, was hired to teach undergraduates at The New School College, and was then accepted to The Graduate Faculty of Political and Social Science of The New School.

After an interview, I was also accepted by the political philosopher Hannah Arendt. She admitted me, all unqualified as I was, to her advanced seminar, "Political Experiences of the 20th Century." I wrote my first paper for her as an attempt to solve a puzzle I did not yet know came from my depths and would, in differing forms, drive me for decades more: how could so many deeply idealistic people, in this case Communists in the early days of the Soviet Union, have failed to see, and to stop, what was happening as Stalin took power? I read journals, memoirs, novels, studies that took readers inside the consciousness of people—even some sent to the gulags who were starved and worked like slaves—who went on believing in Stalin. *If he only knew what is happening, he would stop it immediately*, people said. It was extraordinarily difficult, I had to realize, to think outside of the ways they had for so long thought, to question what they had believed so fully that it had given meaning to virtually all moments of their daily lives. They were not blinded ideologues, though, I also found as I read. They were people who needed to make sense of things, as we all do, who found it exceedingly difficult to do so if everything they had believed in, figured out, lived by was implicated, now, in violently negating its own premises and promises. In short, they were in extraordinary circumstances, horrifying ones, but I no longer found them unusual.

At the end of that course, Arendt asked me to be her teaching assistant, so I continued taking her advanced seminars while also sitting in on her larger lecture courses in order to be able to assist her with them as needed. She was then still dealing with the impassioned criticism of her book, *Eichmann in Jerusalem: A Report on the Banality of Evil* (1963). She took me with her to discussions of the book, as well as to debates in which she participated on the Vietnam War and other hot issues of the times. Arendt's thoughts about Eichmann, a significant perpetrator of the Holocaust, had taken her to conclusions for which many people evidently were not ready. It was not only that there was a lot of disagreement that struck me; it was how vitriolic and highly personalized it often was. Right or wrong in her interpretations, Arendt's thinking had clearly gone off the tracks many people required even to listen. I was troubled and fascinated by blocks to thinking that were anything but "merely" intellectual in their effects. That was what Arendt's "report" on Eichmann explored: what being "thoughtless" meant in the highly specific instance of Adolf Eichmann. Those who could not listen to Arendt's thinking were realms away from Eichmann, of course, as, in different ways, were the Communists who could not stop believing in Stalin, and my family's white neighbors who were so frightened of change in their suburban enclave. Nonetheless, my interest in the version of my question that focuses it for me intensified: *What, how, are they thinking? Are we thinking?*

THE EVIL OF BANALITY

Reflecting on Arendt's work and its early reception by good people who were deeply pained, I found myself reversing her [in]famous phrase and, having done so, thinking that perhaps it would have helped had she spoken, as she did not, of "the evil of banality," rather than—or, as I now think, in addition to—"the banality of evil." To think of evil as "banal" was then altogether too difficult: these were times in which "unthinkable" went with "evil," with the Holocaust—*unthinkable, unspeakable, radical evil*, the very opposite of "banal."

The evil of banality has haunted my thinking ever since it occurred to me, illuminating Arendt's work, especially her use of "thoughtlessness" to describe what was most extreme, most striking, about the man on trial in Jerusalem but then also much more of her work, and that of other philosophers to whom I turned (Plato's Socrates, Heidegger, Husserl, Jaspers, Dewey, Addams, James, Weil, among others). So, whatever else I have been doing, studying, teaching, writing, I have continued since that first paper I wrote for Arendt reading memoirs, novels, interviews, studies that offer the chance to get in close to what and how people caught up in extraordinary events as perpetrators, as resisters, as victims, as immediate observers were thinking—or not—about what they were doing.

Perhaps this focus on making sense, on thinking, is bizarre on my part. I have been told that it is, and all the more often as, in the first decades of our new millennium, so much pressure has been brought to bear on schools

at all levels to "deliver content," to "hold people accountable" for achieving pre-set "outcomes"—in short, for the production of predictable products
measureable by the sort of standardized evaluation methods that are precisely
not suited for the free act of thinking (which Socrates, perhaps *the* Western
exemplar of thinking, likened without contradiction to a wind that blows
everything down; a stinging fly that awakens; an electric eel that paralyzes).
But I realize now that, since my first encounters with dramatic injustices
that did not shatter my own life but that have haunted and driven it, I have
increasingly felt that understanding thinking—and so also thoughtlessness,
and so also banality in its many forms—is for me the most pressing moral
and political quest.

What were you thinking?! we say to a friend, a child, someone we are
interviewing when we just plain cannot imagine how a thinking person could
have done *that*, whatever it was. At root, that is the question of this book,
which is informed by a lifetime, now, of pursuing such questions, many
experiences and conversations, reading, and research. More recently I have
had invitations to talk with wonderfully thoughtful and morally serious audiences in classes, academic gatherings, conferences on genocide, community
groups, and it is that thinking, as engaged as it is with the world and others,
that I bring to you now in the hope that you will join in.

And then I need to say this: one of Hannah Arendt's thinking friends once
said, "I am not duty-bound to resolve the difficulties I create. . . . if only
they are ideas in which readers will find material that stirs them to think for
themselves."[11] I think this could be said as a preemptive excuse, uncaringly
or arrogantly; I hope I invoke it here as a value for which to strive so that I do
not produce a book that is in its own ways self-contradictory.

MEANINGFUL CONTEXTS, LARGER SYSTEMS

I have started by speaking personally and have posed my morally pressing questions about individual thinking. The individual is finally where
moral responsibility lies, and people have been my focus, but it is important
also to emphasize here, at the very beginning, that all the many systems—
governmental, economic, military, social, cultural, linguistic and communications, material and architectural—within which we live our lives matter a
great deal. We have, then, a bit more exploring to do to locate this particular
inquiry if we are to understand each other well enough to think together.

It is what happens when systems are turned rotten by a few people but many
people enable that turn and keep it going—except for the few good souls who
resist, and there are always a few—that I have been trying to understand for
so long. I am not, though, going to focus on the systems. Many have done

that, including Arendt, who wrote *The Origins of Totalitarianism* (1951) very soon after World War II and well before *Eichmann in Jerusalem: A Report on the Banality of Evil.* I am neither a sociologist nor a political analyst, let alone a scholar of the other systems with and within which polities and societies run. I am a philosopher and an educator, and what I want to know of all those people—far beyond the few on top—who enable and perpetrate systems concerns *thinking*, which we do ourselves, but also *meaning*, which we cannot make all by ourselves. So I also ask, *How could they make sense of what they were doing?* If we can understand better that nodal point, the making of sense drawing on meanings shared among individuals, I actually do believe we might learn something crucial about ourselves, first, and then about how to educate the newcomers who join our world so that more of us, more people everywhere, will find themselves unable, when the time comes, to do the work that systems going bad require.

So, while it does not suffice to focus only on individuals as if we live, love, and have our being all on our own, it also does not work to assign all agency to systems, whether conceptual, moral, material, political, and/or economic. We need to consider individuals in meaningful contexts.

Consider these observations by a visitor to Baghdad that come together to raise very large questions:

> To receive this briefing [re: what the U.S. Embassy had, or—as it turned, out, had not—done for its highly vulnerable Iraqi employees], I had passed through three security doors into the Embassy's classified section, where there were no Iraqis and no natural light; it seemed as if every molecule of Baghdad air had been sealed off behind the last security door. The Embassy officials struck me as decent, overworked people, yet I left the interview with a feeling of shame. The problem lay . . . with the politics of the American project in Iraq, which from the beginning had been conducted under the illusion that controlling the message mattered more than the reality. A former official at the Embassy told me, "When we say that the corridors of power are insulated, is it that the officials aren't receiving the information, or is it because the construct under which they're operating doesn't even allow them to absorb it?"[12]

This is astute thinking by an attentive reporter who recognizes both individual responsibility and the system-defined contexts within which we find—or do not find—it meaningful, do or do not accept it, and still there are questions to be raised. "The construct under which they are operating" includes systems of differing but complementary sorts, from actual buildings to professionalized meanings, language, hierarchies, protocols, career paths, and on to individual ways of making sense of what is going on. So I want to ask something additional and a bit different. I want to ask, not whether "the construct under which they are operating doesn't even allow them to absorb it" but, *How, day by day by day, do most of them choose to think within that construct when, as the thinking creatures that we humans are, at any moment any one of them could, like their visitor, be startled back into thinking—really could stop, and think.*

In truth, much as we might rather not admit it, we usually do know what is going on. We just find ways not to think about it, and you cannot care about, and need not take action concerning, something or someone you simply do not take into or hold in your mind. *Don't take it home with you*, friends advise. *Be a team player*, we tell people who start asking uncomfortable questions. *It's not our business*; *I was just doing my job; everyone else seemed okay with it; who was I to question the guys in the big offices? I had a family to support. There was a promotion I could get if I played it right.* There are all sorts of conventional banalities ready to hand that work very well when we choose to avoid thinking about what we are doing within and in service of larger systems.

We might say that systems can be *conditions of possibility*, and so seem possible grounds for *excuses*, but in moral fact, they are not *causes*.

OVERVIEW

Part I of this book is concerned with how monstrous evils actually become normalized, providing the conditions of possibility, and excuses, for the great many perpetrators they require. In chapter 7, about midway through, there is a keystone to the arch of the whole book: I introduce the concepts *extensive evil, extensive good*, and *intensive evil, intensive good.* In part II, my inquiry turns to the doing of good by a few people even in the face of the worst that it seems everyone else is doing: What, how, were *they* thinking? After listening carefully in hope of learning from those who will not collaborate with systemic evils, I have found, among other telling factors, that here too, above all, we need to practice being attentive to the obvious as well as the elaborate, the familiar and daily as well as the professional and technical. Part III then returns to evils—now focusing especially on ways they thrive when places, peoples, meanings have become *enclosed*, by walls, logics, bureaucracies, authoritative "knowledge." These enablers too turn out to be seeded in everyday life.

Among the bolder threads in the patterns of the arc held by the keystone *extensive/intensive* distinction, those that emerge as significant as we move in close to many, many experiences, these also stand out:

Mindlessness enables unthinkable acts. Attentiveness that awakens thinking enables simple goodness.

And then I, as an educator as well as a philosopher, have to say, with breath held:

> *Education can develop either attentiveness or thoughtlessness. There are individual and collective choices to be made. Mostly, I fear, we have made them wrongly. Had we not, the materials for this book would have been far less ready to hand.*

SECULAR MORAL THINKING

My invitation to you, then, is to join me in thinking and rethinking precisely the mindlessness that is perhaps—I believe it is—the most dangerous state of our most dangerous species, considering also what we may learn by reflecting on how we become so thoughtless, but might become thinkers instead. This means, as I understand it, that mine is a secular inquiry into good and evil, depending on and returning to no invocations of deity, dogma, or theology (or, for that matter, any particular schools of philosophy, although I do teach moral philosophy and it is in my mind as I write). There are ways to connect any inquiry into evil and good to religious teachings, of course, but it is not my calling (nor my ulterior motive) to do so, and there are also tensions here insofar as unthinking adherence is of great concern to me no matter to what, or to whom, it is given.

Part I

THINKING THE UNTHINKABLE

Chapter One

Truth and Fiction

Camus' The Plague

I do not know if Hannah Arendt and the philosopher, resistance fighter, and novelist Albert Camus ever spoke, although they may have (I have heard that she admired him). Nonetheless, her thoughts and his have been in conversation in my mind for a long time now. I believe Camus' story will help us imaginatively "trace experiences rather than doctrines," as Arendt suggested we do in our effort to comprehend evil, in quest of goodness.

Among Camus' many written works, it is a novel, *The Plague*, to which I have returned through the years. It continues to provide us with a story, images, characters that simultaneously provoke thought, imagination, and feeling while being at a remove from the more abstract challenges of philosophical writing, on the one hand, and searing historical realities, on the other.

I want, then, to move into our inquiry with *The Plague* upfront so we can return to its evocative fictional truths as strands to follow throughout. The dead rats that herald the arrival of the plague in Camus' novel come to mark among other things the importance of paying attention, and not only to the big but to the apparently small things that seem only somewhat odd, if that, at first.

The Plague is a prolonged allegorical reflection on how extensive evil emerges, takes hold, and finally entirely takes over a small city. We come to know some of the people trapped there as the city becomes, in its profound trouble and suffering, radically cut off physically, existentially, morally from others still living ordinary lives elsewhere who are unaware, yet, of their own vulnerability, of the germs that can lie dormant for years in the most ordinary of places, in drawers, chests of linens, cupboards.

PHILOSOPHER, RESISTANCE FIGHTER

In 1948, Albert Camus—a philosopher who wrote fiction, a member of the French Resistance that struggled against the Nazis, and editor of its clandestine newspaper, *Combat*—published a novel he titled *The Plague*. France had been occupied by the Nazis (May 1940–August 1944) and, under the old French war hero Field Marshall Petain, became actively complicit. Both independently and led by General Charles de Gaulle from exile, Camus and others who opted to resist had to then evade capture, incarceration, potentially also torture and death at the hands of collaborators among their own people as well as the unambiguously threatening and morally appalling enemy. There is heroism in evidence here, and—more rare and essential to action in times of extensive evil—there is evidence of astute moral as well as political judgment of the sort that tends to atrophy when systems go bad. Camus, then, knew firsthand about perpetrators and enablers of large-scale atrocities, and he knew still more intimately what it took for some to resist.

AN ORDINARY TOWN

The Plague tells the story of Oran, an ordinary town on the northern coast of Algeria that is taken over and decimated by an outbreak of something very like the bubonic plague. The anonymous narrator of the story, we find out toward the end, is a doctor who in his professional role sees more of the intimate as well as general effects of this horrific visitation than others. *The Plague* becomes a tale of how differing individuals deal with an unavoidably shared yet profoundly isolating situation in which all that was once ordinary has been turned upside down and inside out, suffering and death become ordinary, and still people must choose how to live, what to do each day while they remain uninfected. When their town is quarantined, they are even more isolated, without hope of rescue from outside and fearful of contamination from all those with whom they are now terribly bonded, from whom they cannot escape.

At the end of this allegorical novel—Camus clearly had the Occupation by the Nazis in mind, but is seeking through it for transhistorical meanings—Dr. Rieux, the narrator and doctor who, at risk to his own life, has quietly persisted in doing whatever he can to fight the plague even though, as he says, doing so once it has fully set in meant "a never ending defeat,"[1] stands listening to the joyous celebration of the townspeople finally delivered from the deadly epidemic that has isolated and, over many months, indiscriminately brought agonizing deaths to children, lovers, friends, strangers, good and bad, cruel and generous, people of faith and of doubt, significant and just plain ordinary people:

> He knew what those jubilant crowds did not know but could have learned from books: that the plague bacillus never dies nor disappears for good; that it can lie dormant for years and years in furniture and linen-chests; that it bides its time in bedrooms, cellars, trunks, and bookshelves; and that perhaps the day would come when, for the bane and enlightening of men, it would rouse up its rats again and send them forth to die in a happy city.[2]

The people of Oran and their officials never wanted to know that there is always the potential for a plague to break out. Still more, they did not want to know what was happening when plague first came to them, to their ordinary city just going about its business. When the first few rats appeared, dead and dying from infection by plague bacillus-carrying fleas, in the streets, in their lodgings, by the docks, the people who found them were curious, but not bothered. *Something odd is going on*, those who encountered the bloated bodies said to each other, and then they went on with their day. They threw the dead rats away so as not to have to look at them, and when the rat bodies, increasing daily in number, kept piling up, they agitated for better pickup services and fussed as usual about municipal government. And then people started dying. Like the rats, there were just a few at the beginning, and little social or official note was taken despite the terrible suffering of each individual.

The first person Dr. Rieux tries fruitlessly to keep from dying is his landlord, who, from the time of the first rat found dead on Rieux's landing, has insisted there are no rats in his building. They must be being put there, he announces, by wicked boys playing nasty tricks. The town officials, told by Dr. Rieux and another, even blunter, doctor that strict and immediate measures must be taken, quibble defensively about whether it really is plague or perhaps something else. Dr. Rieux tells them it does not matter. If they do not act, at least half the population will die. Avoiding the word "plague," the officials finally post signs in out-of-the-way places suggesting halfhearted measures. As always, they do not want the public upset, nor to concern their superiors. Meanwhile, every day more people are suffering and dying.

Dr. Rieux barely lingers on the failures of the citizens to do more than fuss at the inconvenience of it all, of the town officers' choice not to advertise the troubles by taking preventive measures. None of this was surprising. Camus' characters live in an ordinary town in what, before the extraordinary outbreak of the plague, were persistently ordinary times.

They had come to concern themselves mostly with a quest for comfort, and modestly, as he says, "cultivating habits"[3]—visiting in the same cafes after work, strolling the same avenues in the cool of the early night, drinking the same amount too much, loving moderately, indulging in illicit flirtations without fuss or bother—rather than anything as dramatic as virtues or vices. Mostly, the respectable citizens gave their attention to working hard to make more money.

ON BEING UNPREPARED

Their lives, their conventional realities, meant they were not prepared to recognize that a few rats dying oddly in public called for an immediate reaction rather than avoidance, nor were they prepared to choose whether or not to take the mortal risks of caring for the ill, collecting and burying the dead, honoring or trying to flee in defiance of the quarantine that was belatedly imposed on them. Variously, they try radically isolating themselves in hope of escaping contamination; seeking oblivion through drink or anything else possible; muddling on as if nothing has changed. And even as death stalks the streets, people look for ways to profit from the situation.

A mysterious man who seems to have no work but lives discretely among them welcomes the quarantine. We learn finally that he is being pursued by authorities who think him guilty of a "mistake," he says; for him, there is relief and safety in having everyone around him also living as if under an indictment. He welcomes the company. Other people, those who had been living for something other than pleasantly fulfilling success or the warmth of fitting in properly with others, are also caught in the epidemic. A journalist, trapped in Oran by the quarantine and so separated from a newly found great love who lives in Paris, tries at first to escape: he puts happiness over any sense of obligation to others. Dr. Rieux, who knows that we are all always and already vulnerable to such loss, does not condemn him. An admired priest, Father Paneloux, first preaches to his flock that the plague is God's wrath at their failures, a winnowing of the good from the wicked. Even later, when he has watched children die, and friends, the good priest cannot find a differing way to read what is happening without threatening his bedrock faith. He does help remove the bodies with the others who risk their lives to do so, but when plague comes to him, he will not let the doctor even try to fight it. Like the doctor, his life was pledged to saving people, but unlike the doctor, he could not accept defeats, deaths he could not justify. Tarrou, another character who once wanted to save people (in his case, from economic injustices), fights the plague without hope of meaning but still believing that with enough study, the human condition can be, if never justified, comprehended. He, too, dies, but thoughtfully, and without complaint, accepting what his friends try to do for him.

In all the choices, from joining the dangerous body-removal squad, to preaching that the plague is God's flail winnowing the good from the bad, to profiteering or determinedly trying to leave a quarantined city in a defiant quest for personal happiness, Camus presents his characters making choices that issue from their own most familiar ways of being in the world. The plague exaggerates them by its horrors; what is exaggerated, however, was already there.

EXTRAORDINARY

But death by plague, by mass terror, by perverted policy on a scale beyond grandiosity: these are extraordinary events. The mind quails. They are precisely not ordinary. Right? They cry out for antihero perpetrators big enough to match the consequences of horrific deeds, and heroic warriors even bigger to meet and beat such a demonic enemy. It seems so, but Camus refuses to give us antiheroes, monsters, or saints: death by plague is monstrous but its causes are not, nor is the choice to fight it heroic in any romantic sense. It is, the doctor knows, simply what must be done when the plague bacillus does what it does, no more, no less, as do the rats that carry it into the streets. Fighting the plague when it has settled in, affecting every aspect and moment of all lives, is anything but romantic: it is simply the only way to avoid colluding with it.

Camus reminds us of Oran, the town on the coast of Algeria, that it is above all ordinary and cannot be romanticized. It is "ugly. It has a smug, placid air and you need time to discover what it is that makes it different from so many business centers in other parts of the world."[4] Physically, its streets and squares are built so that it turns its back on the sea, the great, pulsating, changing expanse that could give it vistas, character, connections with other lands, other lives than the "doing business" that is its citizens' "chief aim in life."[5] These citizens in this ordinary town are not obvious candidates for the plague, which is so clearly extraordinary: the citizens of Camus' Oran are proud that their merely pleasant lives are so persuasive that "social unrest is quite unknown" among them.[6] How could mere habits, business as usual, minor cultivated pleasures that simply refresh enough to return to one's job prepare people to deal with plague, let alone suggest that they might be vulnerable to colluding with it?

ATTENDING TO THE SMALLEST THINGS

Camus' tale suggests that it is not the dramatic vices that threaten us with extensive evil, nor is it dramatic faith, such as that of his novel's priest, nor quests for justice, such as that of Tarrou, the doctor's friend and former believer in economic salvation, that protect us from it.

> *It is the small virtues and vices that neither religion nor education pay much attention to, those that blink on and off without our noticing anymore as we move through our days, that can make all the difference when systems start changing.*

It is a remarkable thing Camus has done, this resistance fighter, philosopher, novelist, journalist. He has invited us to reflect on how our daily, most ordinary, ways of thinking of ourselves and of acting are more or less already implicated with the most extraordinary harms we can imagine. We might then think: The capacity of the ordinary, the daily, to turn first banal and then deadly needs to be fully attended to, so perhaps, when the first infected rat next comes out to die in the street, we will be ready and this time, perhaps, we will act on time.

A moralist for a modern world in which we know, now, how entirely discrepant causes and conditions can be to their effects—an inherited condition that can lead to great suffering; millions of people enjoying modest comforts contributing to climate change; ambitious financiers finding new ways to profit but crashing global economies—Camus tried to tell us instead to pay attention, close attention, now, here, to the smallest of dangers, the first rat dead in the street of a bacillus we cannot see at all and that cares not one whit about us. He also told us to attend to friendship, to the small pleasures, to the eccentricities that keep us living against the grain: Dr. Rieux and Tarrou, the man who sets up brigades to clear the dead bodies when the authorities fail to do so and becomes an ally and a friend of the doctor, take long swims under the moon at night in the ocean on which Oran turns its back. Tarrou writes in his diary stories of quirky neighbors who manage to remain who they are throughout the plague; he has learned to admire quirkiness, to be leery of convention as of certainties.

Camus also quietly explores the simple reasons there are for doing good things. Joseph Grand, a clerk who, having failed through the years to assert himself enough to ask his superior for a long-promised, never implemented raise, barely supports himself but happily works every evening on improving his knowledge and use of language. He is writing a novel; it is this he lives for. He cannot get past the first sentence, but his dedication to getting language right keeps him going. It is a great quest for him, and he gives himself to it entirely. Each word matters. Grand says, when asked if he will help remove bodies that could still carry the infection, "Why, that's not difficult! Plague is here and we've got to make a stand. Ah, I only wish everything were as simple!"[7]

Despair for Camus in a world that has had plagues and remains subject to them is not absolute, then. There are people who can recognize and fight the plague, and there are survivors, but Camus came to believe that any lessons hopefully gleaned from these few must remain informed by realizations similar to Arendt's: that we are not in control even as we must act; that love must be "the love of persons," not abstractions such as "any people or collective"[8]; and that finally nothing, nothing whatsoever—no ideology, faith, or science; no conventionality, greed, or ambition; no fear, or obedience—justifies collaborating with death, with suffering.

Chapter Two

Thinking about Not-Thinking

> Our darkest feelings do not mind being trusted out of hand. Though immediacy is the true reality, the presence of our soul and our feelings are not simply there like given facts of life. Rather, they are communicated by our inner activities, our thoughts, our knowledge. They are deepened and clarified in the measure that we think. Feeling as such is unreliable. To plead feelings means to evade naively the objectivity of what we can know and think.[1]

I have started with a philosopher, Hannah Arendt, and a philosopher–resistance fighter-novelist, Albert Camus. We have help in trying to comprehend also from others. For some years now, social scientists, especially historians and social psychologists—notably among them, Raul Hilberg, Christopher Browning, Claudia Koonz, Daniel Jonah Goldhagen, Stanley Milgram, Philip Zimbardo, James Waller, Robert Jay Lifton—have been trying to teach us to think of the evils of massive purposeful harm as something we can study not only secularly but empirically. James Waller, for example, cites cross-cultural evidence of purposeful preparations for "genocide and mass killing" by engineering the prior "social death of the victims" through "us-them thinking," "dehumanization of the victims," and "blaming the victims."[2] Preparation is among my concerns as well, albeit not from the slant of social psychology, useful as that is. Journalists, committed to facts and informed interpretation more than proof, have joined in (e.g., Samantha Power's *"A Problem from Hell": America and the Age of Genocide*, and Chris Hedges, the author of *War is a Force that Gives Life Meaning*).

Scholars of the humanities have also recognized as well as contributed to a heightened receptivity to such concerns (notably, Susan Neiman on evil; Martha Nussbaum on goodness), turning as always to philosophy, theology, literature in a quest to discern meaning from events, facts, conceptual framings.

These are excellent studies, offering a rich array of ways to try to comprehend historical phenomena that are often called "unthinkable." My inquiry
would have been utterly impossible without such works, and, of course, it
differs from them. I focus on the close-in *thinking* and the tragically more
common *thoughtlessness*—the failure to be attentive to and reflective about
what we are doing—that keeps us from seeing through the categories, labels,
conventionalities that can be mobilized in ways that Waller, among others,
has aptly described. I see that we can speak of what mass killers do as, for
instance, enabled by "dehumanizing" people, and then I have to ask, *How is
it* that we can go from seeing someone as a neighbor, as many of the Hutus
and Tutsis, the non-Jewish and Jewish Germans were, through various stages
of "social distancing" until finally (and sometimes in remarkably short order)
we can see—and kill—real people, many of them but each also singular?
Without repeatedly asking, *What were they thinking?* I fear that emphasis on
what is now commonly called *Othering* in its differing modes is a description
rather than an analysis.

People do that: they turn people into "others" and then they can kill them.
Yes, but how do they do it, how do they keep doing it, and do they all really
always see each individual they kill as, for example, a vermin, a cockroach (a
term used in Rwanda as in Germany)? That is actually quite a difficult feat.
It is aided by taking away victims' dignity, stripping the fragile significations
of personhood from them—clothes, upright posture, ability to look us in the
eye, to speak and be heard. And still, the indignities themselves must be done
by someone to people not yet so humiliated; once done, they must not move
individual perpetrators to sympathy, to empathy, rather than scorn and distance.
Seeing other humans like that must not awaken conscience, shame. The deadly
distancing must be learned, embraced, integrated, and practiced to be effective,
and, during the months, years, of truly extensive evils, it must also coexist with
an ability to return after work to familiar relationships with other human beings.

Those who have to get the work of massive harm done know very well just
how difficult that balance is. The Nazi leader Heinrich Himmler "ordered that
when executions were carried out in concentration camps, those responsible
'are to be influenced in such a way as to suffer no ill effect in their character and mental attitudes.'" Later, Himmler was proud to observe "that the
S.S. had wiped out the Jews 'without our leaders and their men suffering any
damage in their minds and souls. The danger was considerable, for there was
only a narrow path between the Scylla of their becoming heartless ruffians
unable any longer to treasure life, and the Charybdis of their becoming soft
and suffering nervous breakdowns.'"[3]

Not an easy balance, that, but required if you are to have capable people
doing horrific things over time. There are reports of high-ranking Nazis
being sickened, throwing up, when they saw what their orders were making

happen to people they were nonetheless used to thinking and speaking of as "parasites," "degenerates," threats to the Master Race the Nazis planned to breed from "pure," "uncontaminated stock." All that dehumanization did not shockproof even Franz Stangl, soon to be Commandant of Treblinka, the largest extermination camp.[4] Stangl told an interviewer about his first visit to Chelmno, an extermination camp already in operation:

> "I can't describe to you what it was like," Stangl said; he spoke slowly now, in his more formal German, his face strained and grim. He passed his hand over his eyes and rubbed his forehead " . . . It was a one-story building. The smell . . . " he said, "Oh God, the smell. It was everywhere. Wirth [The officer in charge] wasn't in his office. I remember, they took me to him . . . he was standing on a hill, next to the pits . . . the pits . . . full . . . they were full. I can't tell you; not hundreds, thousands, thousands of corpses . . . oh God. That's when Wirth told me—he said that was what Sobibor was for. And that he was putting me officially in charge."[5]

Stangl was there because he was being made supervisor of construction at Sobibor.

And after that profound shock, what did Franz Stangl do? "The same thing; I continued the construction of the camp. . . . At Sobibor, one could avoid seeing almost all of it—it all happened so far away from the camp-buildings."[6] His prior conditioning did not prepare him; he was indeed horrified, and said he wanted to work anyplace else, to leave. He did not. He continued his work, pursued his career "upwards," to become Commandant of Treblinka, the largest of the extermination camps.

There is more to uncover here. Remember the opening quote of the Introduction to this book? A Hutu *genocidaire*, a killer of Tutsis in the three-month Rwandan genocide, said of one of his victims, "Me, I knew this old man by name, but I had heard nothing unpleasant about him. That evening I told my wife everything. She knew only routine details about him, we did not discuss it, and I went to sleep." Neither the man nor his wife saw a cockroach, an Other, a threat; they knew this man, "had heard nothing unpleasant about him," "knew only routine details about him." And still the killing job went on without disruption by the kind of thinking we call "conscience," the kind that awakens when we become aware of what we are doing—when indeed we stop and think, *What am I doing?* Or, far better, *I can't do* that.

THINKING, MORALITY

I want particularly to note, then, that since the late 1960s we have also had Hannah Arendt's initially scandalizing, now widely accepted (if almost always misunderstood) concept and phrase, *the banality of evil.* She thought it important enough to use as the subtitle for her book reporting on the 1963 trial of the Nazi "Engineer of the Final Solution," Adolf Eichmann, in Jerusalem.

What Arendt's "banal" refers to lies in the vicinity of what Camus was trying to show us with his allegorical plague. Massive in the suffering, death, and almost unbearable moral challenges it poses, the plague is none-theless caused by a mere bacillus and, what is more, a bacillus that persists in our most ordinary possessions and places until again it infects the common flea that feeds off the common rat. Obviously, while this can be said of an epidemic, it can hardly be an explanation of how genocides, mass rapes as acts of war, human trafficking happen: human beings, creatures of mind and heart and imagination—creatures of choice—do these things. Imaginatively, though, it invites us to rethink what *evil* means when we use it to mark off some massive human harm-doing from lesser transgressions.

Some twenty years before Arendt wrote about "the banality of evil," in a 1946 exchange of letters with her former teacher and lifelong friend, Karl Jaspers, we find these two philosophers reflecting on their direct experiences and their still unfolding understanding of the Nazis. Jaspers wrote to Arendt, "I'm not altogether comfortable with your view [of] a guilt that goes beyond all criminal guilt [because such guilt] inevitably takes on a streak . . . of satanic greatness . . . [W]e have to see these things in their total banality, in their prosaic triviality." Two months later, Arendt replied, "We have to combat all impulses to mythologize the horrible and to the extent that I can't avoid such formulations, I haven't understood what actually went on."[7]

Arendt was struggling even then to think about the ordinary rather than the extraordinary conditions of evil, and to do so directly, attentively remaining as open as possible to the most prosaic aspects of realities that even—especially—included mass murder. Later, in an essay titled, "On Thinking and Moral Considerations," she spoke of "the claim on our attention that everything has simply by existing." She also spoke of "thinking without a bannister."[8] We could consider these to be aspects of *free thinking*, although carefully: "free thinking" has many possible meanings. For Arendt, it was a horizonal purpose: to be willing and able to think about anything without being either supported or constrained by conventional concepts; to be able to do that because, and as, we are also willing and able to reflect on our own thinking, to keep it going, to re-open even what seems decided—to lay tracks, as the philosopher Heidegger put it, without ever arriving anywhere. We could then call such thinking *free*, most importantly, because what Arendt meant by *thinking* included it in the few basic potentials for freedom given by our human being. (*Action* is another such potential, as is the human condition of action, *natality*.)[9]

Arendt held that it is this kind of thinking that is required to illuminate "what actually went on," just as it is this kind of thinking of which Eichmann, as she claimed of the "Engineer of the Final Solution," was startlingly incapable.

CRUCIAL CONTEXTS, CHANGING TIMES

Hannah Arendt was a philosopher and remained always a thinker, but her attention was turned by the violations of her times toward the world of action rather than "the life of the mind" that she had previously desired and prepared for in her days as a student of philosophy in Germany.[10] She was clear earlier than too many others that what was happening as Hitler came to power could neither be ignored nor conventionally comprehended.

As the Nazis established themselves, categories of explanation appropriate to other times, even troubled ones, yielded slowly to realities to which they were suddenly inadequate. Few noticed how their language was itself being shifted so that discrepancies, contradictions, changes were less likely to catch attention.[11] Very few, from any walk of life, were willing and able to see that, this time, the rats occasionally found in even the best streets were carriers of a contagion to which only a few people would turn out to be entirely immune.

After the war, when Adolf Eichmann was kidnapped from Argentina (to which he fled as the regime he had devotedly served was finally defeated), he was taken to Jerusalem to stand trial. Sent by *The New Yorker*, Hannah Arendt went to Jerusalem to look, to listen, to try to tell us what she found. An amateur reporter, but one who had by then been thinking against the grain for some time—thinking "without a bannister"—she found herself, she wrote, with a concept. Seeded some twenty years earlier through her thinking with Karl Jaspers, it came to her as she tried to follow the story, the many stories, concerning Adolf Eichmann told in that court. This, of course, is quite different from applying a scholarly or professional method, empirical or theoretical. It was more in the classic philosophical role of a *spectator* that Arendt, like Camus, opened herself to re-experiencing very painful things, this time thinking with a profoundly guilty man in the dock in order to figure out how that mind worked. In the course of taking in, thinking, writing, up came the concept: *the banality of evil.*[12]

It was a phrase that created a furor along with the book for which it became a subtitle. There were other things Arendt wrote that were as, or more, offensive to some,[13] but the contrast between the staggering horror of the Holocaust and "banality" sufficed to evoke outrage. She did, of course, know and say that Eichmann's deeds were "monstrous," but the distinctions she was making between actor and acts, and between "normal" under the

Nazis and "normal" when systems have not been taken so horrifically wrong were rarely heard. Few others had consciously been trying for decades *not* to see the Nazis as larger than life. There was the hold of that powerful, familiar concept, *radical evil.* There was the sheer horror that feels radical in the base meaning of the term: it shakes us to our roots. And, not at all insignificantly, the Nazis were masters of pageantry and costume and propaganda, all used to make them appear to be more than human, a Master Race.

In South Africa, de Kock, you recall, was also widely seen as both sub- and super-human—as "Prime Evil." We could easily proliferate examples of monstrous harm-doers depicted as themselves monstrous, super-sized, from headlines in the media to popular horror movies, electronic games, "comics." No one—not the terrorists who want us paralyzed by fear; not the apologists or analysts who try to make sense of something that does shatter categories; not those who must live afterwards with such acts irretrievably in our histories; not observers near or far—finds it easy to speak of evil as continuous in any way at all with everyday life. Even Camus gives us germs and rats as the carriers of infection. However common they are, they are not human.

STOPPING MINDS

What Arendt was saying almost literally could not be heard as she meant it. This is entirely understandable: in the face of horrors, most of us need whatever help we can find not to be utterly silenced, reduced to wordless weeping, to screaming silently if not screaming out loud. Listen to the painful, heart-wrenching words of community members when a school shooter has killed their children, and to the ways deeply moved, well-meaning reporters try to tell the rest of us what has happened. Almost everyone uses the most familiar of phrases to help them speak of what they cannot take into their minds lest their broken hearts finally shatter. A parent, after requesting anonymity, told a reporter checking in two years after a school shooting:

> "Well, back-to-school was bittersweet. . . . I watched my youngest board the bus. Watched his little face in the window. . . ." His voice trailed off into a whispery human ellipse like the 26 innocent lives that were left suddenly unfinished that awful day when the monster marched into Sandy Hook Elementary School with the loaded Bushmaster AR-15 semi-automatic rifle. . . . "We're not a story; we're a town. With families trying to put the . . . trying to put the bad day in the rear view mirror. Looking ahead."[14]

Arendt reflected[15] that it takes at least ten years for writing to begin to deal with disasters with the unflinching, direct clarity that allows for fresh language and images, and still there are few with the art, the heart, the courage to do so. Even writers, I thought then; so much more the rest of us. Arendt, who rarely used concepts or language of the sort thankfully available to the Newtown parent and the respectful reporter when words yet again failed, was misheard by virtually everyone. She spoke the wrong language, and has since, through the years, been sharply criticized for that, and for the irony she did invoke faced with category-breaking discrepancies: "For all this [Eichmann's trial], it was essential that one take him seriously, and this was very hard to do, unless one sought the easiest way out of the dilemma between the unspeakable horror of the deeds, and the undeniable ludicrousness of the man who perpetrated them, and declared him a clever, calculating liar—which he obviously was not."[16]

Despite all those real emotional and conceptual difficulties, *the banality of evil* is an illuminating concept and, over time, it has ceased being as painful, insulting, infuriating to as many people as it was before. In fact now, when an outrageously harmful event erupts yet again, one can hardly pick up a newspaper or listen to National Public Radio without encountering a reference to Arendt and "the banality of evil." So, in the middle of the thundering oratory by political and religious leaders about evil to which, I am sorry to say, we were returned in the last years of the twentieth century and the first years of the twenty-first—in politics, for example, Reagan's "Evil Empire," George W. Bush's "Axis of Evil"—there remains available that quieter call to think close-in, to refuse romanticism from any side that gives us monsters, devils and saints, and world-scale events to divert our attention from the actual ordinary world that is in our keeping for good and for ill every day.

TWO-FACED EVIL

What I hear when I tune in to secular talk and writing about evil these days is a view of evil as Janus-faced. One face, vividly painted and waved before us by people who want us terrorized—including terrorists (consider ISIS, under whatever name) as well as those who want us mobilized against them—is effectively a Medusa's head, snakes coiling in place of hair, paralyzing any who gaze on it. The actual face that is used thus to terrorize us varies, of course: it depends on whom we are supposed to demonize as The Enemy. In stark contrast, the other face of evil resembles what is taken to be Arendt's portrait of Adolf Eichmann: an Everyman Bureaucrat, a pale office-dwelling worker, a problem-solving engineer in a suit, as at his trial, needing protection by a glass booth from the passionate hatred of others.

Arendt's phrase, coined to capture her realization that what was startlingly *unusual* about Eichmann was "a perhaps extraordinary shallowness," "not stupidity but a curious, quite authentic inability to think"[17] has lost its original meaning, the challenge it poses. Rarely does it lead to Arendt's own question: "Is our ability to judge, to tell right from wrong, beautiful from ugly, dependent upon our faculty of thought? Do the inability to think and a disastrous failure of what we commonly call conscience coincide?"[18] This, I need to note now although we will return to it later, is a philosophical question. Arendt is not asking if "We are all Eichmanns."

However, the ordinary "petty bureaucrat" face of evil is now generalized and variously infused with images of ordinary people doing terrible things akin to those we have heard about in widely read social science studies such as those I mentioned earlier, most notably Stanley Milgram's and Philip Zimbardo's. The former is often referred to as "Milgram's 'Eichmann' study"; the latter, as "the Stanford prison experiment." Both experiments have entered mainstream consciousness as demonstrating that perfectly ordinary people become willing and able to do thoroughly nasty things to other people when in an authoritarian situation—as when an eminent university professor tells you to administer what is staged to appear a very painful shock to another person as part of an experiment; or you are enacting the role of a prison guard, or supervisor, as in Milgram and Zimbardo's studies, respectively. These researchers' groundbreaking works are more complex than that: I am here working with popular understandings, with the "takeaway" phrases that have clustered with "the banality of evil," after being reduced to *obedience to authority* and variants that are to account for our propensity to take on and fully play out whatever social role we are given, including harming other people when authority tells, or a system allows, us to.

Blurred together with such likewise crucial and now common notions, I fear that *the banality of evil* is itself becoming a banality, a cliché, in ways that gut the force of all these realizations. Mainstream press and commentators on the news use these phrases almost glibly, albeit in stentorian tones. The more thoughtful make it evident that they know any such conceptual labels need to be explained, but their explanations tend to be perfunctory. In general, what they tell us is close to what I said just now: that "the banality of evil" means that "ordinary people," and not just Grand Villains, are capable of doing excessive harm.

That is not wrong, but by itself it is utterly inadequate if taken to be an answer we can just add to our stock with no examination of what it does if taken seriously. What, for instance, might "ordinary life" mean if we take that statement seriously? It blends with the common knowledge we have mentioned before, that people are mixtures of good and bad, leaving out of account how very much harder it is to understand how an ordinary human being can also do things that are *Prime Evil.* It also slides toward a notion that *collective responsibility* can be used to reduce individual responsibility unto the vanishing point. *Well, we're all capable of it. . . .* The corollary is not stated but there it is: *so this person, this act . . . well, nothing so special. Could have been you or me.* And then? *Forgive and forget, as I would want others to do for me. . . ?*

As popularly understood, collective responsibility and collective guilt together create an appealing position that acknowledges guilt, but keeps it from turning us inward and isolating us, leaving us alone with our own consciences and responsibility. It gives us company (as the plague did for Camus' character who welcomed it because it meant he was no longer the only one under indictment), and that is a fine way to avoid those dark nights of the soul in which we take account of our lives. So, many people today may rather easily shrug and say, *Yes, "the banality of evil." That racist group: well, we're not exempt, any of us.* That feels good because it doesn't "demonize," and it does recognize and rather nobly, if without any consequences whosoever, seem to share responsibility, to clarify that we know we are not perfect either (as if that were at issue).

But move in close, and we cannot sustain that. Step outside the already clichéd "We're all capable" in order to think afresh. Try this—find out that your loving uncle spent thirty years torturing and killing squirrels in his basement to rid the world of this vermin, and you will not just say, *Ah, yes: we are all capable of that.* With our minds stopped before even more extreme horror, however, we do sometimes use undifferentiated categorical terms. I assure you, though, that, *We are all alike, all "little Eichmanns,"* is not what Hannah Arendt meant. She was struck by how extreme was his thoughtlessness, his enclosure within conventions, clichés, system languages. This kind of avoidance of demonizing Nazis, other virulent racists, exploiters of desperate workers, can be as useless in helping us understand and act effectively as imagining them to be radically different from the rest of humanity in their unmatched monstrousness. It is not an either/or judgment, monster or nonentity, that we need. We are called to think more carefully than that.

ADOLF EICHMANN, SADDAM HUSSEIN

The headline of the veteran reporter John F. Burns' report on Saddam Hussein's trial in Baghdad was "Judgment Days: From Banality to Audacity." I will quote from the piece at length; it has several strands of interest for us here. Burns wrote:

> During Saddam Hussein's remorseless harangues from the dock last week, one
> spectator sitting in the glassed-off viewing galleries found his mind moving

back more than 40 years, to a court in another Middle Eastern country where a man accused of mass murder stood on trial for his life.

The man was Adolf Eichmann, and the venue of the court was Jerusalem. His was a trial memorialized by Hannah Arendt's famous phrase, in *The New Yorker*, about the banality of evil—Eichmann was an almost pitiable figure, a man so ordinary when stripped of the trappings of fear and power, who in fact saw himself as so ordinary, that he seemed quite out of proportion to the slaughter of millions in which he had been among the most lethal practitioners.

In Baghdad, Mr. Hussein has been monstrous in his lack of pity for sobbing witnesses and their tales of torture, rape and execution in the gulag fashioned to sustain his power. Day after day, until he refused to attend at all, he commanded the court to attend to the outrages committed against himself—as a captive of the American "occupiers" and as a man who for 30 years had been "your leader," as he admonished the chief prosecutor, and synonymous with Iraq.

But pitiable he has not been. Tragic, perhaps, in the sense of a man incapable of the repentance that might lend him at least a glimmer of humanity in this, the extreme passage of his life; wildly deluded, too, in his insistence that he is Iraq's legitimate ruler. . . .

But of a reduction like Eichmann's, to a figure so commonplace, so insignificant, that he seemed inadequate to his grotesque place in history, there has been no sign.[19]

Even John Burns has misunderstood. The evil Arendt called "banal" after observing Eichmann's trial does not refer to the deportment or style of dress, nor to the self-perceptions of the person presenting himself through these as well as other enactments of self. That oddly theatrical reading of character suggests the old romanticized notion, the idea—perhaps actually the hope—that *those people* are so radically other than you and me that it must show, no matter how cleverly they try to hide it. Eichmann was not remotely, let alone "almost," "pitiable." Indeed, people rarely speak of "bureaucrats" or "bureaucracy" with anything but scorn unto contempt, even if they themselves work at an office, or in a cubicle, in a large organization. Would you pity a dry, tight, self-absorbed, bumblingly inarticulate, self-contradictory man whose bureaucratic skills and ambitions were key to what made the extremely difficult work of murdering millions of people possible? If he seemed inadequate to deeds as horrific as his actually were, that is not grounds for the kind of pity we feel for someone who has blundered into bad deeds, who somehow got in "over his head," or fell into "bad ways" after being badly treated herself. Eichmann was good at what he did, and ambitious, not reluctant.

An impulse to pity can express a need to understand something that we are still trying to comprehend, something that sends us in quest of concepts and familiar emotions ready to hand. When we find one—*The poor unfortunate child; the wounded; the lost soul; the man in over his head*—it can protect us from really dealing with the person before us. If this is not within your own direct experience, ask anyone with a temporary or lifelong disability if people who pity them are open to who they really are. But pity could be a call to stop and think, and think again, if it moves us to try, as the philosopher Immanuel Kant put it, to think in someone else's place. Yes, *think*, not only unreflectively *feel*. Arendt was not inviting us to feel for Eichmann when she observed his extreme thoughtlessness, his need for "edifying phrases," for cliché: she was observing a radical failure of thinking, of a basic human capacity for freedom. And when we renounce our capacity for freedom, we are also effectively trying to escape responsibility.

OUT OF TOUCH

What seems more useful as a thought-line in comparing Adolf Eichmann and Saddam Hussein is that Eichmann, however differently he comported himself at his trial, like Saddam Hussein was startlingly, radically out of touch with the realities of his victims as well as his prosecutors. While Saddam went on claiming to be the Iraqis' leader and demanding a kind of respect a defeated tyrant in chains cannot realistically expect, Eichmann went on worrying that he had not been promoted within the Nazi hierarchy as he felt he should have been, even as he, too, was on trial for his life.

The man who captured Eichmann in Argentina also had the chance to talk with him while he was being held captive before being spirited out of the country. "What was I hoping to hear?" Peter Malkin asks himself. "Even I didn't know. Maybe a trace of real sorrow, a sense that he felt something about it beyond regret at getting caught. . . . But, never, not once, did the man convey anything but the feeling that everything he had done was absolutely appropriate. Not nice necessarily, or even reasonable, but absolutely correct in context. There was a job to do and he did it."[20] It is that bizarre out-of-touch quality so startling in both Saddam Hussain and Adolf Eichmann, these doers of terrible deeds, that should, I believe, help us see what they share despite their vast differences in style as well as the different levels of power they achieved in their times and places.

But knowing as we do that these men had all too sustained, real, deadly effects in the world, how can I say that they were *out of touch*? That, too, seems utterly inadequate. A temptation then is to equate "out of touch" with "insane," or in contemporary parlance, "sick," which would at least seem to be on a scale somewhat more commensurate with their actions, and is increasingly often where we go when we cannot fathom how someone could otherwise have done what they did. Students in my moral philosophy classes often say, when confronted with an example of someone who has done something truly cruel, "That's just too weird!" When I try to explore that (wondering if there is a moral sentiment there: *weird* meaning in such usage morally troubling and inexplicable), often their next categorical choice turns out to be "sick."

But insane people cannot be as effective as Saddam Hussein and Adolf Eichmann were. Their being out of touch with the meaning of their actions to other people, with the meanings of many other people beyond their immediate circles, did not hinder, it helped them do what they did. This does not feel like banality, but a main function and effect of banalities is just that: to protect us from being in touch with realities, as sometimes instead of being overawed by the magnificence of a mountain range stark against a pale and distant sky, we see a picture-postcard image and so experience the merely picturesque rather than the sublime.[21]

SELF-CENTERED

Those who are not thinking about what they are doing are often concerned about themselves. They can also get their feelings hurt when the world fails to see them as they see themselves and, because they remain out of touch, keep trying to tell their side of the story—or, as Eichmann also did, adopt the conventional terms of the charges against them, as if, Arendt suggests, he was still showing people what a good team player he was. People who are not thinking can do such startling things because they are not imagining how they might sound to other people. That requires thinking, and specifically what the philosopher Immanuel Kant called for in his *Critique of Judgment*: developing "an enlarged mentality" by practicing thinking in the place of others.

Saddam Hussein and Adolf Eichmann's "self-centeredness," in an extreme but apt sense of the term, can also seem startlingly petty, ordinary, not something we expect of people who have done truly monstrous things. It seems utterly inadequate to say that Idi Amin or Eugene de Kock or a school shooter were "self-centered," no? But Saddam Hussein could and did listen to wrenching stories from devastated, sobbing witnesses without taking in their realities. By his lights, he already knew who they were, what they were, what they meant to him, and that is what he persisted in trying to tell the Court: his view, his reality, his position. If anyone was not being listened to, or was misunderstood, it was, to Saddam's mind, evidently he himself, thence his anger, his sulks, his tirades. Eichmann apparently was not at all dissimilar either during the trial or in doing his evil work before it, despite the fact that he, an underling unlike Saddam, tried to go along with superiors, rather than ordering everyone around, although he did that, too, when he was the more powerful one: it was all a matter of roles, hierarchy, whatever doing his job required, and allowed. And, in captivity still in Argentina, Eichmann responded to hearing about the fate of his guard's sister—the Nazis murdered her and her children—by falling abruptly silent, and then asking, pitifully, if Malkin was going to kill *him*.

Both, bizarre as it may seem, showed us during their trials that what caught, held, and dominated their attention was almost exclusively their own efforts to be treated rightly by the world, to get what was theirs, to be respected for the hard workers they actually were. Both got easily aggrieved on their own behalf. No, I do not mean that they were narcissists or any other diagnostic type, similar as they may seem. How many narcissists could do what either of these men did? Although one of the best studies I know, Elisabeth Young-Bruehl's *Anatomy of Prejudices*, shows a way to make use of psychoanalytic categories within historical, political situations that enable differing psychological pathologies in particular ways, I fear that diagnostic categories too readily serve as another way of avoiding attentiveness particularly when applied to historical individuals the analyst has never met, or interviewed, let alone analyzed. We diagnose, and that is that: done. Nothing more to comprehend politically, morally. *Torturers? They're all psychopaths.*

A CONTINUUM OF ATTENTIVENESS

Eichmann and Saddam could together be said to mark the extreme end of a continuum of attentiveness to the realities we can experience. At their end, there is obtuse, closed refusal to recognize as significant anything but what one has already categorized, encapsulated, settled with regard to oneself and demands it might make on one. On the other end, we take in—we sense, perceive, apprehend something, someone—with full consciousness. We reflect respectfully, remaining open to new encounters, to the uniqueness even of the familiar. Imagine being in the country, falling silent and coming, slowly, to hear sounds you have never paused to listen to. Imagine interviewing a person you have disliked for years but never before really listened to. Imagine hearing her, staying with what she says, trying to discern what she is wanting to mean. We may then find ourselves with new insight, shifting categories, reconfiguring interpretations that continue to unfold: thinking, and not merely sorting through possibly applicable categories. Reaching for fresh language, too, as poets may.

On the encapsulated end, we do not take in: rather, we put out onto the world what we have already decided, foreclosing any possibility of encountering uniqueness, whether of the familiar or, indeed, of the radically strange that ought to capture our attention. This end of the attentiveness continuum is too easy to imagine: we all have prejudices, prejudgments, that keep us from meeting the actual person who looks like a "kind" of person that, say, we believe to be more prone to violence, or stupider, or smarter than we are. But daily, most of us move back and forth along the continuum, differing in how characteristically attentive or inattentive we are. We also differ as the work we do rewards or punishes unoriginal thinking, or as the times in which we live do, in how far toward the extremes we go, and how persistently we stay there.

What was unusual about Eichmann was not that he (like Stangl, the Commandant of Treblinka as we earlier found, and the Hutu *genocidaire*) could sometimes be out of touch with the realities of what he did, but that he appeared before, during, and after his trial to be *unable* to relate to the world attentively, to think at all if "without a bannister." Arendt saw him as filtering through conventions and clichés to figure out what he was supposed to do when he was on trial for his life rather than sending other people to theirs. His captor, Peter Malkin, reports several quite astonishing examples: Eichmann keeping his eyes shut when they finally removed the blindfold used during the actual capture—until ordered to open them, which he then did immediately; Eichmann refusing to eat when offered food until, again, ordered and only then hungrily doing so; even, Eichmann awaiting permission, for which he did not ask, to relieve himself. I join my students here: this is *weird*. And it is of a piece with the man who went on arranging for the death of Jews even as the war had been lost and other Nazis were preparing to pretend no such thing had been done, or if it had, they were not responsible. Eichmann was an extremely reliable worker, quick to obey but, once sure of his job, seems to have been capable of doing it on his own. In the game of being a prisoner, that meant doing what you are told, and only that.

This is how conceptual banality works: like the kudzu plant, it spreads quickly over the surface until there appears to be an eerie quilt over landscapes once defined by their differing plant life, the contours of their ground. It is hard, then, for anything new or different to make its way through into the sunlight and air.

Arendt reported that, standing under the gallows on the day of his own execution, Eichmann delivered himself of edifying words appropriate for someone else's funeral. He needed conventions and clichés to know what to think, what to say; lacking any such things for a gallows speech, let alone his own, his mind produced eloquent words suited for death. Close enough for him: he gave his speech without being startled back into attentiveness and thought even by his own imminent death. Arendt writes: "That such remoteness from reality and such thoughtlessness can wreak more havoc than all the evil instincts taken together, which, perhaps, are inherent in man—that was, in fact, the lesson one could learn in Jerusalem."

And then, to keep us thinking, she wrote, "But it was a lesson, neither an explanation of the phenomenon nor a theory about it."[22]

We are not, then, done with *the banality of evil.* We need now to focus on how daily clichés, conventions, and other ways of going on autopilot can actually do the not-so-easy task of disabling our minds, and so our consciences.

Chapter Three

Changing Minds

There is no one sort of banality; almost anything can become banal if we use it so often that it prefigures the world for us without our even noticing anymore. Not only clichés and conventions: insider jargon, technical terms, field-specific logics, and scientific, political, military, economic, psychological, religious, and other domain-defining categories can function as entrance requirements to our attention. Thus, Lakeesha becomes *an ADHD kid*; a Christian named Maria becomes *an infidel*; a friend who gets fired becomes *a loser*; a nation becomes *the enemy;* a whole generation becomes *millennials*; all unhappy families become *dysfunctional*; destroying communities in pursuit of more profit becomes *creative destruction.* There is so much we need not think about once we have used the right conventional or technical term, and there are so many people who will reward us with their attention if we use code words that show we too are insiders and ready to chat safely within the fences of our proudly shared expertise. None of this is unusual, and indeed it has its functions; that is why it is a ubiquitous human phenomenon.

In extreme instances, however, we know that we humans can shift our minds into making sense of and accepting things that, before we became insiders of utterly distorted systems, we would have found impossible to imagine ourselves approving of, let alone doing. Among other evidence, we know this by the sheer number of people involved in carrying out genocides, slavery, colonialism, exploitative labor practices, child pornography, sex trafficking, and other profoundly shocking harms. After the fact, if we survive and become able to look back on ourselves or on what others did, we might well say to those who were not there and are now judging those times and actions, *Well, but that's not how we thought of it. We were so obsessed by [whatever—perhaps, serving the Queen and her Empire; now, going global; growing the economy; joining the one percent; developing the latest big thing]*

41

that we did things we'd never ordinarily do. We were just part of something. We never meant to do harm. Even that can be hard to say, heartfelt, and in its way, accurate. It is, however, neither an adequate explanation nor an excuse.

It is, rather, an arrow pointing at the heart of our inquiry. How was it *possible* to avoid thinking and reflecting about what you were doing when you actually were murdering, inflicting harm, using people up and tossing them away to profit a few, demeaning people on whose service your good life depended? It ought not to have been. To those never tested by direct experience with radically unjust, violative systems, it is genuinely hard to imagine, and so to believe, that *They didn't know.* Or, *They didn't mean it.* But it is not only possible, it is to be found offered as some kind of excuse throughout testimony gathered in trials, memoirs, in conversations, and in interviews of all sorts of people who are later held to account. Here is one we have already met, Commandant Franz Stangl, in charge of a Nazi extermination camp, when asked years later how he could have continued his work after, as he had admitted, he knew—could no longer avoid knowing—about the thousands upon thousands already murdered as ever more trains into which Jewish people had been forced kept arriving, said, "Yes, that's what we know now, what we can say now. But then?"[1] Another deadly meaning for "the unknown known."

Experientially, how can we be functionally unaware of what we do know? We do not seem to be encountering something held in the inaccessible reaches of the unconscious. There are connections. *Not being aware* of *what we cannot avoid perceiving* is itself an act of consciousness, and cannot be done once and for all—or, if it is, has become a pathology that lessens effectiveness, and we are asking about people who did indeed do their jobs, often well enough by then dominant standards.

TRANSITIONING

A survivor of the Rwandan genocide suggests with his testimony that being radically out of touch with what you are doing even as you continue to do it can be practiced beforehand. "Innocent" (that really is his name) says of the killer of his family:

> I've known him since our school days, and we later became colleagues and friends since we were both teachers. [Even when] we were in opposing camps . . . that did not prevent us from sharing a Primus [beer] and some laughs.
> Still, as I said before, his character changed completely after January. If I came into our neighborhood *cabaret*, he'd stop talking until I left. If our paths crossed, he would change direction and look away. . . . We hadn't quarreled

about anything. . . . He preferred putting in hours at closed meetings with influential people.

What I think now is that he didn't know the tiny details of the genocide, such as the day and the exact agenda. But he certainly knew three months in advance that he was going to kill me, and my wife and my child, with whom he had shared pleasant times.[2]

And so the killer-to-be moved to the extreme end of the attentiveness continuum, taking in what he was told at closed meetings in order to *not see* his friend even when he was indeed right there, before his very eyes. As we have reminded ourselves, experientially this is actually not at all easy, and it is also common where great harm is done. There are many observations from Germany too about changes in social relations as their system was being turned so very wrong. It does take time to go from thinking of a man as a good drinking buddy to seeing him as someone you are going to kill without flinching, which I have been forced by now to think may well be far more common than recategorizing your old friend as Other, as a cockroach, as a lower life form. Those are in effect cover stories; the killer-to-be can and often does know perfectly well that that person, "those people," are friends, neighbors, fellow citizens, professionals—which, I venture to say, cannot readily be said of cockroaches.

Studying historical instances of evildoing, we can, however, see changes being made in speech, often initially through propaganda, that, as they take and spread, begin to change peoples' perceptions, thence feelings, and finally actions toward others. Consider, for example, blaming the to-be-victim by speaking of her/him as part of an international plot against you and your kind; always preceding references with belittling, or worse, terms such as "primitive," "depraved," "lazy," "corrupt," "sneaky," "parasitic," "animalistic"; denigrating not solely one individual, but his/her "kind" usually marked as such by race, class, sex/gender, ethnicity, religion, mental capacity, these being the "kinds" all too ready for such use, carrying their own histories of unjust hierarchies within them as they do. Still, when you are faced with an old friend, no matter what dehumanizing term you have learned to call him, what does it take to murder him, close in, while actually looking at him? Slave drivers knew the individuals who were enslaved; they worked, whipped, killed people whose faces and names they knew. Bosses who worked, and work, children for long hours can also hand out toys for Christmas, celebrate Diwali with them, recognize and call the children by name. What does it take to see people like that, and continue violating their bodies, hearts and souls, their minds, their standing as fellow humans?

They often used machetes in Rwanda; in Nazi Germany the *einsatzgruppen*, mobile killing squads, in some cases started out using pistols, close-up, even face to face, shooting people one by one. Those who sell children into service equivalent to slavery today? They see those children; sometimes they are their own. In "honor killings," men kill their own daughters, sisters.

I regret pressing this point, but I have found that if I do not, we avoid it by moving to abstract explanations too quickly. I understand that. How could I not? But our explanations have done nothing to lessen the outbreaks of the plagues of massive harm. Surely we have to keep trying.

We remain challenged to move in close enough to discern how peoples' minds are and are not working, making sense of and carefully interpreting as acceptable the egregious acts by which they ought to be utterly appalled as they prepare to do them—beforehand, but also anew each day. Aspects of our question unfold: How are vices turned into virtues, virtues into vices? How are realities turned into pale, wan things with no unavoidable claim to recognition? How can an adult personally and repeatedly, with breaks in between to go home, to see children, friends, neighbors, continue to slaughter children, seeing *Catholics, Protestants, Tutsis, Jews, Armenians, Gypsies, blacks, Muslims, Infidels, enemies, cockroaches* (categories, from the polite to the insulting), but also just plain people, including people the killer knows, people evidently like those the killer knows, people with whom eye contact can often be made, people the killer had many friendly beers with, people who are known *not* to be radically different, inferior, people who can speak, cry, bleed?

When I asked a Rwandan at an international conference on genocide how the Hutu knew who was a Tutsi and who was not, he said, *Oh, that wasn't hard. We were neighbors; we knew each other.* Mostly all were Catholic, too, and spoke the same language. There had been a lot of intermarriage. Despite deeply troubled relations at differing times, these were not people who had alienated themselves from each other to such an extent that they did not know their neighbors were real people, and individuals. Remember the earlier quote from the man who told his wife about the old man he had killed that day? The killer knew the man, had nothing against him, killed him, and told his wife, who also remembered the old man. They had dinner, and slept. He did not see that old man as some disgusting animal or someone he had learned to have something against, worthy of killing him. He just did it, did his job—as, he told his interviewer, did the South African Eugene de Kock, the one called "Prime Evil." As did Eichmann and Stangl—and thousands and thousands more.

Those who do the work of violating others even unto death are not entirely unprepared: there was a lead in, a transitional time, for many of them (as, importantly, we will also see when we turn to reflecting on the doing of great good: preparation, lead-in time, can be crucial there too). The man who was getting ready to murder his old friend, "Innocent," among many others, "preferred," in the time leading up to the genocide, "putting in hours at closed

meetings with influential people" (as we have heard). In a quite literal sense, he chose to resocialize himself in order to be, as he saw it, ready to be on the "winning side." Notice that, whether or not he had heard those with whom he aligned himself call people he knew "cockroaches," there is no evidence that he was on a personally motivated killing spree to rid the world of them. He had chosen sides, and he wanted his side to win since that is, indeed, why he chose to join it. Unfortunately, his old friend was on what he now, preemptively, thought of as the losing side. He was not thinking about what he was going to do in a direct, attentive way. He was thinking about those meetings and the powerful people he liked hanging around with, and he looked forward to being rewarded for his troubles.

In part III, we will look far more carefully at what can shift and how it occurs in times of transition from, let us say for now, friendship or neutrality to a deadly absence of mind. I have to mark as with a deep red dye a strand of the weave that has reemerged here, as it will throughout, though. The statement, which we have no reason to disbelieve or discredit experientially, that *It was my job, and I did it*, recurs hauntingly, along with some not uncommon corollaries, a taste for status, ambition, money. As I said, when times are changing, the usually small everyday vices and virtues can make all the difference. They do so for good as well as for ill: we will explore that too.

REVERSING

Faced with many such examples, I have discovered that there is a great deal to learn from my reversal of Arendt's concept as a way to go deeper into the on-the-ground meanings of *the banality of evil*. It holds before us *the lack of congruence between monstrous acts and the petty people who do them, between the horrors of plague and its cause, a mere bacillus*. And then, well before we get to the actual doing of evil when systems have gone bad, we encounter and have to face up to *the evil of banality* that makes so many of us vulnerable to being thus changed.

Here, too, we have to reflect on meanings. Neither of these phrases—*the banality of evil, the evil of banality*—at first seems quite right by our more common use of these words, as reactions to Arendt's concept keep making evident. There is nothing at all "banal" about what we want to mean by "evil," and it seems absurd to attribute "evil" to the "banal." The faith that there is a moral, epistemological, and ontological chasm between the dully ordinary and the monstrous extraordinary recurs here, as it does every step of the way. We cannot just change our minds about that once and be done with it. Arendt herself, as we have seen, struggled for decades to understand the insight that she shared with her teacher and friend, the philosopher Karl Jaspers. Ways of thinking that I believe can turn out to function as a kind of excuse—key among which is the conviction that evil is by definition and always radical—persist because they do work for us.

In good enough times and places, unreflective assumptions, including those we make about the chasm between good and evil but hardly it alone, shield us from the tiring daily demands of realities on our attentiveness, and so from a felt need for moral reflection. In rotten times, unreflective assumptions shield us from the searing realities with which even silence makes us complicit—and right there, in such shielding in good as in rotten times, lies a germ of their complicity with the evildoing that requires many of us to happen at all.

We are all, if to varying degrees, practiced in avoiding awareness of things that might divert our attention from a task, irritate us, trouble us emotionally, challenge us morally. We practice allotting our attention daily. If we did not, we would find it hard to get through a day, to do our jobs, to focus on a friend, a child, learning a new computer skill, deciding whether to do this rather than that in response to a friend's need.

We are also therefore all too able to see in the first dead rat in the street nothing but a bother, an embarrassment to our establishment, another sign of the ineptitude of our municipal service providers. Even if the rat spewed blood from its mouth, staggered, died at our feet, and evidently ought to have caught our full attention, we can manage to keep walking and remember it later only as a bit of gossip to tell a friend over coffee so we can enjoy sharing a *frisson* of shock.

A German diarist, the linguist Klemperer mentioned earlier, attuned to observing even small shifts in meaning, wrote one day early in the rise of the Nazis, but *not* before there was evidence of their brutality: "On the way home from the theater, [I] noticed a colleague who was 'anything but a Nazi' wearing a discreet swastika lapel pin. Why? I asked. 'Well! Why not? I'm no risk-taker.'"[3]

When the majority of basically decent people do not refuse to go along with the early small changes by means of which regimes, social orders, cultures, economic systems, historical eras, religions take over definitional power of "good," of "decent," of "ordinary," a very dangerous slide has already begun. There is no awareness, no judgment—or, awareness is only as processed through no longer apt categories, and thus no effective judgment. As in Camus' tale of a city struck by the plague, most of us, forced finally to see what is happening, then call on the kinds of judgment we have learned to depend on—as Camus' character, Father Paneloux, judges the plague to be the act of a just God winnowing the good from the bad among his flock.

Thinking about *thoughtlessness;* the *out of touch* end of the thinking continuum; the role of clichés, conventions, insider concepts, prejudgment categories; people accepting early, lead-in system changes; deflected awareness—these together suggest a relation of *banality* and *evil* at *all* times.

This—the implication of what seem very small things with the worst of all—brings us to the very heart of the matter.

THE HEART OF THE MATTER

Having dramatically said that, I have to observe that in the dominant tradition of the West, we want the "heart of the matter" to be almost anything other than thinking or its opposite, thoughtlessness. Pale and wan, thinking, is it not? Really not the sort of thing that could possibly enable good, strengthen us to go against the grain of a difficult world, let alone in its absence as thoughtlessness actually enable evil. We need to change hearts, not minds, not thinking, to make people really care for each other, the environment, justice, peace, do we not? Perhaps I have gone off on the wrong track.

I am often asked, *Why do you not speak of love? Isn't that what really matters?*

I do invoke love and its failures sometimes, but not, in any case, without a whole lot of attention to thinking. Thinking is how we make sense of what is happening, what is before our eyes, in our memories, in our hearts and bodies. It is the activity of consciousness, of awareness, and we cannot develop consciences that attune us well to the world and others if we are unaware of—inattentive to—our thinking. Nor, when we become aware, can conscience develop further to become illuminating (if never a certain guide) without reflexivity and reflection, without our being thoughtful even about our own thinking.

Love and care can go as wrong as reason when we are not thinking, being attentive, reflecting. We are as responsible for thinking about our feelings as about anything else. "I loved . . ."; "I hated . . ."; "I desired . . ."; "I feared . . .": these are every bit as complex, or superficial; clichéd, or profound; apt, or wildly inappropriate as any other report from our consciousness we might make. Feelings too can be the result of inattentiveness; unthought-through, they too can be banal—and deadly. Both Eichmann and Stangl spoke to their interviewers about their lack of hatred for Jews, of their respect and fondness for some people who were Jewish. Stangl, out of touch as he was, even got his feelings hurt when a young Jewish man he thought was a "nice boy" when he knew him as a forced worker held in Treblinka later testified against him. These Nazi murderers seem to have thought their lack of personal hatred for their victims mattered, and that people needed to understand that about them.

I would suggest that having felt respect, friendship, fondness for people who were Jewish when that was a death sentence they themselves were carrying out helped them do their job with a clearer conscience and contributed to protecting them from the overwhelming guilt, and the shame, they so strikingly did not feel afterwards. They felt themselves to be good people. They had not descended into ugly, crass hatred of their victims; they make a point of telling us about the crude men they encountered who *did* hate, marking themselves as superior. Morally superior. Because they continued to have the feelings of decent folks while they did horrific harm. No, I do not think feelings, including love, are a more reliable prod to moral reflection and action than attentive, reflective, free thinking.

THOUGHT EXPERIMENTS

What were they thinking, those white medical establishment people, when black men, never told what was going on, were used as research subjects infected with a deadly virus? (I am making a thought experiment but yes, there is history here: the Tuskegee syphilis experiment.) What were they thinking when each of those individual men who had been turned into experimental subjects without knowing it was met by other individuals carrying out the work of the study? When food went from that real hand to that other, known person's hand every day, with exchanges of pleasantries, what was the one who was fed, the one who knew, thinking? When researchers came to know each other, laughed together, kept public silence about key provisions of their research through the years that the research stretched on, what were they thinking, each of them, all of them, those who funded them, those who read their reports, those who actually knew, and those who suspected?

What were we thinking when we felt exultant and cheered on hearing reports of deaths, of massive destruction to a densely inhabited city halfway across the world (consider "shock and awe," and Baghdad), in the same way we cheer ourselves on in video games when we zap The Enemy? If we had been thinking of—not about, but *of, with*—what was actually happening, actually being done, really being experienced by individuals, how many of us would still have cheered, whether we approved of the war or not?

What were we thinking when they worked on an explosive device capable of obliterating huge numbers of individual human beings, each and all unique and irreplaceable? Many people have worked on those atomic and then nuclear bombs, from eminent scientists to those who fed the workers at the research facilities, and their families. Many people in the surrounding communities, public officials, congresspeople who funded them knew. *How did they all manage thoughts about what it would actually do to people and places and the future of warfare and the world in which such things are possible?*

It takes some time to do these things. It takes concentration, effort, sometimes great skill. What do we think about as we do things in our labs, at our desks and computers? What do we think of our work over lunch, at the end of a hardworking day? We should ask ourselves those questions; we can also ask them of others, from apparent bystanders to the highly visible agents and leaders of great wrongdoing.

How we think and how we avoid thinking about what we are doing are always relevant moral questions. Jobs do not exempt us: a paycheck is not a moral pass. Neither is a cause we consider good.

Consider this: "In wartime Berlin, Hitler's chief architect and director of armaments production, Albert Speer, would pass large groups of forlorn people standing at the local railway station. He chose not to think about the terrible fate that awaited them. Years later, he recalled, 'I had a sense of somber goings-on. But I was rooted in the principles of the regime to an extent that I find hard to understand today.'"[4]

In the present and then the future, looking back, when we continue radically to divide extraordinary human actions from ordinary ones we may be acquiescing in a willed failure to comprehend, just as Speer and so very many others did in the many daily moments of the doing of what we now, as if it were one, singular, sudden, all at once thing, call "the Holocaust."

The extraordinary, the ordinary: they pull away from each other as if mutually repellant, opposite in their very being, but failure to try to comprehend the smallest of steps, the conceptual blinks that daily allow us to shut out what is right there before us can go hand in hand with failure to figure out what it is that makes an individual, a group, a nation ultimately responsible. And if we do not keep trying to locate responsibility more aptly and justly, we also cannot continue trying to understand how to keep extraordinary actions, extensive evils, from once again gaining purchase among us, in our ordinary lives, and not just off there, among Others. Nor can we notice what happens to the few who do ask questions, who will not just go along, most of whom never become whistle blowers or rebels but just quietly say, *I can't do* that, and quit, or are fired, leaving their colleagues a bit more anxious about their own jobs and so, perhaps, even less willing to stop and think. Doing good is also more than a matter of feeling.

Chapter Four

Escaping Explanations, Excuses

There is a catch-22 right at the heart of what we are doing through this inquiry that I do have to pause to recognize. I have found that when I speak about genocides and other "unthinkable" human-perpetrated horrors, there are a familiar few, user-friendly conceptual categorizations I hear people muttering to themselves or dropping into a comment or question addressed to me after my talk. Some but not all come from the key thinkers in this area I have already mentioned. Unfortunately, even those important categories can be turned into clichés that stop, rather than activate, our minds. The concepts and phrases I use, too, the ones that both capture what I have found and can be used to illuminate other situations as categories can—especially *the evil of banality, the continuum of attentiveness, thinking, mindlessness, thoughtlessness, out of touch*; and those not yet introduced, *being on time* and, notably, *extensive evil, intensive evil* and *extensive good, intensive good*— are not exempt from being used for precisely the opposite function than that for which they are intended. We are capable of turning anything into a cliché, jargon, a banality. Since we cannot do without categories, it is crucial that we remember that their use is for thinking, no more, no less. This is one of the reasons one can be very knowledgeable and still thoughtless: categories are achievements and building blocks for knowledge. *Ah, yes: that is a microaggression.* Done; we know what it is. But at first that was a fresh term that made us think about and not just with it, and such categorizations can always be questioned, refreshed again, if the knowledgeable do not enclose their turf. To be both knowledgeable and in touch with our messy, changing worlds, the point is precisely not to settle and contain thinking by invoking familiar categories but, on the contrary, to startle us back into thought, to inform and renew thinking.

When we are actually thinking, we will not fall back into concepts that can block us from apprehending reality, from being open to experiences, because thinking, as Hannah Arendt puts it, *unfreezes concepts*—even those we have discovered, or created, ourselves. After citing the philosopher Immanuel Kant's observation that "our mind has a natural aversion" to accepting even its own conclusions as settled once and for all, Arendt says:

> From which it follows that the business of thinking is like Penelope's web; it undoes every morning what it has finished the night before. For the need to think can never be stilled by allegedly definite insights of "wise men"; it can be satisfied only through thinking, and the thoughts I had yesterday will satisfy this need today only to the extent that I want and am able to think them anew.[1]

Please excuse me, then, if I seem to repeat myself: I am not assuming you did not understand the first time. I am turning concepts this way and that, revisiting them, unfreezing them, so as to keep thinking with, about, through them. In quest of, and to keep practicing, fresh thinking, I am trying to avoid just adding another couple of conceptual pens to our mental holding areas.

CATCH-ALL PHRASES

Here are several of the ways I have found people responding to, *How could they?* None are wrong; they have their significant uses. As always, the issue is whether we use them to stop thinking or to further and keep it going.

Compartmentalization is common among these explanations: *Ah, yes. You are talking about* compartmentalizing. *We all do that, put what we are doing over here, in this box, as if it has nothing to do with anything else. That's how we avoid guilt.* Quite right, but when we have said, *Ah, that's compartmentalizing,* we have not yet done anything more than capture a flock of meanings in an already-labeled pen. We may not have thought much as we did so, nor continued thinking carefully afterwards. It is an irony approaching a catch-22—but also the moral conceptual heart of the matter—that the very effort we make to understand can protect us from doing so, as we have noted in today's misuse and overuse of "the banality of evil" that threatens to reduce even that startling concept to a banality.

On occasion, someone recurs to a very different sort of prepackaged category such as ***original sin***. More often than to religion, though, at least in comments made out loud in the secular settings in which I am more likely to be talking about these matters, people turn to the sciences that may stand in for religions as authorities on human nature for a lot of people today. *Genetics* are invoked, for example, sometimes as used by evolutionary psychologists. In neither case, "original sin" or "genetics," am I sure what the speaker means, and I fear that when I ask, I have most often encountered a retreat to the authority of religion or science rather than efforts to understand. For example, I hear that so-frequent phrase, "studies show," with no further information concerning *which* studies, by *whom, when, under what conditions*, let alone information that might give us a chance to evaluate the pertinence, soundness, scope of their findings. I will risk saying that "studies show" is thus akin to multiple variants of, "The minister/the sacred book says." Authority has spoken; we can stop thinking.

It's original sin, or, *It's genetics, et al* may satisfy our desire for something not only authoritative but neatly causal, insofar as both are understood as naming something that unavoidably and significantly shapes who we become, what we do. These satisfactions are also problematic, though. Without some knowledgeable theological or scientific discussion, what we are left with is another excuse available to anyone, anywhere, no matter what: *They did it because humans are weak and sinful creatures; they did it because they were genetically programmed, because we are hard-wired to—say, fear The Other.* We have then in one leap sailed right over the whole realm of human mind, choice, responsibility, not to mention the universe of our differences.

More commonly, though, I hear, **They were just following orders**, which carries with it as a given, **because they had to, were afraid, would have been killed had they not**, all of which is to say, **They did it because they had to.** This one also worries me because it so evidently denies choice and so also responsibility. In truth, although someone can threaten me with death if I do not murder my child, they have tempted rather than forced me to do something very wrong. I may not be required by ethics, law, or my society to do so, but I *could* choose to refuse.[2] Furthermore, it is not even factually the case that everyone—or even many—of those who did the work genocide requires for the Nazis, or the Hutu in Rwanda, or anywhere else, or those who are slave drivers, or factory bosses in sweat shops, or soldiers raping and plundering, actually were under threat of death, or torture, or even, I have to say, consequential disapproval. You could not get a genocide or any of those other massive harms done if you had to provide guards with guns to force the perpetrators to do their work every day, every time. I am afraid it turns out that people will do that work for far more mundane reasons.

I hasten to add that I do not equate even evidently thoughtless uses of *the banality of evil, obedience to authority, compartmentalization* with *they did it because they had to.* It is, however, among the most common explanations I am offered, not for those at the top giving orders, of course, but for underlings with whom more of us are more likely to feel uneasily implicated.

In *Ordinary Men: Reserve Police Battalion 101 and The Final Solution in Poland*, Christopher Browning gives us access to the testimony of a policeman ordered, with his battalion, to murder Jews—not abstractly, not one of these days, not from a distance, but immediately, face to face. Without ambiguity, the policeman says:

> It was in no way the case that those who did not want to or could not carry out the shooting of human beings with their own hands could not keep themselves out of this task. No strict control was being carried out here. I therefore remained by the arriving trucks and kept myself busy at the arrival point. In any case I gave my activity such an appearance. It could not be avoided that one or another of my comrades noticed that I was not going to the executions to fire away at the victims. They showered me with remarks such as "shithead" and "weakling" to express their disgust. But I suffered no consequences for my actions. I must mention here that I was not the only one who kept himself out of participating in the executions.[3]

You see? We cannot trot out our usual generalizations to explain how they could have done it. Some actively resisted; some did not do it; some found ways to do less of it; some did it for a while and then became unable to continue; some just went on doing it, one way or another; and a few enjoyed it (and were on occasion therefore stopped from continuing: unreliable, that sort). We must not overlook the lack of coercion to murder, to exploit, to rape: there is by no means always certain, unavoidable punishment awaiting those who refuse to do so.

Painful as it is to admit, but in full awareness that there are other ways of getting people to do both bad and good things than by direct, mortal threat, *They made me do it* is not necessarily an adequate, and so not quite a credible, explanation or excuse.

Furthermore, the thing about obedience, whether by a conventionally docile soul or a strong one who has directly been coerced, is that it can be withheld, refused, rejected from one order to the next. Mere obedience is simply not reliable. As the famed military strategist and theorist Otto von Bismarck is said to have observed, *You can do anything with bayonets except sit on them.* You can take over peoples' lives and force them to do things, but you cannot then expect them to stay obedient without the provision of indubitable, constant threat for each and every one.

Everyone was doing it then. What about another familiar line, proffered not so much as a full explanation but as a kind of moral exculpation: *Everybody was doing it. Nothing special that I did too.* Well, no, everyone did not do it, as we have seen. One way or another, whatever the evil we have in mind, there were some who did not become, or remain, victimizers. As just illustrated, at some point or other—and especially when actions must be carried out over time and in many places because of their sheer scale and scope—there will be times and ways to slip out, to refuse without even taking a stand, by avoiding. How easy it is to avoid doing what one is being asked or told or invited to do at such times of course varies enormously. No easy generalizations here. Nonetheless, we do need to know that even in the belly of the beast, some do manage not to join in, and more important still, we need to realize that early on, when evils are spreading but are not yet normalized, if more people simply turned away from doing the work involved, histories would be quite different.

Hannah Arendt used to observe that soldiers and others who do the work of legitimated state violence can choose to put down their guns. Each one individually picks his/her weapon up; each individually can put it down; and the group consciousness that can encourage us to do bad, unto evil, if others are doing it can also encourage us to do good. One soldier, one guard putting down a gun can break the spell, kick individual thinking back into action. Choices with groups are not guaranteed moral, though. Officials, police, soldiers can refuse to help just as they can refuse to harm: point is, they have each and all made choices. *Everybody was doing it* is not factual. It is also never a moral argument. How many children have tried that one and heard, *If Mira stuck her hand in the fire, would you?* If we do not accept this effort at an explanation that might pass as an excuse from our children, how odd it is that we do tend to invoke it when faced with a time when great numbers of adults did terrible, terrible things.

Self-defensive fear drove them. Yes, it can—but carrying out and then perpetuating, defending the massive harms and violations that last beyond, say, conquest, as enslavement has, and colonialism, take more and other than any kind of lashing out. As Gandhi realized, fighting off protestors or revolutionaries face to face in the line of duty wears its doers out physically after the first adrenalin rush of fear and, perhaps, anger, or excitement at doing battle, wears off. British colonial officers sometimes literally became so exhausted that they had to quit beating Indian people trained in *satyagraha*, soul force, "passive resistance" (which is actually not passive at all, of course). Exhausted by fending off people who just kept coming, who walked right into range of their crowd-control weapons, the soldiers' arms dropped, they stopped, and more than before saw the people around them who were not harming them, not threatening them physically—just persisting in doing what they claimed the right to do (such as getting essential salt from free sea water). It became hard for some of those officers to go on doing their jobs. Passions can be sated, run down, become boring; the body simply wears out, the mind wanders, the spirit quails—in most of us. Not in all: there are genuine murderers (as there are secular saints) among us. They just do not suffice for sustained action on a significant scale.

These were outbursts of personal, tribal, or ethnic hatreds—or, *Those people were cold-blooded, entirely unable to feel for any other person.* I have had to set aside, with the picture of rabid haters reveling in the slaughter, visions of some equally confounding people proceeding to do great harm with no feelings at all. Systemic evils are more complicated than that, as the Nazis certainly knew, or quickly learned. Among other meanings, "the final solution" carried with it not only its central meaning—that the only way to rid the world of "the Jewish problem" was to rid the world of Jews entirely so there were no more to breed new ones, ever—but also the notion that a solution had been found to the *how* of genocidal murders that did, after all, take a toll on the killers. The gas chambers were designed to make it less difficult for the people right there who did the work of mass murder to persist. *Method* is at work here, and neither passion nor its opposite explains it.

If those who plan and benefit from such monstrous systems know that their success depends on making the work doable for ordinary people over time, surely we, whose moral sanity depends on comprehending and working against these evils, must also think about that *how*. As Loraine Hansberry wrote in her preface to *A Raisin in the Sun* "I have given up on the *why*: it is the *how* that matters."[4] Yes, although I think some important aspects of the *why* are revealed and realized in the *how*.

Gandhi, the leader of India's struggle for independence from Great Britain who became known as *the Mahatma* (Great Soul), also knew that it was the *how* that mattered, and those who have worked with his ideas most actively (best known, perhaps, Dr. Martin Luther King) have thought a lot about how to protest, resist, change harmful systems so that the doers of harm, each and all, are invited and helped to stop doing the work of those systems, to put down their guns, to walk away from their posts. Had more of the ordinary men in Police Battalion 101 done so, what might—and might not—have happened? Had more of the colonists of the Americas refused to betray, remove, slaughter the people they found there, what might have happened? What would happen if more people simply would not do some jobs?

Mass harms are enactments of prejudice. To our shame, prejudices are common, but they are by no means all deranging, virulent motivators sufficient to sustain many people over time in doing horrific things to many other people. Such preformed attitudes can stem from ignorance, stereotype, and biases that are not very hard to change once pointed out and informed, but can also form stubbornly settled prejudices, clear onto (more rare) virulent *categorical* hatreds. Issuing from some brew of these, there are what are now called *hate crimes*, extreme, horrifying examples of which include murders of gay people such as Mathew Shepherd, who died on October 12, 1998, after being tortured just for being who he was. But the relation between the ugly reality of prejudices ramped up into virulent categorical hatred and massive harm extended over time is not causal, and certainly not singularly so.

Prejudice can indeed be part of conditions that enable extensive evil, but alone it does not suffice. There need to be social and other provisions to support it in many senses—to normalize it, formalize it. Then, when it has become openly systemic, official, conventional, and often covered over by scientized knowledge from which it is aberrant to dissent—*Those people are crazy perverts, abnormal: just look them up in the diagnostic manual for psychologists! (This is why removing homosexuality from the DSM mattered so much.)*—it can indeed enable the doing of enormous harms.

And then there is this explanation: ***Mass murder was and is possible because all of us can be turned into killers given permission and safety (e.g. by anonymity or, conversely, a high status position) to let loose our deepest, darkest (perhaps "most natural," "animalistic," "unconscious," "sinful") selves.*** It is questionable whether there are such selves in all of us, all the time, to the same extent and in the same ways, but even if there are, when decent systems provide expectations of decent behavior as the norm, most of us most of the time do not do terrible things repeatedly. Pervert those systems utterly, and many of us are also likely to go along with the perverted systems—but not as the ravening, Id-driven, devil-possessed sorts this explanation apparently expects. No, we go along with perverted systems as people who can do the work, ride the train, feed our dogs, love our children, pull the switch or swing the machete, or sign off on the safety of a factory that is a fire trap, well enough to get the task done and continue through our days and nights. Even during times of extensive evils, our worst selves have to be kept under control; a regime, a leader, a system has to help us control ourselves enough to be effective agents of its horrid work.

Ethnic cleansing is possible where there are old "tribal" hatreds that have never quite died out, and/or: "Primitive people" are more prone to slaughter each other than "civilized"/"we" are. Same as immediately above, with racism or other stratification codes built in. It is "those people" who are defined as "closer to the animals" who are being picked out to be blamed, obviously, as if "civilized" people were incapable of collapsing into terrible warfare, have never run economies based on slavery, have never used weapons of mass destruction, have never worked people to death, have never raped, have never killed to "protect our honor," have never profited from child-labor, have never tortured and slaughtered people of different faiths. History and the present give the lie to that self-deluding position.

And yet, I have heard the "tribalism" explanation quite often; "primitive," fortunately, has decreased in frequency. These are explanations that discredit themselves.

Economic self-interest is always ready to rise to the level of greed. We all turn out to have a price, and anything can be done if you pay enough. Indeed, greed is astoundingly evident in the doing of massive evils—from neighbors turning in neighbors in order to get their slightly bigger apartment; soldiers destroying ancient monuments and museums without qualm as they also send a bit of loot home; to the biggest of bosses taking in huge amounts of wealth as those who do actual productive or service work are increasingly impoverished. But most of us, even in extraordinary times, are not dramatic creatures. We are, if you move in close and follow us through our days, just trying to get by. We are not even all that greedy; for a decent salary, some status, some job security, we will do a very wide range of things. Colonialism, for instance, made a few very wealthy, but most of those who did its work—including the killings, mutilations, horrific working conditions for "the natives"—just made what money they could. Greed, it seems, is indeed and importantly a motivation, but except for a few, it is not an overwhelming passion that can explain, or explain away, monstrous acts. It is harder, I think, to explain why it is that so many of us will do such horrific things for quite so little.

On another level, economic systems that sanitize, unto sanctifying, greed can be a different matter. Like any other system that perverts basic, decent human values, in which a very few empower themselves while normalizing the growing disempowerment of many, such systems once launched can indeed go very wrong indeed. But it is not *greed*, understood as a passion, a lust that trumps rationality, common decency, and empathy that characterizes the many people who make such a system work.

People under the influence of a charismatic leader, an all-explaining political ideology, will do things they would not otherwise even imagine. No question that, as the founder of psychoanalysis Sigmund Freud observed, we are capable of putting a person and/or an ideology in place of our conscience, our super ego—but then I want to add: up to a point. Tarrou, one of the main characters in Camus' *The Plague*, confesses to having allowed himself to overlook murder by the people with whom he had aligned himself in trying to put an end to poverty. Himmler told SS men to substitute for Christianity's "neighborly love, humility, and pity" the higher virtues of "hardness and self-discipline"[5] of the sort needed to do even the—admittedly offensive, said Himmler—work they must do to save the *Volk* (the folk, the "real" Germans) from destruction from within. Too true that too many did so, on the record. But still there are ineffective charismatic leaders and ideologies aplenty. Charismatic leaders can be found preaching in pulpits and running corporations and nonprofits; ideologies can be found contending for dominance of mainstream political parties, and among professionals in many fields. None of them necessarily or even often produces demagogues capable of virtually hypnotizing otherwise decent people into doing, over and over again, terrible things to other people. After a mesmerizing speech, most people come to and get on with their lives, not at all moved to leave everything and become saints or killers. (That, *over time*, meanings and norms can be changed to enable good or ill is another point, as we have seen.)

Fear of the Other: This is the explanation I have heard most often in recent years. I cannot credit it; it avoids too many questions. Why, we have always to ask, is *this* group "othered," and whom and what does fear of that group, rather than a different one, derive from and serve? And if there is in humans a primal hatred and fear of groups different from their own sufficient to explain genocides, enslavement, virulent prejudices, economic exploitation, how can we explain the pleasures of cosmopolitan cities; trade beyond the neighborhood; communities that had lived together well before ethnic cleansing started; even just the pleasure so many people take in travelling, in reading about different people, places, times, in taking the children to museum collections from other lands and times? After the fact, when we need to explain horrific deeds, *fear of the Other* functions, I think, rather as demonizing and romanticizing do: clearly, we want to say, *something* primal broke through here. Which is to say: nothing of the ordinary could explain this. But that does not stand up to scrutiny, I fear.

NO GENERAL RULES

Pointedly calling *the banality of evil* "simply factual"—meaning usefully descriptive, not a theoretical construct, not a theory—Hannah Arendt tried to teach us that:

> Particular questions must receive particular answers; and if the series of crises in which we have lived since the beginning of the [20th] century can teach us anything at all, it is, I think, the simple fact that there are no general standards to determine our judgments unfailingly, no general rules under which to subsume the particular cases with any degree of certainty.[6]

Insofar as that is true, which I think it is, it holds for explanations as well as for social and moral principles turned into rules. I do know that such a position creates great anxiety in some (*If there are no general rules or theories*

I can use, how can I know what is going on at all?); moral tremors (*How do we know what is right and wrong if there are no absolutes?)*; invitation to sin, to licentiousness (*If moral/religious dogmas are not certain, then all is permitted*); as well as presenting a crucial challenge to think independently (*If there are no general standards I can learn and then just apply in any and all circumstances, then I need to be able to think so as to be able to make good judgments and choices on my own).*

Without exploring all that studies of history and our own experiences suggest in this regard, may I just say that, when in doubt, we can choose to embrace as liberation a loss of dogmatic standards, rules, codes of behavior *and* ready-to-hand explanations of their breach, or we can bemoan it as loss of quality, order, even morality. In either case, such a loss entails being thrown back into ongoing experiences not only without rule books to consult (where we might find, say, *stealing is wrong*) but without an interpretation key to tell us what, in the real world, we need to sort out how to act (*That* act is *stealing*; *this* one is not).

AS SPIDERS SPIN WEBS: ABSTRACTIONS

We emerged from infancy into social creatures significantly by learning how to share in the meanings of those around us—abstract, generalized meanings, such as "ball" for that thing over there; "throw" for something to do with it; "broken" for an effect of that throwing; "bad" for how big people feel about what happened that seemed sort of neat until we were jerked away from playing by an angry parent. Abstractions, generalizations on differing levels, remain crucial to how we make sense of the world at all, even before we come consciously to judge it. Reality is, in fact, already categorized, interpreted, evaluated in many ways by the time we, as newcomers, come into it in the first few years of becoming socialized, learning languages of word, tone, gesture, act.

Indeed, language is nothing if not informed by choices, evaluations, judgments: that a language has a word for something at all already reveals judgments, choices. We do not have words for the things we have not considered important to notice: once there were no "blue collar workers," no "yuppies," no "fallout," no "rappers," no "social media," no "selfies," but once these phenomena had been called to our notice by someone who helped us see that they mattered, and what they meant, they became as real as, say, an arm, a cousin, meat, fire.

In short, as spiders spin webs, we humans make generalizations and categorize. If we did not, we would not even be able to use nouns: they would all be names of just one thing ("table" would not allow me to look at many things as having similar functions; it would be the name of one such thing, as if I had called what I put my plates on *Gwendolyn*).

The trick, upon which, with Camus and Arendt, I have come to believe lives depend, is not to lose ourselves in any set of abstractions, from familiar generalizations to technical languages, from social conventions to insider/outsider-creating ideologies or faiths, all of which can render us *out of touch.*

Thus, in Rwanda the Hutu called the Tutsis "crocodiles," "cockroaches." We know this technique; it is usually a part of mass harms. But a person does not look at the person he or she is about to murder and actually see that person as a cockroach: that is an abstraction we have to collude with for it to have any effect, and before that, we have to have already learned to think of cockroaches as disgusting and killable, crocodiles as dangerous and killable. So, too, do we collude with the usage of other epithets that are used to reduce individuals to members of a group, and a group to a "kind" that is defined as inferior, exploitable, expendable. Up close, we have to be determined always to see an abstraction (which is what epithets are) when before us are individuals.

That it is indeed more difficult reliably to see a (put in an ugly epithet for a "kind" of person) than an actual individual may be one reason why oppressed people who live close to their oppressors learn not to draw attention to themselves. A man determined to see all females as inferiors, as not much more than sexual prey, is not likely to respond kindly to a woman he suddenly realizes could be capable of judging, or resisting, or (worse?) laughing at him. The violence that can follow such moments reveals the effort it takes to protect against them, to avoid them. Those absurd epithets and characterizations would not need to be so fiercely defended against disproof if we were not using them to cover over, to suffocate, any fresh apprehension, any real experience in a highly variegated world.

RECONFIGURING MEANINGS

Alphonse, interviewed about the genocidal Tutsi murders in Rwanda in which he played a role as an organizer, said: "You were either pushed into flight by cowardice or drawn to your machete by obedience."[7] But what we are looking for, between resistance to being a murderer (called "cowardice," you notice, and choosing to accept the job (called "obedience," the same terms we find in testimonies of Nazi killers as well as other militaries) are multiple sorts of translation, from how we apprehended and thought about things when we were constrained from doing harm, and how we need to see things to be agents and enablers of harm. For genuinely horrifying acts to be performed by many ordinarily non-cowardly, conventionally good folks, anchoring notions of what is taken simply to be real for us, the ways things are in accord with common sense, personal identities, social acceptability, and, crucially, criteria for success, have to be reconfigured.

The testimonies of perpetrators such as Alphonse overflow with examples of just such a process, one we will focus on again later. But it is not that people only trade one set of abstract conventionalities for another, evident though it is that that has happened. It is also that their minds replace perme- able, falsifiable, non-locked-in generalizations and abstractions with new, rigid ones through which experience cannot penetrate precisely so they do not have to think what they are doing. *Once, a man saw women and could feel desire aroused by the very idea of a woman without failing also to recognize that each woman is different, that each is a person just as he is, that he can- not, ought not, and does not want to have sex with any woman who does not choose to be with him. And then, when systems have gone bad, that same man can see* a woman/a female, *and join other men in raping, mutilating, killing without all those second thoughts.* Desire, like hatred, can become terminally abstract when we lock up our minds.

With those warnings about conceptual pens, rigid generalizations, blinding abstractions, it is time for more thorough definitions.

Chapter Five

Meaning, Truth, Rationality, Knowledge, Thinking

If we are to think together about the ordinary and the extraordinary phenomena that we call "good" and "evil," which are themselves generalizations, categories, abstractions, we do need to tune and to attune our meanings. I do not presume—indeed, I cannot want—definitively to specify, to limit, the ranges of meaning, the uses, of these crucial terms, but rather to try to be clear about how I am here using them, along with other terms, so that you know what I want to mean (whether or not you then agree or disagree).

Having invoked *meaning*, I should say why it matters for this inquiry. Meaning sustains and is renewed through coherent, shareable converse with others. I might say that it enables us to check, confirm, negotiate our realities with them. If I say, *I like to eat rainbows. I had a fine one yesterday. Did you?* it is going to be difficult for you to respond without figuring out what on earth I mean. If you kindly do not think me crazy, you might decide I am being poetic, or trying in some odd way to be witty or funny—but while you do not know why my reality seems incoherent with yours and others', we cannot have even a minimally meaningful exchange. To do that, we have to negotiate through our disconnect, repairing the breaks in the fabric of meanings that holds us together. We often do that, questioning each other, responding— doing something very basic to us as the communicating, social species we are: we are the creatures who say, *Say what?!*

Because we need meaning to relate and to get on with life, we will do a great deal to refind coherence with those around us when the social order we knew how to negotiate changes more notably than is usual. At such times, to be part of a community again, we will sometimes overlook lies, even big ones. This can be very dangerous, of course, but truth alone is not at issue when meaning is lacking, when things just do not make sense anymore. Your first thought when I have spoken of eating rainbows—or, of discovering that

redheads are the spawn of Satan, or that there are aliens breeding among us—
is not so much likely to be, *Is that true?* (unless you were already inclined
to believe it, of course), but rather, *What does she mean?* And if I can then
persuade you that it was a meaningful thing to say, and, better yet, that you
reveal yourself to be a deep and poetic soul, a loyal citizen who will not be
sent to Siberia along with your neighbors because *you* understand, you are
perhaps unlikely to stand up and say, *She's lying!* Or, *That's utter nonsense!*
There are small and sometimes large rewards for finding meaning where
there is no truth even in daily social life; all the more so when injustices are
to be justified.

Thus, speaking about less dramatic times (but with them in mind), Hannah
Arendt said, "The need of reason [specifically, thinking] is not inspired by
the quest for truth but by the quest for meaning. And truth and meaning are
not the same."[1] We can find an untruthful statement meaningful, and revealing *(The sun stopped in the sky when first I saw you.* Or, *We do not sacrifice
civilians to our war aims)*, and lying is not itself a meaningless act. We can
talk together about it, at least as long as lying has not replaced truth-telling as
utterly as, under radically distorted systems, it usually does. We can also fail
to find the meanings in truths, which does not mean truth is meaningless: it
reminds us that truths need to be humanized, talked about with others, made
sense of for our lives. *Einstein's theory of relativity: what does that mean for
us? Is* everything *relative?* Or, *What does the fact that we have nuclear bombs
mean? Can we still want to bring children into such a world? Are there other
uses than military? Should we spend so much? Can we make them safe? How
has this power we now have changed us?*

Words, concepts, acts, facts—all come to have meaning (good or bad;
difficult or clear; shocking or comforting; interesting or banal) when we
can think and speak together with and about them fruitfully. Human beings
suffer greatly when such connections cease: *It's just all meaningless* is the
cry of an isolated soul, perhaps even a suicidal or otherwise potentially
violent one.

If we are not thinking, it becomes difficult to share in the meaning-making
of the society around us and we can lose touch with human realities. If a
whole society becomes thoughtless, the danger escalates hugely. Speaking to
a gathering of Hitler's Storm troopers, a Nazi expert on the still new radio
carried on about how this wondrous tool enabled the regime to reach everyone, everywhere, at virtually any time with its message. And that message,
he believed, would then shape what all those very different but lonely, alienated people would welcome as meaningful, true, and good: "Modernity," he
said, "bred cynicism and anomie, but it also offered the means to re-create
community on an entirely new scale. The modern man 'longs to be one of a
crowd of people who think, feel, and react in the same way. The listener feels

he is a part of this great entity that is not torn between countless differences of opinion, but revolves . . . around a central concern.'"[2]

CLARIFYING THINKING

Thought is not what inhabits a certain conduct and gives it its meaning; rather, it is what allows one to step back from this way of acting or reacting, to present it to oneself as an object of thought and question it as to its meaning, its conditions, its goals. Thought is freedom in relation to what one does, the motion by which one detaches oneself from it, establishes it as an object, and reflects on it as a problem.[3]

Having already so often used "thinking" and "thoughtlessness," I should refocus on what I want to mean by those elusive and critical terms (I will do more with them throughout, key as they are). Foucault gives us a good start as well as a crucial point: thinking is not here used as a generic term for reasoning, calculating, intuiting, imagining specifically or all together, as if whatever we do with our minds is thinking, a familiar use of the word that is more inclusive than its meaning here, or for Arendt. Thinking, here, refers to what we are doing when we practice our conscious capacity for freedom—our ability to reflect on, about, around something, including ourselves, including our own thinking.

Thinking, we might say, opens a space, a gap, in consciousness between the thinker and whatever she is reflecting on. Think about it: An aspect of the freedom implicit in that gap between I and me is that, although I can ask, *Who am I?* there is even less of a final answer to this: *Who wants to know?* The thinking ego, as it is sometimes called, is neither subject nor object: it is both, and more.

A long time ago, in the fourth century, the theologian and philosopher Saint Augustine of Hippo, having reflected long and painfully on his desires, drives, aspirations, and failures—not thoughtless, Augustine—observed that it is a truth of the human condition that we are questions to ourselves: *Questio mihi factus sum.*[4] Questions are open; answers are meant to end them, to close them off. *Who am I?* asks the child. *You are Victoria Slonim*, says her father, firmly. True, but not usually a meaningful answer to a question she will ask throughout her life and never answer. If nothing else, as soon as she lights upon what might be an answer, the gap opens again: she is right then thinking about who she is and so is also outside of that identity.

When we are thinking, and reflect on the experience of thinking, we may understand why something else relevant to moral and political concerns has also been observed for centuries, in the dominant Western tradition at least since the Stoics and clear unto today: *They can lock up my body, but not my mind.* Which, although it recognizes the mind's given capacity for freedom (in our ability to think even about our own prejudices, for example) is not as true as we want to believe. Minds can also in their own way lock in when we have stopped thinking. As the great liberator of enslaved people Harriet Tubman is said to have proclaimed, *I could have liberated a thousand more slaves too, if only they had known they were slaves.*[5]

Because we can think even about ourselves, become questions to ourselves, think freely even when politically unfree, we can become two-in-one, as Socrates put it, and so dialogue with ourselves. We can then be in solitude, but not alone. We can also think with many others: we are not stuck within ourselves, our own minds. Once we become conscious (*con* means *with; scientia* means *know: consciousness is knowing-with, being aware of*), the fall from oneness/unconsciousness opens us to knowing-with others in all sorts of ways. Thinking is in this sense inherently public even though it never as itself appears in the world.

It is not always a happy experience, but remember when you were so caught up in something that, when someone spoke to you, you jumped and "came to" with a startle reaction? When we "come to" like that we experience close-in the gap that thinking opens: I was entirely and utterly without self-consciousness—I had no awareness of myself—and then I became aware that I was there, I was doing something (like not paying attention, as a teacher, or spouse, might say). This is like and is related directly to social self-consciousness, when we are aware of ourselves through the categories of others, aware of ourselves as being looked at, evaluated, typed—or perhaps, just seen. That this can be uncomfortable, that we often seek to be unselfconscious, is related to the discomfort thinking can cause, and a desire to avoid it. But, like reading something we wrote and being able to see it as if someone else wrote it in order to edit, to make it better, such awareness allows us to change. So does thinking, *I am not thinking; I need to think!* Very curious, and a truly remarkable ability, our ability to open a gap within ourselves that allows us to think about ourselves as well as about all sorts of other things.

As noted, I will do more with this crucial, freedom-giving but often felt to be burdensome ability of ours later, but for now what is important is that when we are *not* thinking, not practicing this reflexive, reflective ability to be aware of, rather than entirely submerged in, ourselves and whatever else is going on, we are not free to observe. We are also then not free to evaluate or to choose: we are on autopilot, letting what we can do unreflectively carry us along.

We already know there are problems with such unreflectiveness. When we say to a child, *Don't be so thoughtless,* what we mean is *pay attention,* and usually we mean, *to someone other than yourself*: *You didn't thank your grandmother for her wonderful present because you were so wrapped up in yourself.* Thoughtlessness is rude, which even on a small scale is troubling because it means something more than not being mannerly. It means not recognizing someone's claim to be taken into account, a very basic moral right. On a larger scale, it is very serious indeed. To act without taking others into account because you are on autopilot, or you are simply not thinking about them or what you are doing, can lead to both physical and moral accidents, among other things. Worst of all, as we have been exploring, it can allow us to participate in, even to directly do, terrible things to those other people, to those animals, that forest—whatever we "simply" do not think about.

A NOTE OF CAUTION

Here I have to say that rethinking evil, offering definitions and distinctions even as we also remember experiences, engage imagination, memory, empathy in quest of useable conceptualizations, is a task that must proceed with particular caution. There are habits and convictions about acceptable ways of thinking and speaking in these fraught vicinities. In some, only initiates (by overwhelming suffering; by religious conviction; by scholarly immersion, for example) are welcome at all, and these can be exclusions that we want to honor out of profound respect for the need we humans have for boundaries. Some boundaries around meanings of *evil*, though, justify a comfort-protecting thoughtlessness, so it does need to be said, with care, that avoidance of thought here can, tragically, protect precisely what ought to be exposed.

We cannot know enough to decide for each other, or even for ourselves, all that is at issue with renewed inquiry here. We will simply have to be careful, and as honest as possible. If we can clear some pathways, move around more freely, glimpse meanings we can share, we may even go on a way toward making ever more sense of what at first many dealt with by marking it off as "the unthinkable." Meaning, explored together, makes human life for social creatures of language such as us sustainable; like physical health, it enables a future. I will try, then, to say here what I think "evil" means.

BEYOND BAD: MORAL HORROR

I think we usually reach for the concept *evil* when we are confronted with something so harmfully violative that every other category we have fails as ludicrously inadequate to capture it. "Evil" thus used means, *This is so far beyond the ordinary that I cannot even call it "bad" or "wrong." It is beyond such judgments, beyond comparisons, beyond categorizations. Nonetheless, it is so evidently destructive of all that is normal and good that not only I but anyone I could consider sensible, sane, decent can be expected to judge and condemn it, even if by a shudder of our being rather than a conclusion that can be expressed as a statement.* Thus we invoke *evil* when we experience a swamping intensity of moral horror—*this* no one, ever, anywhere, for any reason should ever suffer; *this* no human should ever do; *this* (wounded souls have also cried) no good, powerful, all-knowing deity would ever allow. For *this*, there is no excuse, no justification, and most of us then feel that there can be no forgiveness let alone exoneration. *This* is self-evidently morally repugnant, beyond wrong; it needs no argument to establish that it ought not be done, ought not happen. We feel as much as think such things: thinking thus is itself terrifying.

"Unthinkable," "unspeakable" used in these contexts are experientially apt terms. Words do fail; minds do stop. But the moral horror from which "unthinkable" and "unspeakable" arise is important to our very core as moral beings. I believe, then, that it is risky to accept these terms as meaning not only that we were reduced to silence, but that we really ought not think or speak about anything that could do that to us lest we suggest continuity with meaningful life. That, too, is comprehensible, but I fear that it leads to abdication that leaves us with nothing but a void, too often then reinhabited by old habits, conventional meanings, unilluminating categories and explanations. In Camus' terms, such silence and/or restrictions on acceptable speech together can leave us still vulnerable to infection rather than at least somewhat more immune to the plague for having been exposed.

For instance, after being so appalled, we may even later find it hard not to think that evil *must* be the appearance, the effect, of sub- or supra-real forces, of unearthly eruptions into ordinary lives to which they are entirely alien. It becomes, then, very difficult indeed to think of acts done by ordinary people, no matter what the circumstances, as evil. I repeat—because this is one of the more deeply rooted but misleading conceptualizations many of us remain entrapped by even when we think we are not—that we want, we need, the agents of evil to be so far from the ordinary, from us, that they must be as "unthinkable" as what they did.

Nonetheless, this—an understandable reaching for something big enough to be named as cause, to be used in explanation, to withdraw the horror from anything ordinary—turns around and betrays us. We were trying to comprehend, but our craving for a cause, a condition, an actor equal to the moral horror we feel has instead given us the opposite of what we sought: *unspeakable, unthinkable* mean, of course, *incomprehensible.* What is wrong with that? Such terms mark the very limits I just said have been transgressed by anything we call "evil," rather than "bad." If no explanation suffices to bridge the horror and the world within which we are seeking to understand, then what is before us actually must be "unthinkable," no? That is what "evil" *means*.

Always, we must be very careful here. "Incomprehensible," we say—but we are left, then, unable or unwilling to think at all about what really happened, about what, if we still choose to live in a shattered world, may be one of the most important things of all to comprehend (along with astounding good, about which we also find it difficult to speak in familiar, ordinary language).

It is a scary thing to say, but is it not possible that then, rather than honoring and protecting the ordinary by radically severing it from evil we have, instead, left it ever again vulnerable? Slamming the door, locking it, guarding it does not make what is outside go away, nor keep the rats from inconveniently dying on our own front steps. It does not make us, inside, safer, freer. Psychic survival sometimes requires such barricading, but that is a tragedy, no more or no less. It is not a prescription for other people, or for other times. It is not even a prescription for those who dwell with the ones who know what is outside that door but have not themselves ever seen it face to face. They, along with the most shattered who may have little choice but to refuse to remember, may suffocate. Returned soldiers know this; as a society, we are still learning how to deal with the defining need we humans have to find meaning with other people. In solitary confinement, too long in silence, we break. And even an informal conversation with others who have been through what you have can help. *It's not just me*: such a relief to say, even when on the face of it of course "it" was not only me, or you: confirming coherence and communication with others can return the belief that meaning—a kind of secular communion—is again possible, and on that our life really can depend.

If we can, we do need to think, to speak, to comprehend. That we cannot take these givens of human life for granted is one of the things experiences we can only call "evil" leave with us. But not taking them for granted is not the same as a protective embrace of their loss.

RATIONAL, IRRATIONAL, ANTIRATIONAL

We believe that people choose to be bad. We call what they have done "evil" only when we cannot approach the idea that a human could choose such acts, even if she or he is "sick," "mentally incompetent," or a "misfit" and "loner" as people tend today to mutter about a young man who has done something violent and shocking. Evil is invoked when any other recognizable exemption from moral responsibilities just is not strong enough to carry the weight. Then we say, instead, they were "possessed" or some other term that says, *This* is

beyond rational, and even the irrational: *this* is antirational—although intentional, a kind of antirational that partakes of rationality's ability to choose
and to guide action. That this is curious is a clue that our thinking may be on
a wrong track.

I have to say that I fear we over-compliment reason in this notion that
rationality and not doing horrific harms usually go together. I am anticipating
here a later discussion of *extensive evil*, but allow me to use it to underscore
just how far rationality as it is generally understood—following a set of rules
of thought, from formal logic to socially acceptable strictures—is from keeping us safe from evils.

As we know all too well, a crucial element of the particular horror of the
Holocaust is that it was planned and run so efficiently, so *rationally.* It was
extraordinarily rule- and hierarchy-defined. The core of the SS and SD were
young men, some 60 percent of whom held university degrees and who
prided themselves on being "rational," "objective-minded men."[6] Worse, it
was done by people who were consciously making rational choices that could
and were then claimed to be according to conscience. As Claudia Koonz has
found after exhaustive study, " 'The Nazi conscience' is not an oxymoron"[7]:

> Mobilizing citizens in a modern and enlightened nation, Nazi rule relied not
> only on repression but also on an appeal to communal ideals of civic improve-
> ment. In a vibrant public culture founded on self-denial and collective revival,
> ethnic Germans were exhorted to expunge citizens deemed alien and to ally
> themselves only with people sanctioned as racially valuable. The road to
> Auschwitz was paved with righteousness.[8]

Right along with the ugliest of racial stereotypes and fearmongering, the road
to Auschwitz was also paved with clear, rational statements that made a case
for it as righteous *and* scientifically based, and so justified. This was the time
of eugenics, of theories of race, genetics, and of evolution in an unholy blend
that led eminent scientists, public policy makers, intellectuals, and many others (by no means only in Germany: in England and, perhaps most of all, in
the United States) to argue that there was now the hope that we could breed
superior humans on purpose just as we could chickens, pigs, horses. There
was nothing irrational, let alone antirational, about these arguments: they
accorded with logics respected then as now. They failed to stop at the human,
moral limits of logic, but that does not make them antirational.

And given the common blithe conflation of "rational" with "educated," it
is important again to recognize that those "ethnic Germans" were not mostly
uneducated, and/or mostly marginal, fringe, or "brutish" sorts of people who
might be expected to be "less rational" than their "betters." A 2003 study of
The Social Bases of Nazism 1919–1933 found that:

On the eve of its acquisition of power, the Nazi Party represented a microcosm of German society . . . In the course of its rapid expansion from the late 1920s, the party had penetrated into all corners of Germany and mobilized support from all "Christian" persuasions, from all classes, irrespective of whether these were resident in isolated rural areas, or in heavily industrialized regions, or in urban sprawls . . . [Its] remarkably heterogeneous . . . rank-and-file at the branch level is particularly striking.[9]

Also worth noting: "The typical Nazi leader . . . was a secure, rather successful professional, official, or businessman with a history of considerable upward mobility before he had joined the movement."[10] *Before* the Nazi party took power, it was *not* made up primarily of the uneducated, or of the resentful unsuccessful, thugs, malcontents, or—pick your prejudice—*petit bourgeois* or working class or aristocratic people, or unassimilated, alienated immigrants. It grew exponentially, from barely in the thousands to hundreds of thousands, as what its proponents liked to call it, a *Volkspartei*, a peoples' party for everyone, glorying in its claim to move beyond the old divisions within *the people*.

Those with supposedly differing blood lines, or genetic make-up, were quite another story, of course: scientized—that is, rendered rational in today's most authoritative form—the stark racism, of which eugenics did not purge itself, was invoked, and *the people* became a category for some but not all human beings. What, then, are humans who are defined out of the category of "people"?[11] Not only lesser but by definition a threat to the right and proper and real race should interbreeding, sex with or without marriage, continue to be allowed, so soon enough under the Nazis, it was not. It has also to be observed that much of what I have just said could be applied with appropriate adjustments to other doers of extensive evils such as slave owners, and those grown wealthy off the labor of powerless workers.

In short, the doers of extensive evil cannot safely be described as irrationally, or antirationally, "possessed" in any sense, I fear. Were they so, their deeds could not have been so effectively carried out over such lengths of time by so many and such varied people from, as they say, all walks of life, including scholars, scientists, doctors and others from among the most "respectable." Eichmann, less well educated than the majority of the SS and SD, nonetheless "had the right objective, problem-solving, and managerial outlook."[12]

But for the victims and still-thinking observers of evildoers, a subcultural or whole culture's normalizing and rationalizing that make horrific acts possible make one shake one's head and say, *This makes no sense: this is really irrational.* Many said just that when, around 2015, people indiscriminately calling themselves "terrorists" proudly posted videos of astoundingly cruel killings of journalists, among others: *This is insane; how can they do it? How can they post it? How on earth does that draw them more recruits? This is beyond all rationality.* Tragically, that really is the wrong category, and can be paralyzing. No order, system, organization, polity that is on the way to being or already is established is utterly insane, however some of its most mind-stopping acts appear. There are decisions being made, rewards and punishments decided on and meted out by individuals who may well have chosen that role, deals for essential money being made, strategies worked out, plans laid.

There are also backstories that are morally agitating but do not thus paralyze our ability to find meaning and rationality because they are, humiliating thought this is, all too familiar. As the historian Koonz also observes:

> What surprised Jewish Germans during this period [1933, when Hitler became Chancellor] was not the cruelty of kleptocrats, fanatics, and malcontents, but the behavior of friends, neighbors, and colleagues who were not gripped by devotion to Nazism. Most Germans fell into this category. Jews sadly noted their mundane lapses: the silence of a store clerk who refused to answer an inquiry, the politely worded requests to drop their memberships in leisure and civic associations, or the embarrassed silence that greeted them as they walked into a favorite café.[13]

These "small" lapses, which seemed at first to make no sense, in fact indicated what seemed to non-"risk-takers" rational choices not to "make waves," not to "cause trouble," to "go along." These were, in Camus' terms, the reactions of proper citizens upon encountering the first of the rats coming out to die of a bacillus they could have recognized, had they paused to try. They—officials, citizens, business people, the poor, priests, some doctors, travelers caught there by the plague, young and old—did not choose to listen to those doctors who did speak, in part because *it made no sense* that their ordinary city should suddenly become the site of plague, and so they did not think about it. And for others, elsewhere, the first small steps, sometimes not yet even in their own cities, seemed aberrations, and then, closer by, risks to be avoided by keeping your head low—or, instead, by joining in some small capacity that gave them standing in the emerging order. Seemed like common sense, until it did not.

This familiar pattern can be seen in a front-page story in the *New York Times* in 2015 titled, "For Isis Women, Fraught Choices." In it, we meet a woman who lived in Syria in an area taken over by the Islamic State. For two months, she worked for the Khamsa Brigade, "the all-female morality police of the Islamic State." She did so, she says, because that role, one of the very few open to her, gave her some new and welcome "authority" in her family as they all adjusted themselves to this new order. She did her work reporting other women until finally confronted with the severe whipping of her closest friend. The punishments meted out had escalated as so often they do: effective leaders of horrific orders know to give people time to adjust—and adjust, and adjust. This is not irrational. (In this case, the woman and her friend managed then to flee, but they remember and know how lucky they have been to have been shocked into awareness early enough to find permeable borders still available.)[14]

Belief in rationality plays out differently, then: What is done makes no sense, radically so, to the victims, but the many who enable and then move into doing the deeds are, on the contrary, *just being sensible, not making a fuss, going along, achieving some authority*, as the former Khamsa Brigade woman said. They are being rational people choosing cautiously to believe their leaders, protect their families, enhance their careers. They are remaining connected to their society by using its new meanings.

As economists not only know but, it seems, positively embrace, "being rational" can also mean, is indeed often defined by, just such self-interested calculations, and specifically (as in Camus' Oran) by marketplace exchanges to maximize profits. In his study, Gotz Aly underscores the efficacy of such rationality in enabling evils:

> Nazism secured the compliance of the German people not because of Hitler's charisma or Goebbels's propaganda, nor because of its anti-Semitic policies or the Gestapo's ruthlessness. A majority of Germans were not seduced or scared by the Nazis. On the contrary, their loyalty to the regime was bought and paid for—quite literally so.[15]

They made a calculation that was by market realities then rational: it maximized their profits, income, wealth. One need not accept Aly's dismissal of all other motivations to feel the force of his revelation of where validation of profit-seeking as a prime meaning of rationality can indeed lead.

Rational people can cause unique individuals translated into standardizing economic terms to suffer radically, to die, simply by following the logics of rationalized systems. Ordinary people do their jobs; kindly people turn their heads; people make "rational" economic decisions to get a bit of the plunder a deadly system is extracting from its victims; good peoples' consciences are re-formed by knowledge validated by "expert studies" of racial, of sex/gender, of ethnic, of class, of religious "inferiority"; the "laws" of economics, of history, are pronounced known, rendering ethical objections to change moot; and deformed systems get work done through all these conceptual collusions until they entail doing what no one could have imagined, in better times, that he or she could or would possibly ever do, no matter what.

The ordinary can be quite rationally subverted until the majority of us are doing
mad things for which logical arguments can be, and are, made.

We actually do know the line is thin here: we speak of "rationalizations,"
and mean excuses and self-protective explanations that are both rational and
dishonest.

INCOMPREHENSIBILITY AND THE UNIQUE

The experience of a massive horror that stops the mind is also said to be
"incomprehensible," although nonetheless our minds stubbornly do continue
working and coming up with *something* that might return meaning to our
worlds ("incomprehensible" is also a category, after all). But it is not unusual
then to say that the experience of horrific acts is also unique. There is emotional truth to that, obviously. But if *there has never been anything like it*, then
of course our generalizing, language-using minds turn off the usual search for
comparisons, for which we need to find some related good-enough categories.
Turning from what is unique in quest of something familiar can feel like a
betrayal of our moral horror, our core sense that *this* is like nothing else, cannot be allowed to be like anything else. Those who have been seared to the
core by a moral horror may not then want to find a category for it. They, we,
want it to remain outside our worlds, unintegrated, so it will not shatter all else
we thought we could believe in, count on, think—not only outside as *monstrous*, but as *unique* and so incomprehensible, and so also, again, antirational.

It is true that "unique," like "evil," marks a boundary of anything ordinary.
But again we need to be careful: it is dangerous to define and protect the ordinary as *antithetical* to uniqueness. *It's nothing special; I'm nothing special.*
We're just ordinary people. Now, Einstein—or Michael Jordan, Shakespeare,
Pavarotti—well, that's a whole other thing! One of a kind, no doubt about it.
We thus reduce the ordinary to the replicable, comparable, sometimes standardized, and on to the conventional, clichéd, banal. The ordinary need not
be thus reduced. An ordinary sunset can astound; a standardized sunset—an
artifact of imposed notions of what a sunset is or ought to be—does the opposite. There is another turn we can make, though, and—anticipating: we will
explore it when we get to part II, on goodness—it is to remain open to what
is unique in each and every person and most of the phenomena we meet in
our worlds, each tree, each dog, each cloud, chicken, insect, reptile, puddle,
rusted old motor part.

The Nobel prize-winning Polish poet Wislawa Szymborska, who knew
something of mass horrors, thought it important to say this to us: "Granted,
in daily speech, where we don't stop to consider every word, we all use

phrases such as 'the ordinary world,' 'ordinary life,' 'the ordinary course of events.' But," she wants us not to forget, "whatever else we might think of this world—it is astonishing."[16] And that astonishment—which I believe is a wellspring of the attentiveness to, the interest in, that which is here and now before us as we act and thereby enables any morality at all—is, Szymborsa rightly says, "an epithet containing a logical trap. We're astonished, after all, by things that deviate from some well-known . . . norm, from an obviousness to which we've grown accustomed. But the point is, there is no such obvious world. Our astonishment . . . isn't based on a comparison with something else." For those who, like poets, calibrate the relation of their words to their perceptions very carefully, "nothing is usual or normal. Not a single stone and not a single cloud above it. Not a single day and not a single night after it. And above all, not a single existence, not anyone's existence in this world."[17]

Our conceptual as well as other boundaries (rules, fences, national borders) do hold our existence and if appropriate, can make it daily more smoothly negotiable, but their very obviousness can make them the enemy, and sometimes the deadly enemy, of the good as well as the beautiful. The singular, the individual, the particular—the unique—ought not always be clothed such that we never even try to see below the conventionalized surfaces we impose so as not to be stopped by wonder, terror, or just the awkwardness of confusion.

In tightly managed systems aimed singularly at previously set outcomes, the unique is, of course, a great deal more than a source of confusion (and something quite different from wonder, or terror: highly inappropriate in an efficient bureaucracy or business, the unique).

The unique, the individual, belongs to different spheres of being, meaning, value, and experience than effectively rationalized systems.

What matters here is that we pay attention to the systems within which we live and work, aware as history ought to make us that their rationales—whether evidently highly emotional, or strictly rational—may be fine where appropriate, and ineffective or even horrifying when they transgress those limits.

To be attentive is to be able to be startled back into thought, to become again able to be in touch with the originality of all that is around us, and so also to be aware of what we are actually doing, here and now.

THOSE WHO KNOW

Those who are established as knowers in good and bad times may not equally value thinking, or the questions we raise when trying to understand its meaning for us and our world. The poet Szymborska also said in her Nobel Prize acceptance speech:

> [T]hey "know," and whatever they know is enough for them once and for all . . . But any knowledge that doesn't lead to new questions quickly dies out: it fails to maintain the temperature required for sustaining life. In the most extreme cases, cases well known from ancient and modern history, it even poses a lethal threat to society.[18]

A use of "unthinkable" for the horrific that shatters all negative judgment categories we have; for extreme, saintly good that does the same for positive judgments; for the ordinary, if we have really apprehended its uniqueness, ought not allow us to stop questioning—which is to say, to stop thinking. There is knowledge that has justified lethal programs—eugenics, scientized racism, and history—but it is not the knowledge that does the killing. It is our failure to think perceptively soon enough to realize we must act to stop those who would use such knowledge to legitimate the doing of harms from which we would otherwise flinch.

POLITICS OF FEAR, TERROR

"If lawfulness is the essence of non-tyrannical government and lawlessness is the essence of tyranny, then terror is the essence of totalitarian domination."[19]

Evil is an epithet that simultaneously disables and takes over the usual role of explanation. To use the extreme language of militaristic force, using *evil* as an epithet is conceptually, imaginatively, and emotionally a *blitzkrieg*. It is intended to shock and awe us. When something or someone is called "evil," observers have been reduced—if the invocation is spread popularly—to the base sameness of gaping, terrorized onlookers. The epithet *evil* then becomes also a mental occupying force: if all normal categories and judgments are not big enough for *this* (whatever has been called *evil*), we cannot act, we cannot speak unless something moves into, takes over, the space emptied by our incomprehension but filled with something terrifying, and so also with threat.

Politically, "fear itself" is not "the only thing we have to fear" for these reasons. The sorts of anxiety and fear that we all experience now and then usually are, after all, more or less realistic. They have real or at least plausible objects: a truck that may be about to stop abruptly right in front of our car on the highway; an odd-looking raccoon starting to move with erratic gait toward our child; footsteps behind us in a dark alley. Give us a shot of adrenalin, and we become more, not less, alertly attuned to realities of the situation, watching out for what might actually threaten us so as to be ready to deal with it effectively. Invoking evil, however, turns us away from immediate realities: the normal, that with which we can at least hope to cope, is precisely what transfigures or disappears before our very eyes. Imagine a real cat. Imagine a real cat that is frightening you. Then start again: imagine an evil cat. The belief that that creature is evil literally means that nothing we might normally do if scared by a cat has a chance in hell of protecting us.[20]

Terror is therefore a lot more morally and politically dangerous than fear, and one sure mark that it is terror someone is trying to push us into is the use of "evil" (rather than "bad") as an epithet. When both fight and flight, the quick reactions of our body/minds when we fear something, are reduced to absurdity as they are in the face of evil, we can feel unable even to try to escape. How even think of it, when the mind is stopped?

Perhaps most important, we do not, while terrorized, turn to other people in order to think about shared meanings, seeking either the comfort of solidarity, the sense of shared perceptions, the possible security of common judgments, or help in seeing better than we can alone possible shared strategies for action. These are the warp and woof of regular public life. Even after intensive evils such as a gang going on a rampage, killing, raping, leaving severed heads by the roadside, we rush to reweave such a shareable public life, going out of our way to help others, to *reach out*, as we say, *to those in need, those who have suffered and lost loved ones.* But when the possibility is presented to us that such appalling evildoing is likely to come again and again, that our whole daily world has become infected with insidious, unpredictable threat—that the gangs have made our town their headquarters—we can become radically isolated from each and all others. During the Reign of Terror (1793–1794) after the French Revolution; when the East German secret police, the *Stasi*, turned all sorts of people into spies reporting on their families and neighbors; when Senator Joseph McCarthy and the House Un-American Activities Committee charged, arrested, jailed Americans for their political views, people did not join together in public, in common cause. On the contrary; in all sorts of ways and for quite awhile, they withdrew. And so the few in power took over more and more of public life, space, meanings.

If thus pushed beyond fear into paralyzing, isolating terror, we can become desperate to accept whatever the Authorities say we, and they, must do. If what we are told is that we should be terrified of evil in the form of terrorists, the script moves from obvious to blatant: what can one be, faced with evil "terrorists," other than terrorized? All too obviously, mere anxiety and fear are not as effective in thus producing a hollowed-out state that can leave us politically passive, obedient, docile.

Evil, when invoked by others to whom we listen seriously, thus turns us away from the ordinary world in which we count on making some degree of sense with those around us, those on whom we do to some extent depend as they do on us. In the ongoing social as well as political world, we have to try out our own interpretations and take responsibility for our own explanations and consequent actions. Before evil, all that fractures, melts away, leaves us existentially naked, shivering, alone with the abyss.

This is why, politically, we should always be frightened of, hence super-alert and ready to act to protect ourselves against, anyone who tries to terrorize us, even about the "terrorism" of others. People whose categories of judgment of good and bad have been trumped by invocation of evil can become incapacitated for meaningful moral and so also for social life; people who have been rendered speechless because all talk and possible actions have been rendered superfluous are incapacitated for political life. And it is vanishingly rare for people to stop and think when terrorized. This is one of the very real consequences of our having romanticized evil: we paralyze ourselves, leaving the field open for even the pettiest of people to do its work.

INTENTIONAL

When we encounter what someone has called "evil," we are not faced with the sort of acts that get people corrected by parents, friends, colleagues concerned about our and perhaps their social acceptability and standing. We are not thinking of the disruptive acts covered without much social disagreement by informal manners and mores, by formalized rules and regulations, or even by official laws—acts ranging from polite lies to theft and even, if you'll excuse this, understandable (I do not mean acceptable) murder (to save your child; in self-defense; in war). Nor are we talking about those things done by someone who was, by virtue of what we call generically "mental illness" or "incapacity," unable to understand our codes of right and wrong.

Across both more and less religiously flavored unto entirely secular moral conversations, I think we persist in using "evil" for the big stuff, the radically violative, harmful wrong that is nonetheless done—this is key as well as startling here—*intentionally.* A volcanic eruption can be devastating and do great harm to many people both short and long term, but the volcano is not evil. Genocide is intentional; so is the intensive evil of a murderous cult. Nonetheless, we have a very hard time thinking that something so extreme can be done, really, by fully conscious, rational people who intend to do what we cannot even comprehend doing. This is understandable, even as it causes us difficulties in thinking clearly. After all, as we have said, to merit the label "evil," harms must be so extreme—so, as we say, "mind-boggling"—that usual moral words—"bad," "wrong"—become inappropriate, almost silly (being silly, laughable, notably marks a boundary of moralisms we find it hard to transgress). Thus, to say, for example, *What Hitler did was bad*, seems ludicrously not so much tame as categorically wrong, almost laughable, like saying that a massive earthquake is inconvenient. Which, of course, it is, by usual meanings of "inconvenient." The inadequacy, rather than inapplicability, of such usual terms is what tells us that we categorize some acts, situations, individuals in quite another way when they are radically excessive.

There is a point at which quantitative change becomes qualitative. As water gets colder and colder until at some point it loses the fluid characteristic of water and becomes solid ice, there is a point at which intensification and extent of badness crosses over into something for which we need a different word entirely. But that cannot mean that evil acts that are indeed intentional even if they seem to us incomprehensible are not subject to moral judgment. Again, we need to be very careful here, lest we hand over moral along with political and social agency and responsibility.

The problem morally is clearly akin to the problem with invoking evil politically: by disabling our usual socially understood and efficacious categories, *evil* leaves us isolated and paralyzed. Being stripped of our own sense of intentionality—that we can and do choose purposefully—we can also cease looking for the intentions of evildoers. There they are again, then: monsters, supra-human or subhuman, insane, mad, irrational—none of which means they are morally responsible as indeed they must be.

BREEDING GROUNDS

Leering "comic" book characters, blood-soaked slasher movies, technology-enabled "games" of dismemberment and slaughter, best-selling "studies" of serial killers, Nazi-themed parties, restaurants, weddings (yes: just do a search for "Nazi themed" to glimpse the tip of this iceberg) suggest that there is something appealing in being thus utterly appalled. Check out the closest electronic game store online or elsewhere. Check out those pictures in porn magazines and books and films of highly sexualized women and men decked out in Nazi costuming, or a get-up that signals *torturer*. We cannot ignore such an array of evidence that a tamed evil still sizzling with a bit of hellfire, romanticized and intense, flourishes in the darker, and I fear not so darkened, corners of society, simultaneously stereotyped and so familiar, alien and, especially, illicit.

Evil, reduced to cultural specter with which to scare ourselves silly as well as theme for playacting transgressive acts, can provide a kind of vacation from the frustrating bonds of convention and consideration of others. Sometimes, then, people seek release and relief in safely crossing those boundaries into a super-dramatic fantasy, a break from reality from which they easily return to acceptable social lives. Pressed into service by a system going wrong, however, what was known to be transgressive can be transmuted into, rather than used as defiant escape from, the conventional.

As the crumbling Roman Empire used free bread and circuses with deadly sport to keep the masses from turning against their leaders, modern societies may benefit—on purpose or not—from our own versions of the same sort of entertainment. A congruence of playing at violative harmdoing and terror, and actual situations in which such things are really happening can have effects regardless of intent. Consider this: "In World War Two, when the Marines hit the beaches, a surprisingly high percentage of them didn't fire their weapons, even when faced with direct enemy contact. They hesitated. Not these guys [in Iraq]. Did you see what they did to that town? They fucking destroyed it. These guys have no problems with killing."[21] The author also notes that, "Many are on more intimate terms with video games, reality TV shows and Internet porn than they are with their own parents."[22]

With the rise and spread also of pop psychology and a plethora of professional experts at the ready, along with many crime and violence TV shows and movies with their increasingly common and even sometimes sophisticated uses of psychology, we are hard to shock into utter speechlessness, and we are quick with explanations. Many of those explanations are actually just used as labels that feel like explanations (like those we discussed earlier, such as *obedience to authority* and even *banality of evil* when used unthinkingly) in that they allow us to wrap the subject up in something familiar, to contain it and file it: "Well, he's a product of his culture"; "alienated youth." Each of those is actually very complex, of course, as is the effort to explain—but when our minds do not want to take something in as it really is, the complex can be rendered simplistic with remarkable speed. How not just a few but very many of us can be prepared to kill without qualm as if it were just a job, our duty, a game, is of course a question we must ask, and also pursue further and deeper than *violent video games*, say, in order to find out, close-in, *What were they thinking?*

"DON'T LOOK BACK"

From the perspective of evil, if I may for a moment speak that way, hiding things away, encouraging secrecy, suspension of spontaneous shared speech and thought for lengths of time—wherever it is done: in school, at work, in housing that isolates us, by spending hours paying intense attention to video games and electronic devices—is likely more welcome than brutal public entertainments. The detritus left when human consciousness has been for a while seriously inattentive—the undescribed acts and untold stories; the evaluations and judgments avoided; the emotions unreflected upon; the memories unintegrated; the desires unmodulated—can make it harder and harder to think, to question oneself, to reflect. I think of the advice attributed to Satchel Paige, the great African American baseball player who reached the peak of his game when baseball was still systemically racist: "Don't look back. Something may be gaining on you." As I said, this can indeed be good advice to get through what cannot be changed or undone.

But I believe it can be the case that when we are isolated from each other in all sorts of ways (including being in competition rather than collaborating) and moving too fast, it can come to feel as if something is indeed gaining on us and so we have to run faster, think less. This does not seem to me safe for many of us to do in a world that has many ways of going desperately wrong.

STOP, AND THINK

The claim on our thinking made by experiences that break our usual categories is greater, not less to be honored, when those experiences are shocking. It is hard to think just then, as we saw when exploring terror as distinct from fear, and still it remains the case that we actually can think, alone and together, about the evils we call "unthinkable." After all, even as we say that it is impossible to comprehend the "unthinkable," the "unspeakable," we have already thought about it, whatever it is, enough to have rejected other categories in order to choose this one. That is, "unthinkable" and "unspeakable" are terms available to us as descriptive of real reactions to an experience. They serve to save our minds from utter lock-up: faced with that for which our categories are inadequate, faced with that which shatters all faith we are aware of having and holding to get through life, our minds may well go still, alert but silent, waiting. And then, as minds do, they kick in again and allow us to name even that experience: it is *the unnameable.*

Romanticized, that could be an ontological statement asserting that the Unnameable exists, but in another reality, a different dimension. Not romanticized, such anti-categorizing categories are more like warnings than descriptors. Rightly so: Do not, we mean with them, slot this horror that is before you, even at the safer remove of my report to you, into a category utterly inadequate to it. Do not chatter on about this to keep your mind occupied even as you are desperately aware of inadequacies of understanding: that is as unfruitful as it is disrespectful. Stop and think before that of which it seems you cannot speak.

Stop, and think: when you can, risk as open an attentiveness as you can abide, and then, with feelings as prods, guides, alerts—think. When we do not know, still we can think. And yes, thinking in these vicinities is about as hard as it can be. Being the word we have for violative harm that defies description, *evil* is a word that contradicts, counter-speaks, itself. Nonetheless, in recognizing that it is "unrecognizable," I am, whether I am aware of it or not, already refusing to yield to wordlessness and the utter meaninglessness it threatens.

To call something "evil" can be, then, also to *do* something: to invite ourselves and others to seek the meanings, and limitations, of our ordinary moral terms in ways that can call us into thought afresh. *That gang doesn't murder individuals; they execute the competition, and traitors to the gang. But "execute"? They're breaking the law, not carrying it out. They're eliminating obstacles; they've turned killing people into just that, only that, no more, so they just go and erase them. It's worse than "cold-blooded murder," and it isn't any of the lesser charges, either. It defies the moral basis of law. These are political as well as ethical crimes.* Such efforts to understand what is going on here, what it means, what it asks of us, are the opposite of an isolating, conscience-protecting choice *not* to think, which is all too akin to what it takes to do rather than try to comprehend horrific things: "I built a wall in my mind" says an Albanian soldier remembering, and trying later to explain, what he did to living prisoners from whom he extracted organs to sell on the international market.[23]

Chapter Six

Romanticizing Evil

Camus most likely had fascism, and specifically the Nazis, in mind when he wrote his novel, but it is evidently not the monstrousness of those virtually archetypal modern doers of evil that he felt compelled to illuminate with the truths possible in fiction. His novel explores the ways very different characters react to a plague, to something directly caused not by human choice, human actions, but, as we have already observed, by a bacillus that, Dr. Rieux remembers, is always there, "dormant . . . in bedrooms, cellars, trunks, and bookshelves."[1] Where is Evil, with a capital "E," when the killing of innocents is done by an amoral organism fulfilling its own biological imperatives, no more, no less? Is this Camus' version of blaming a system, rather than the people who make systems work? Or not even a system but something utterly out of our control, such as Fate? Where, then, is human agency? Does Camus want us to pay no attention to those searing issues of responsibility that do—and should, must—trouble us not only during but for generations after massive harm-doing, murders beyond numbering?

Camus, like the very few characters in his book whose way of making sense of their lives survives the epidemic along with their bodies, is radically antiromantic about both evil and good. It is precisely not abstractions such as Fate, Sin, or Monsters that he is interested in. It is how we lead our ordinary lives before the plague, and how that prepares or fails to prepare us to deal with life and death when an epidemic emerges through no direct choice of ours to which he wishes to call our attention. In a stark juxtaposition, he links the conventionally happy life of Oran—a port town that has turned its back on the unruly sea, whose solid citizens cultivate their habits rather than vices as harmless diversions from the business of making more money—and the horrors of plague. These are not people driven by power lust, ideology, fanatic faith, monstrous desires. On the contrary, quite on the contrary.

Camus does not want us to look around for singular villains: no one or few humans can directly cause, let alone carry out, vast harm to many people over time. For such an epidemic to set in, many must become allies of death-dealers directly and indirectly, perhaps for some passionately, by choice, but more commonly and more dangerously, while they continue to be thinking of something else.

With Arendt, Camus observed a link between a superficiality that pauses for no depths, is stopped by no dark nights of the soul, deflected by no pangs of conscience, startled back into attentive thought by no real experience, and an ability to convert from ordinary goodness to conventionalized evil that can be sustained over time.

But if the questions before us—*How could they do it? What were they thinking?*—take us by various routes back to superficial meanings that can spread over, suffocate, lay waste a great deal and a great many, why now take up as a problem our tendency to *romanticize* evil? Why did Camus evidently work so hard not to do so? One reason is that it is our persistent inclination to romanticize evil that protects us from paying attention not only to its undramatic causes, but to the conditions that make it possible on such a grand scale.

Still, this seems odd: we abhor evil, so how, why, would we be romantic about it? And yet, what else are we doing when we depict evil and evildoers as extraordinary, demonic, other than heightening their stature, exaggerating their traits, attributing sub- or supra-human qualities to them? A remarkable amount of our storytelling does just that, and it can be as breathless and, I fear, titillating, as any of our pulp tales of romance.

> She stood thunderstruck, rooted to the spot, as the creature emerged from the bog. . . . Evil incarnate stood before her, ancient, hideous, defiant, a force so much greater than its form that she knew even as her eyes locked on to It that It was not even then nor ever would be only as it appeared. It was no one thing; it could be anything; it merely adopted some shape now and then to visit and wreak havoc upon us, to play with us, to enjoy its utterly destructive power.

Romanticized evil is common; it sells; it is even fun to write (I enjoyed doing the bit above). Really scary, even terrifying, movies, books, magazines, campfire stories, even many of the old fairy tales and myths draw us, thrill us, and, *as actual experiences of evil do not*, bond us with each other. In those forms, such hyped evil—odd notion as that is: "evil" is already "hyped"—is not my concern now (and we touched on it in chapter 5). What is troubling is the persistence of such overblown drama when we try to comprehend the extreme, violative harms that real people do to each other. Camus has started us off with an antidote to the infectious *frisson* of terror at a distance.

His book is not a blockbuster movie waiting to happen. It is the opposite of romantic. There is defeat throughout, and the heroism is of the few who will not collude, who do what they can just because what else are they to do, keeping their attention on what gives their lives meaning, whatever a world they cannot control brings. They help out, and they go on, that is all. As I said, the opposite of romantic, both the evil and the good.

"THE NONWICKED EVERYBODY"

And still: evil knocks us off our feet. Awareness of where we put our feet as we walk simply through our days surely has nothing to do with it, so it is not surprising that we romanticize it. Romanticized good can strike us blind, too: no one can quite see an angel, or quite comprehend a saint. There is experiential reason for such romanticizing. We go along, speaking when we must of *bad* and *wrong*, *immoral* and *illegal* acts; of *sick* and *crazy* and *insane* acts—and then sometimes something manifests before us that so stuns mind, heart, spirit that we are, as we say, "shattered." We fall silent or are reduced to the strongest exclamations we have, which tend to carry religious roots with them, and/or collapse into the infantile, anal, erotic, the obscene: "Lord god!" "Oh, my god!" "Holy fucking shit!" The transcendent, the most debased: either, both, seem alone to be available when our minds frantically reach for something to capture experiences that are felt to obliterate what we take to be normally real. Reality and extremes in tension, in collusion: how to find meaning, form, sense?

> *Unearthing one skeleton did not stop him, nor the next two or three, but when he realized there were more in there—more and more and more, right there in that one man's suburban backyard—he froze, the shovel falling from his hands, his mouth open but able to emit no sound at all. One word lit his mind: Evil. And so said the neighbors as the word spread. Nothing like this happens here, they said. We are ordinary people, a quiet community. He was just a neighbor, someone we saw now and then at the grocery store, at the post office. How wrong we were. The man is a monster, a devil incarnate. Our community will never be the same. Nothing can be the same.*

Such things do happen now and again. Serial killers are caught, their hideous careers suddenly public. A neighbor's child climbs a tower on a campus and shoots down fellow students. A friend's spouse turns out to have been a torturer. Such acts are particularly both shocking and mysterious, troublingly so: beyond the horror of the acts uncovered stands someone who is very hard to romanticize. There he or she stands, looking familiar, ordinary, entirely human and unremarkable. But that is flat-out unacceptable: this is someone we suddenly do not know, cannot even imagine. Not knowing what else to do, we encapsulate the doer of such deeds by recategorizing her or him: "Monster," we say, feeling outrage and lingering terror that we could have been so fooled. "Completely insane." Neither works, of course: if he or she actually was a monster or completely insane, by definition normalcy would hardly have been a sustainable act. But that is what we do: we categorize the acts, and then move the actor into the same category.

Those who actually have experience with purposefully, professionally doing harm to other people not only do not thus categorize themselves but also tell us that "monsters" are no good at such work. Professional harm-doers are the opposite of romantics. Says an "interrogation expert"—someone who knows about torture: "Only a psychopath can torture and be unaffected. You don't want people like that in your organization. They are untrustworthy, and tend to have grotesque other problems."[2]

With encapsulated evils like those I used above as examples, we are dealing with some of the images, stories, experiences that we tend to use to define evil. We lump these and other examples together, in part led to do so by their press to be romanticized as extraordinary, incomprehensible, even, ironically, unique. But there are very serious problems caused by doing so. It is time now to sort out some differing meanings in the broader scope of *evil* that allow us finally to think unromantically and so, I believe, far more effectively not only about what we are up against, but how we might work against it. A quote from Hannah Arendt to pull together some threads while, as always, pressing us to keep thinking:

> We were here not concerned with wickedness, with which religion and literature have tried to come to terms, but with evil; not with sin and the great villains who became the negative heroes in literature and usually acted out of envy and resentment, but with the non-wicked everybody who has no specific motives and for this reason is capable of *infinite* evil; unlike the villain, he never meets his midnight disaster.[3]

Chapter Seven

Intensive Evil, Extensive Evil

The vignettes I just used depict what I have come to call *intensive* evils. They differ in crucial ways from *extensive* evils such as the Nazis perpetrated and that are my major focus. It is time to clarify this distinction. I believe that lacking it has had seriously skewing effects on our efforts to understand the evils that humans do, and so what we might do to render them less likely to happen.

Intensive evils *are great harms done by one or a few people. In that sense, they are contained: they stand in shuddering contrast with the lives others are leading around them in their times. When they burst into our lives, almost all of us are genuinely spectators, not participants, not enablers, not perpetrators.*

If the evils that concern Camus, Arendt, and Szymborska, which I call *extensive*, spread like plagues, *intensive* evils in the body politic are more like poison: they do their great harm to a few, leaving lasting effects among others when they cease, but they do cease and they do leave clear lines between the poisoned and the unpoisoned. This is why this kind of evil, intensive evil, tempts us to romanticize it so much: there *are* antiheroes, terrifying individuals and groups that actually did identifiable things in direct, obvious defiance of still-prevalent norms that everyone else can and does use to condemn the aberrant actors and acts when revealed. Systems have not gone bad; people within them have, so the people who did terrible things do stand out in stark contrast. They are precisely not ordinary.

These evils are indeed intensive: exaggeratedly distinct from our usual more scattered and mixed lives as, say, an all-consuming, obsessive, intense passion differs from the love we feel for a long-term partner, or—moving away from the drama—as "intensive study" is differentiated from simply learning.

But there is another kind of evil too, and it is importantly different.

They were asked what they had seen when they returned from the war, what they had seen at those camps, and they would look down, look away, look lost and say, very quietly, "It was unspeakable: we saw the evil of which humans are capable." Not 15 skeletons in a suburban backyard: hundreds in a pile, thousands in pits, millions altogether and who knows how many entirely? New terms were coined: "genocide" entered the language, a project using murder to render a whole "race" of people not only dead, but extinct. Terrifying pictures, films of mass rallies, of goose-stepping automaton soldiers, of flat-eyed men in jack boots with whips, and huge red swastikas proliferated as the hideous silences of heaps of bones, of gold dug out of teeth, grew.

There really were the slave ships, those terrifying slave ships, human beings jammed together below decks, in chains, taken to markets where people—people with families, people with friends, interests, purposes—bought them, shackled them, took them to labor with less care and respect than their oxen and horses.

These are extensive evils, *the massive, monstrous harms carried out by many, many people for significant periods of times—months, years, decades, and more. They are the evils of which we would not speak, of which we so often say, "unthinkable."*
Extensive evil, which precisely in its distinctiveness from intensive evil is my primary subject, can also be romanticized, but it ought to be harder to continue to do so when we turn from the horrific acts on a grand scale to the actual doing of it. Extensive evil is not contained; it is widespread. It does not stand out in stark contrast to persistent ordinary lives, normally decent people; it is enabled by the turning of whole systems until it is ordinary to do terrible things, to benefit, or to go on living as if "We didn't know." Extensive evil requires that it be conventional to do its work as one's job, daily, day after day after day after day, with supper at home and picnics on the weekends.

It is hard to see the ordinary in Charles Manson or Hitler himself; they can indeed be made to seem demonic. It is actually not so hard to see the implication of the ordinary when we think of the vast number of people it takes to do extensive harms. Step back from the most dramatic moments, and we realize that mass harms actually carried out depend on a lot of work reliably and persistently carried out over time by many people doing their jobs.

He sighed and shook his head when he received the orders. They were not entirely a surprise, not really, but still he had hoped. . . . He took his glasses off; polished them; poured himself another cup of coffee. He sat down, took up his pen, and started drawing yet again a map he knew very well, a map of the train routes from the city to the quieter, more private, semi-rural areas surrounding it where already Jews were being held in concentration camps. Now, with the order before him, he needed to figure out how to make the transport of millions, not just hundreds or even thousands, of people to the camps not only possible— lord knows, a huge challenge already—but efficient, effective. The logistical dimensions of The Final Solution, announced now as state policy, were huge. He focused on the first obvious problem. Interesting, *he found himself thinking. After a bit, he also found himself beginning to smile.* He could do this. They, *his superiors, had asked* him, *not anyone else, to help; they had turned to* him *to get the hard job done. There would be recognition, no doubt a promotion. He worked late, kept going by a new exhilaration.*

Such extensive harms—some of which continue for hundreds of years, some of which are still with us after millennia—can become so woven into the fabric of lives that individuals enact them with a sense that they are simply serving or protecting a good, even a necessary, way of life:

Sue, mistress of the house, knew the woman well. For years, Ruby had cleaned the house, minded the children, helped out in the garden. She was hard- working, warm, respectful, even funny. She was also, the older woman who was her employer knew, smart, although she didn't show it much to other people. It was part of the bond between them, a secret they could enjoy, or so Sue was sure. The white mistress of the house took pleasure in saying that her black maid was, really, her friend, and loved her and her children. And then Sue heard: instead of going to church one Sunday, Ruby was caught going around to register others in her community to vote, walking around with one of those outsiders, those troublemakers. Of course, Sue fired her on the spot, knowing that now no one else would hire her either, that Ruby had no other income, that she was not well, and her children not yet grown. Thereafter, now and again she saw her former maid in the street. Each time, Sue looked away, quickly walked on. If she felt a momentary twinge of sadness, perhaps even of shame, she remembered that that woman had so cleverly pretended to be a good maid but was really a snake, a traitor, insinuating herself into her superiors' good graces when she really hated them. A close call, Sue thought, hugging her children to her as she explained what a threat those people are to all that is decent. You cannot give them an inch, she explained, even if they fool you into thinking they are all right, the exception, even your friend. Really, they can't help it: they're just closer to the animals than we are. So, I know you miss Ruby, Sue said, but she is dangerous and she will not be back. Then she hugged them again, and gave them cookies she had even, this once, baked herself.

To the fictional composite Sue, to those who "defended our way of life" against Civil Rights workers but, when pressed, did not approve of the Ku Klux Klan either, what they did was not evil, nor, probably, would many of us romanticize Sue, as distinct from the extensive evils of which she was a worker ant. She was not important enough to seem to be evil-incarnate. She simply had her explanatory categories at the ready and they did the work for her. She upheld the conventions of her people in her time, and nothing about that then made her seriously stop and think. There are no excuses there: Sue failed to remember all she really had glimpsed in Ruby, what she knew about Ruby's life, her own basic moral principles, when remembering all that would have forced her to think about what she was doing. She chose to remain privileged and conventional. Others did not. But Sue was simply not up to the job of thinking for herself as, in this case, her heart as well as her mind could very well have asked her to. Perhaps she had some sleepless nights, and perhaps that made her feel better because then she was angrier at "those people" for disrupting her life.

Sue was certainly less powerful than Eichmann and could not have done what he did, not in a million years, but she in her numbers was and is more essential to the actual, on-the-ground doing of the work of injustice on a monstrous, potentially and often actually deadly, scale.

Both of the imagined (but not, shall I say, entirely made up) people in this set of examples were carrying on systems that enabled and justified massive violations, horrific harms to many other people over time. Both actually thought of themselves as doing something ordinary. Both, in fact, thought, really, only of themselves, about what was done to, asked of, expected of them. No questioning of the system, no reflection about their acts, no imaginative empathy for the others affected by their acts (such thoughts, which probably did intrude now and again, can always be squelched). Both were, in short, ordinary, well-behaved people nonetheless deeply complicit in genocide in the one case, slavery mutated into exploitative, violently enforced segregation in the other. Not good people, then. Cape-swirling monsters? Not really. What they are is determinedly conventional people who do not, in astonishment of any kind, find themselves stopped, startled back into genuine thought by what they are doing in carrying out requirements of systemic evils from which, for a while that they do not see ending, they benefit. They are out of touch with what they are really doing, but they are entirely in touch with the operative, reward-conferring conventions around them. They have no desire to lose those rewards. They have no serious difficulty thinking about what they are doing solely in terms with which their times and places provide them, and their friends and superiors approve. It is good to be a team player and admired for living by such clear rules.

So, yes, we can, and certainly do, romanticize the doers of extensive evil as we can those of intensive evil, but it is harder and falsifies a great deal more. They are not monsters so much as they are the material of, have chosen to suppress themselves into being, well-rewarded stereotypes of "one of us," "a success," "a loyal Southerner," "a good German."

There is a problem with thinking within systems of extensive evil: as egregiously unjust organizational, societal, economic, political systems spread and establish themselves, the unique, independent, original becomes ever more risky, and ever more minds pull back into themselves. Much more of life becomes banal. As Camus wrote, "By reason of their very great duration great misfortunes are monotonous." "The truth is that nothing is less sensational than pestilence." [1] But it kills or damages many, many more than sensational intensive evil.

Where our minds want to stop is all too often precisely where and when we need them most of all.

So, my need to make the distinction between *extensive* and *intensive* evil has a special urgency because I fear that its lack keeps us from understanding the extensive evil that is by far the greater threat of the two. On a complementary and parallel track (in part II), I want also to think through what it might do for us to distinguish between an intensive goodness "that passeth all understanding," goodness that is "not of this world," "saintly," and an extensive goodness that arises when doing good is, for the doers, simply the thing to do and so can be and is something that can be done by many over time: "I'm not a hero. No. What else could I have done?"

Let us, then, gather some threads we already have and go deeper into meanings of these terms, to see what sort of work they can do for us as we try to understand "the unthinkable" and what more we might do to make conditions less hospitable to it.

FOCUS ON INTENSIVE EVIL

It is this kind of evil—for instance, of serial killers, cult murders, "shooters," lone bombers of public buildings—that can, and I believe much too often does, dominate our thinking, thence our comprehension, our explanations, our defensive acts and plans and provisions pertaining to *all* evils. The lack of this distinction, I am now convinced, distorts our thinking about the large-scale, extensive evils such as genocides, slavery, endemic sexualized violence against women and children, deadly exploitation of workers, millennia of anti-Semitism, that entail the scattering, isolating, slaughtering, raping, exploitative violations of millions and millions of people in many countries and times. Thinking of all evils as if they were intensive—taboo, smacking of possession, shocking to still-functioning conventional society, hence readily felt to be antirational—blinds us to the on-the-ground realities especially of extensive evils that are enabled, instead, by such familiar motivators as careerism and greed, social conformity, a desire not to rock the boat.

There is a similar confusion of differing kinds of deadly harm captured in these lines by the poet Charles Simic:

> There are one or two murderers in any crowd.
> They do not suspect their destinies yet.
> Wars are started to make it easy for them
> To kill a woman pushing a baby carriage.[2]

I have to respond, Ah, yes: There are a few murderers always among us, whether or not they have had their chance yet. Still, I am afraid that murderers are a risk, not a bonus, for the military even in wartime. They are out of order, inappropriate: intentional violence against others does not become a *war* until a very large number of non-murderers are also killing, and many more have become complicit in all the daily ways that enable frontline people to do their work. Murderers make poor soldiers, since the actual purpose of soldiering is not to kill but to do as ordered toward the end of winning an armed conflict. Bloodlust can get in the way of trained obedience and skill. The poem, then, may express truths about intensive evil, but is quite wrong about extensive evils, for which, as for wars, *reliable* workers are needed.

In contrast, *intensive* evils are horrific, episodic rather than sustained acts *by individuals or small groups*. One person or one rather small group is directly responsible for such acts. The acts may stretch through time, but they do not infect many people: typically, they are carried out in secret, in isolation, because they are not normalized for a whole society or polity. On the contrary. They are bounded, sharply defined and identifiable by striking deviations from conventionalized behavior even though, within their bounds, they do have their own cultures of explanation and legitimization. They are intensified by their very boundedness, their isolation from, defiance of, all that surrounds them as normalcy, as ordinary. When discovered, they cut through the protective wrapping of the ordinary like a laser: central to their power to appall and paralyze us is precisely their revelation of the utter uselessness of normalcy to protect or to inure us to them.

Stories of what I call intensive evil go something like this:

The woman who opened the door to the man who was already a serial killer might have been able to talk a merely twisted, merely troubled man out of what he intended to do to her, but she stood not a chance in hell of talking her way out of what this man had so carefully planned. He had practiced. He had been successful with other women who, as she did, fit his criteria. He was proud of having fooled everybody for so long, and believed himself superior to those who blundered about trying to figure out who was killing so many women, and why,

and how to stop him. He smiled charmingly at the woman holding the door and
began to talk himself into her home.

Most people remain outside of, unimplicated in, acts of intensive evil. When they come to light—a telling phrase—we become in our numbers their appalled (for some, also titillated) voyeurs. This distance between "us" and "them," the perpetrators, is a recognition and a felt experience of the shared understandings by which social orders, cultures, legal and political systems, religions draw lines to demarcate the acceptable, the punishable or actionable, the taboo. In encountering radical violations of those shared understandings of limits, we reaffirm rather than violate them in our gut reactions of moral horror perhaps even more than our expressions of shock and outrage.

"EVIL"? OR "BAD," "SICK," "ABNORMAL"

We may actually know that we could ourselves under some extreme circumstances commit, say, murder (to stop someone from stabbing an old man; to end years of sexualized abuse our world colludes in refusing to see; during an insurrection), but we do not usually call such murders *evil*. We might do so if a culturally needed norm were violated—if a mother murdered her child, if a general killed his own troops—because then the supposedly normal, conflated with the normative, has been radically exposed as vulnerable: *that* is beyond "bad." Understandable and, we believe, explicable bad acts, including killings, done by rational-enough people we nonetheless hold morally responsible are quite, quite different. We can understand killing in self-defense without threatening the very pillars of our conventional worlds, and while to understand, we know, is not necessarily to excuse, it does keep actions on the other side of the line from evil. We also provide for so-called insanity defenses, thereby recognizing that there are wrong actions, including killing, which we may not understand as congruent with *normal*, but for which we do have categories. Doers of categorized, non-normal acts may not then be held morally and/or legally responsible—for example, because they were judged incapable of knowing right from wrong. Again, these acts are not called "evil" because they are not, in good-enough times, *anti*-normal. More specifically, I do not think them to be intensive even if they are aberrant.

Both rational and irrational acts (so judged) can be categorized and dealt with, however more or less well, justly, or fairly, but dealt with: our systems, conceptual, moral, legal, are not paralyzed by them. Even a planned, murderous, and suicidal binge of killing by one person for which no organization "claims credit" (an odd phrase indeed) may not cause some of us to invoke evil anymore as long as it is contained, singular, entirely over with when the killer kills himself (far more rarely, herself). We are now more likely, as a society, to call in the social scientists, the psychologists and social psychologists, to explain to us how that particular individual became "sick," when and how that could and should have been known, how to be more effectively protective next time. That is, we are not rendered helpless by such acts: we think we ought to know what to do, ought to have done it, can do better.

In our psychologized age, what we call evil with the characteristics of intensive evil in mind may be a shrinking category even if not a shrinking phenomenon (would that it were). Still, intensive evil disproportionately haunts our imaginations, our popular arts, and dominates meanings beyond its rather narrow useful scope.

CROSSING FROM "WRONG," TO "TABOO," TO "POSSESSED"

What is important to observe now is that the evils that are usefully considered *intensive* are acts that are more akin to those that have been called "taboo" rather than "bad." They are individual and/or small group acts that isolate the perpetrators from all that their audiences can consider normal enough to be categorized in some explanatory way, even as clinically abnormal. The idea of a devil, shall we say, is not of a clinically psychotic individual whose biochemistry or neural wiring and/or childhood sufferings could adequately explain his malevolence. In a key scene in the movie *The Exorcist* (1973), the little girl possessed by a demon, perhaps the devil, is to be treated by a psychiatrist. He approaches her with careful but apparently kindly concern. He questions her. Suddenly, her head spins around and the little girl lets loose with a blast of sound, of sheer malevolent force and, as I recall, profanity, that knocks the presumptuous psychiatrist clear across the room. That which has taken possession of the girl, we are to recognize, is something way, way beyond the puny human psyche, however deranged. Something way, way beyond human knowledge has revealed its presence right here, now, but such that even time and place are transfigured: No place, no time marks limits to its potency.

What being "possessed" means changes through differing eras of religion as of social sciences, but something like that notion characterizes what we persist in calling evil and that I am distinguishing as of the intensive sort. We picture a person (or people, but in an identifiable, limited group, such as those at Jonestown who passed the deadly Kool-Aid even to their own children) who is not only not thinking but is radically out of control, or, while doing something horrific, is so controlled as to be incomprehensible and therefore all the more terrifying. Finding no ready connecting points in our own experience with what faces us, we can be rendered temporarily unable to think, in effect blasted across the room like the psychiatrist questioning the possessed little girl. In that weird, frightening, void state and its appalled aftermath, we reach for, we welcome, labels that point beyond themselves to the extraordinary: *the devil, a monster, zombie-like.* Such labels, which can be heard when observers of intensive evils try to speak, are really opt out signs: Here There Be Dragons. Do Not Enter.

The life that goes on when the monstrous acts of intensive evil, in their radical, isolated, abnormality, flame out is actually the hero of such tales, or the comedy (in the classic sense) to their tragedy. Eruptions end; spring and love and other gifts of regular life return. This is unheroic on the face of it, but, seen starkly against intensive evils, ordinary life grows in value to us, revealed suddenly as not dull and daily, but infinitely precious. It is not unlikely that part of the appeal, the titillating invitation to romanticize the tragedy of intensive evil, is precisely that both when we are faced with it and in its wake, banality is banished.

Things are quite different, more complicated, even contradictory with extensive evils. In their aftermath, which is very long in coming, a "return to normalcy" has quite a different ring to it. If we lose trust in ordinary life because we know it can be ripped apart by intensive evils, still we come also to value it. If we lose trust in ordinary life when an extensive evil has finally ended, it can be because we then know that the evildoing had itself become common, not exceptional but integrated into dailiness. Not a few white Southerners in the United States considered efforts to end slavery and, after Abraham Lincoln's Emancipation Proclamation of January 1, 1863, further efforts to empower former slaves, to be *attacks on our way of life.* We do not hear such responses to efforts to stop a serial killer.

Recognized ordinary virtues such as modestly doing one's duty; working hard at an established job; being respectful of established political, cultural, social, and moral authority; being self-interested (a "realist," "economically rational"); acting unquestioningly on the basis of presently legitimated knowledge—all of these can be flipped to become the very qualities that enable daily the work of extensive evil. This is not the case for intensive evils: serial killers, cults, shooters drastically violate just such qualities and virtues.

NOT JUST CRIMES

Consider the starkly contrasting movies *Dead Man Walking* and *The Silence of the Lambs.* In *Dead Man Walking*, a murderer on death row becomes, as we get to know him through the visits of a nun in the days before his execution, not a mysteriously evil figure but a desiccated, frustrated, angry, un-self-knowing, swaggering but weak man. He becomes, not Evil/Other/ Devilish, but pitiful and, in fact, pitiable—although not innocent. He is hurt, he has become weak, he has done a very bad thing indeed, but to the nun and by the end of the movie, to most of us, he is not evil. A challenge this movie issues us is thus to recognize that explanation and understanding may not alleviate guilt, nor remove from us the burden of choosing whether and how to mete out appropriate punishment to someone both pitiable and guilty. A nun can forgive, but can a society based on law do so? Such genuine and important quandaries can, as they should, arise when romanticizing is avoided, as in this film: we can sort out a crime with its attendant legal issues from intensive evil, and there is no suggestion of the contagion of extensive evil.

In *The Silence of the Lambs*, on quite the other hand, there is a kind of stunned fascination that only grows as Hannibal Lecter is revealed through his conversations with a woman (interesting gender themes there, too) as worse than we can imagine. He becomes hypnotic, fascinating—romanticized as both horrible in boundary-shattering ways and, a key point, superior. As the behavioral psychologist says to the young woman he is sending to talk with "Dr. Lecter" (and she does use his title), *Do not let him into your mind*. Locked up for eight years, under constant surveillance, this evil man can still overpower us lesser creatures. He can even kill, as he does the man in the next cell, just by talking.

This is intensive—encapsulated, super-ordinary—evil romanticized, and all the more so for the gendered dynamics involved: super-dominant maleness with the power of both rationality and death are Dr. Lecter's to use, his to abuse. "Hannibal Lecter" evokes lecturer, reader, and lecher as well as Hannibal the Conqueror. The very field that provides labels by which "modern" folks seek to contain sheer horror in the face of what humans can do, psychiatry (no mere psychology for Dr. Lecter: he is a physician *and* a shrink), is romanticized into a tool an evil person can use utterly to destroy normal, good people. Or at least come close enough to give us a vicarious thrill of simultaneously sexualized and infantile terror. The revenge of the psychiatrist, perhaps: blown across the room by the devil in *The Exorcist*, he returns as an evildoer himself.

FOCUS ON EXTENSIVE EVIL

The evils I am suggesting we call *extensive* are distinctively different: they are massively violative harms kept up over time that—simply, factually— could not be done by one or a few people. Such acts—following from, carrying out, state and colonial genocides; creating, continuing, refusing to alleviate large-scale famines; undertaking to wipe out a whole class of people; arming and rewarding men for terrorizing, killing, raping all possible people in a large area that is to be taken over; silencing whole nations through policing all expression, arresting, torturing; basing economies on labor by enslaved people, on labor by radically exploited people, by children, by non-citizens with no protected rights—these things must be done by many people. And they must be done by many people in a sustained fashion, which is also to say, the doers must be reliable, not out of control, possessed, irrational, filled with murderous hatred or frightened for their own lives.

RELIABLE WORKERS

These are not crimes of passion any more than they are the acts of insane or "sick" people, or super men, either. Many ordinary people must get up, day after day after day after day; have breakfast; go out in daylight among others; and once again directly themselves do and/or participate knowledgeably in enabling others to do horrific things on purpose. The doers must take regular care of themselves in ways that genuinely keep them going as they continue to do such work in the world. There are still differing kinds and levels of complicity and guilt among the many doers and enablers of extensive evil, of course, *and these do matter*, but from enabling bystander to frontline agent of horrific harm there is a web of mutual implication. Extensive evils require them all to continue to show up and keep playing their roles, doing their work.

OBJECTIONS

What on earth, you may say: people don't purposefully, as part of their everyday lives, repeatedly do or directly enable horrific harm to many, many other people. Something is wrong with them if they are doing that: *sane* and *civilized* people don't do such things; rational people don't do such things; educated—fill in your preference or prejudice—people don't do such things. Unfortunately, trying to define what a majority of people do daily and on purpose and in accord with a prevailing system as "insane" or its dangerous cultural equivalent, "uncivilized," is not at all helpful. Whatever else "insane" means, it includes inability to function as normal people do, and under systems gone badly wrong and committing extensive evils, it is the few who resist who seem (and have historically been treated as) insane.

As Hannah Arendt put it, in her report from the trial in Jerusalem of Adolf Eichmann, the Engineer of the Final Solution, the judges dealt with a case that:

> rested on the assumption that the defendant, like all "normal persons," must have been aware of the criminal nature of his acts, and Eichmann was indeed normal insofar as he was "no exception within the Nazi regime." However, under the conditions of the Third Reich, only "exceptions" could be expected to react "normally." This simple truth of the matter created a dilemma for the judges which they could neither resolve nor escape.[3]

"Sane and civilized people don't allow torture," I have heard it said in the United States, even as the US government was indeed having people tortured: records are emerging indicating that the practice was forwarded under the George W. Bush administration but hardly his alone. *Oh, well,* some say. *That's because you have to treat those people the only way that works with them. Terrorists are not rational. They are religious and political extremists,* which is to say, *They are all insane.* I fear this is prejudice—pre-judicial, sweeping group categorizations impervious to contrary evidence or reflection. We also, however, make such dangerous errors in part because of a conflation of intensive with extensive evils. No, a planned series of attacks that are "successful" in wreaking havoc, displaying the reach of your power into the very heartland of your declared enemy and doing so again and again is not evidence of intellectual incapacity. Nor, I fear, is torture as state policy.

I also have to say that, when I speak to European-Americans about the Rwandan genocide, the idea that it was caused and is explained by "tribalism" is working more or less behind the scenes in more than a few post-talk comments. Need I point out that there are deeply ingrained prejudices at work in such "explanations"? (*Those people are not really civilized. The veneer just came off. They reverted* can be right there, unspoken but efficacious.) Not surprising, and dangerous: where our minds want to stop before things that horrify and terrify us, they all too readily produce prejudices we may even have thought we had rid ourselves of long since. Preventing us from being in touch with the individual, complex realities of people who have been defined by those in power as less than fully human is precisely the function of prejudices.

What needs to be fully realized now is that conventional biases, assumptions, prejudices can be turned from aberration into normalcy during periods of extensive evils, when "sane and civilized people" of many sorts in differing times have indeed reliably gone about torturing, slaughtering, raping, exploiting, stealing from others as part of their daily lives, and jobs. It is *intensive* evil that seems mad, utterly abnormal, to most others *in its own time*.

We cannot understand and so cannot realize that, and how, we might act to stop extensive evils if we keep thinking of them in ways only appropriate to intensive evils.

Deep at the heart of the horrific shock of the Holocaust remains, I repeat, the thought, so dear to the dominant Western tradition, that "we" don't do such "primitive," "insane" things as mass slaughter, extermination camps, domestic enslavement and/or sexual violations of females, or literally working people to death. We have criminals; we have "sick" people; we have the occasional monstrous eruption of intensive evil—but these actually are all exceptions, so admitting that they do happen goes safely under exceptions that prove the rule: *We are not like that.* Tragically, though, I am afraid "we" have indeed done those other things that, while they went on, were the rule, and not exceptions. Consider the treatment of Abolitionists in the United States, of early union organizers, of Civil Rights workers: these, opposed to mass, normalized, horrific harms, were the outliers, breaking the law, at risk of beatings, deportations, murder. To be moral then was to be abnormal, and that I fear is always risky.

Extensive evil cannot be understood if we keep using the categories we use for crime and for intensive evil for it, much as we clearly want to. Lingering desires to depict "them"/those barbarians, insane, extremist, tribal, primitive—need I go on?—people as inferior to "us"/civilized, rational, moderates ruled by law and always-kindly religions are, I fear, not viable: entirely to the contrary. They are seeds as they are fruits of racializations and other categorizing devices that remain available and useful for extensive evil everywhere and among us all. This is all ugly. It is also indulgent nonthinking precisely where we need the opposite.

Most simply, and challengingly: comprehending extensive evils specifically requires us to think about how massive harms actually can and do get done by the many, many ordinary people without whose active, persistent, consistent, and so also necessarily purposeful participation such evils could not get done at all.

With *extensive evil* before us, we are not, then, asking about a person or small group acting in radically aberrant ways, as we are when working with *intensive evil*. We are asking now about *almost everyone*: extensive evil requires that uncomfortable shift. No one person, no few people, can commit genocide, keep a slave-based economy going, or a worldwide child pornography trade. It simply is not possible. And we already know that there are not enough monsters to do the work of extensive evil in some way that would cut way down on all that work, all that need for reliable personnel.

"A MURDEROUS RAGE"

A hate-filled mob can do great harm, but the fuel of active, murderous, prejudicial rage burns quickly. It cannot be sustained daily in one let alone many people for months and months and months. Even if present, it has to be sublimated: it takes other drivers to get the work of extensive evil done. Anti-Semites, for instance, may fully believe their racialized fears and hatreds are justified (all racists do: that is what we mean by "racist"), but extensive, fully public, horrific deeds carried out over time as a normalized thing to do require something other than flare-ups of even long-nurtured passionate hatred.

Remember some time when you were filled with rage and wanted to annihilate someone (which we will trust you did not actually do, but most of us have indeed wanted to at least a few times). Could you have sustained that rage for a full day? Sustained and acted on it for three days? A week? A month? Three months (the length of the Rwandan genocide; the Nazis' took years, as did, and does, slavery)? Could you have murdered, close-in, often face-to-face, hundreds of people, thousands of people, on the strength of your unflagging rage alone?

If it always required blinding rage or another equal passion to overcome the taboo against murder, extensive evils would not have happened; some intensive evils would; but mostly, we would have had no more than crimes "of passion"— not even "murder in cold blood."

There are, though, intensive evils that are part of extensive evils—for example, some rapes, lynchings, castrations, beatings, beheadings, stonings. These, which can occur as onetime outbursts, as crimes, can also become intensive evils when they break the bounds of even those deeply shocking actions. Hard to imagine, I know, but think of a killing that is prolonged to keep the victim suffering which, when we discover it, leaves us utterly undone. *Not just a murderer: a madman, a monster did that.* If such intensive evils then recur, even take on recognizable patterns as they also become very widely known—horribly brutal killings videotaped and posted for the world to see, perhaps—something else is also going on. What recurrently shocks us as intensive evil can keep us from realizing that here we may instead have extensive evil because these are evidently not, or no longer, the acts of singular monsters when they are publicized, repeated, and not stopped or punished by legal systems or the horror of conventional society that would once have done so. By shattering ordinary constraints and boundaries with impunity within a system that ought by prior standards to have reacted as we do to outbreaks of aberrant, horrid acts, these apparently intensive evils mark the presence of and do work useful to extensive evil. They keep us thinking, *They must be mad!* for too long.

REVEALING RESISTANCE

Gandhi's revolutionary technique of *satyagraha* (*soul force; nonviolent resistance;* or, as he called it also, *experiments in truth*) is in part as original, and was as effective, as it was because he understood so well that the repressive British imperial Raj depended on thousands and thousands of individual people calmly and effectively doing their jobs in its service. Gandhi and the growing number of people who wanted their freedom thus took on the task of making those daily jobs—and not directly the most visibly powerful ones held by very few—more difficult to do. They did so purposefully, without providing the doers, the jobholders, the loyal colonialists, with ready ways to continue avoiding thinking about, facing up to, having feelings in relation to what they were doing and to whom they were doing it. Thus, in some actions, *satyagrahis*, nonviolent activists, walked up to and faced directly the people who were supposed to stop them from crossing a barrier—and then went on across the barrier unless physically stopped. However prejudiced and fearful the colonial officers trying to stop oncoming *satyagrahis* were, they could not keep on for long bashing unarmed, nonviolent person after person. Their arms got tired; their spirits quailed; their obedience failed: they were given too many chances to realize what they were doing, and just plain wore out in the doing of it.

Gandhi thought of this aspect of his technique as turning conflict, during which both sides are trying to win, into ethical communication concerning choice: "The objective is not to assert propositions, but to create possibilities. In opening up new choices and in confronting an opponent with the demand that he make a choice, the satyagrahi involves himself in acts of 'ethical existence.'"[4] Similarly, Dr. Martin Luther King wrote in his *Letter from Birmingham Jail* that nonviolent activists were trying to increase tension to the point at which those who had refused to negotiate would become open to talks after all.

I do not think this remarkable kind of political action was and remains so effective, as it is so often claimed, because it was the British or US Southerners and not Nazis being challenged to choose differently. Hardly: that is for non-Germans a self-congratulatory prejudice that overlooks historical evidence of what the British (and not they alone, then or now) could and did do–for instance, in Africa, in Ireland, and, yes, in India, where, some 350–1,000 pilgrims and nonviolent protestors were shot and killed by British troops in the Amritsar Massacre. But the key point for now is that the Indian revolution against the Raj and in its ways the Civil Rights movement in the United States demonstrated, among other things, that where great harm is being done by ordinary people over time as if it were normal, it may be combated by ordinary people refusing to stop being ordinary—if there are enough, if they are ready, if they, like the doers of harm, are able to understand what they are doing as part of a system that they are serving. In March 1930, to protest an onerous tax on salt, Gandhi led a great march to the sea to make salt as one of his more dramatic revolutionary tactics. He thus stayed close to the everyday, to where colonialism was hurting many ordinary people directly rather than focusing on the most dramatic of harms. As noted, he also called the revolution "experiments in truth," and called off actions, including his own hunger strikes, if they seemed to be more coercive than persuasive. He was changing minds, not harming bodies. Which makes me want to say that it is another startling failure to think that leads us to continue to believe that harming bodies changes minds. But the immediate and pressing question is this:

> *Why do we want to think it impossible to get many people to* resist *horrific harm when altogether too much history, not to mention contemporary movements, proves that it is not impossible, not even terribly difficult, to get many people to* do *horrific harm?*

Extensive evils are done, and we do know can also be resisted, by many, many people. We will explore such resistance, and what it takes, further when we turn to discussion of extensive good.

IT REALLY IS THAT BAD—AND
THAT COMMON, AND EASY

People who think of themselves as normal, ordinary, sane and civilized have done and are still doing some kinds of massive harms to many people as part of ongoing daily work and social orders around the globe, and "we" are no exception. The United States was born in its unjust, often horrific, rising to genocidal, treatment of Native Americans (a shameful story hardly yet finished), and built slavery into its foundations. The disenfranchisement of all women from all groups made a lie of the claimed-to-be-generic "men" from the beginning: Neither all men nor all people were created equal as citizens.

People are still being sold into slavery, including the sex trade, including children, all over the world—something like 27 million people (The Borgen Project gives 29.8 million as its figure) are enslaved worldwide[5]—and some privileged, normal, often well-respected Western white men, among others, are taking special "sex tours" in underdeveloped countries to "enjoy" the "services" of enslaved children and women.[6] Workers are laboring for wages paid by some of the biggest names in hugely profitable corporate America that can barely keep those workers or their children—who must therefore also labor, sometimes for people to whom their parents sell them—alive. And everyone knows and openly says that *Of course employers go anywhere to find and use the cheapest of labor.* Why "of course"? After long struggles, we passed child labor laws in this country: we know it is morally wrong on many grounds. And, while there is general agreement now that slavery is morally wrong, arguably it is still practiced in the United States, too, among other ways in use of the labor of prisoners—who are obviously not free—from which not they, but the private, corporate-owned prison that is already paid to incarcerate them, profits. This is quite standard practice now. Communities compete to have private prisons, penitentiaries, and detention centers built in them; profits are made; stockholders "of course" care not as long as our investments pay off. "Of course"?

Well, economists say this is "rational behavior": this is the "free market," the "sane and civilized" way to behave. It is all part of normality, and it is not done by devils incarnate. It is done by respectable citizens and jobholders right out in the open, with legal and political support. There is resistance, too; always, there are people who do not go along.

NOT "BAD APPLES"; PERHAPS GOLDEN ONES

"What occurred at Abu Ghraib is deeply disturbing and Americans, individually and collectively, need to ask, How could this have happened? How could our sons and daughters, good kids from Pennsylvania, Virginia, New Jersey, Maryland, engage in this conduct? How could so many have looked the other way? What happened at Abu Ghraib was not the work of a few bad apples."[7]

This is real progress from romanticizing and defending ourselves by blaming "bad apples," and from familiar assumptions that all Nazis, say, were moral monsters, every last one of them; that any owners and bosses whose workers are horrendously exploited are sociopaths; that rapists are never nice frat boys, noble soldiers, family members, boyfriends, but are always sex fiends, out of control, despite the ugly facts that tell us, for example, that one out of every six adult women in the United States has been a victim of rape or attempted rape. The absurdities of romanticizing the doers of sustained horrific acts do persist, however, as we think of extensive evils in terms only appropriate for intensive evil. That, I fear, is among the reasons that Nazi paraphernalia are also now sex toys, and there are skinheads with swastikas marked on their skulls. These are small people seeking to lose themselves in the romance of taboo, of powerful, possessing evils: they do not playact Eichmann, the man in the suit and tie in the glass booth during his trial in Jerusalem, speaking about his frustration at not being promoted even though he worked hard and did his job well.

If we told the truth about evildoers, separating the reliable workers of extensive evils from criminals, sociopaths or other "sick" people, and from the doers of intensive evils, what would happen to the ways we think of them, of ordinary life, of conventionality? Harder still: If we told the truth about evildoers, what would happen to our romantic fantasies of conventionally successful strivers willing to do what it takes to make the big bucks, get the next promotion, even if they are profiting from the labor of factory workers in Bangladesh working in buildings that can and do collapse, can and do burn to the ground, killing hundreds and more over the years? (As in 2013, two did.) It is never to be underrated, the degree to which material rewards motivate most of us, from the poorest for whom they can be a matter of survival, through those for whom they pad the hard edges of life, and onto those whose growing "wants" are regularly reinterpreted (with the help of status-driven societies, advertising, etc.) as "needs," clear to the radical excess of "the 1 percent" who profit proudly from systems that are destroying, among other things, the middle class any democracy must have to continue. And such people are romanticized too.

In the ongoing quest for an explanation sufficient for the magnitude of extensive evils, good old-fashioned grabbing for money and goods has not often made a significant appearance. It is now beginning to, and this, I think, is very helpful. We encountered a study of Germans following their "rational self-interest" into the Nazis' orbit earlier. Here it is again, filled in enough to show just how familiar their motivations could be:

> [N]othing more than an unremarkable pursuit of self-interest led most Germans to pledge allegiance to the Nazi regime. Germans wanted their children to have nice Christmas gifts. They wanted to set aside money for retirement. They wanted to send a special someone back home a pretty sweater from Holland or perfumed soap from France. Citizens were sated with decent wages, generous overtime pay and innovative pension plans—that is, through the establishment of a complex, if absolutely amoral, welfare state. [8]

Call it a "welfare state" or not (this can mislead, to say the least: hardly the welfare of all), it was a state that plundered as it murdered and used the plunder to turn its citizens into stakeholders in genocide:

> [M]illions of care packages of plundered items were sent back home from the occupied territories by Wehrmacht soldiers who were themselves given hearty rations and plenty of disposable cash. Clothing and household objects that had once belonged to Jews were sold at affordable prices at government-organized public auctions, or simply handed out free as emergency relief. And the Nazis also introduced a progressive income tax that shifted a far greater tax burden onto corporations and the very rich.[9]

There is nothing simple about this; people of differing political persuasions can obviously pull differing strands to emphasize our usual points. Here, I want simply to underscore that we can, and on the record do, allow a focus on our daily, personal well-being to blot out from our moral horizon what that well-being (from survival, to fancy presents) depends upon—and, on the record, can and have done so even when our own well-being is depending on the purposeful, sustained murder of millions of people, some of whom were once our neighbors and friends.

Writing about the "mostly senior officers of the SS, the paramilitary formation that would later organize and carry out the murder of the Jewish people," Dan McMillan observes that, early on, these men did share in Hitler's racist view of Jews as less human than "real" Germans, but then adds that, "Equally important, these men saw that they could advance their careers by taking the initiative to radicalize policy even without orders from Hitler."[10] That is, whatever their ideology, these ambitious, largely highly educated (60 percent held university degrees) men picked up on what the boss might want and tried to get themselves noticed, and so promoted, by advocating and doing more than was at all required—in this case, murderously.

This is the suffocating spread of banality into extensive evil. The ordinary—a thoughtful desire to make a decent living for oneself and others one cares about—flattens into banal greed that suppresses thought about what one is doing, warding off reflection. Getting that promotion blocks out what you do to get it, and then, should we have moments of concern, Leave it at work, colleagues, friends, family, counselors, say. You deserve a good life. Go for it.

Large-scale, extensive, sustained evils must—to be possible, to persist—be socially sanctioned, and that is an aspect of why blaming "bad apples" (a platitude itself) who can be marked off as "exceptions" is inaccurate and so also ineffectual with regard to learning lessons for the future. That these doers are not radical aberrations in their times and places makes them very hard indeed to think about effectively and is part of the weave of reasons we so stubbornly think in terms of intensive evil when faced with the realities of extensive evil.

I need to repeat: one thing not to do with such a realization is to leap straight into, *We're all guilty; all "little Eichmanns"; all the same.* That is too quick, too easy, and as Arendt insisted, it is not true. There were not, and are not, that many Eichmanns. Unfortunately, that does not suffice to avoid extensive evils. Leaping to "all little Eichmanns" keeps us from stubbornly asking about the many, many others without whom he could not have done his work, either, and the ways so many decent people can fail to think what we are doing.

There are two immediate problems with trying to clarify and come to grips with key meanings here. One is how to speak of that which violates our categories of the ordinary, the daily, the normal and normative. The other—and this is my main focus now—is how to speak of that which violates such categories but is in fact made possible by having replaced their usual content with its own, such that killing is turned into an ordinary daily act, a job requirement perhaps; enslaving and/or working people to death is turned into a reasonable business practice; denying females liberty, equality, education, safety from sexualized use and abuse is admired as the act of a rightly ordered society, a demonstration of proper manhood; killing large numbers of ordinary people of all ages randomly as they go about their daily lives is justified as a religious and/or liberatory act.

Again, then, we cannot overlook the fact that such normalizing of the abnormal is not likely to work unless whole systems have gone bad. As they can. Religions have organized people into sustained killers of other people just as scientific theories have been used to justify sterilization of people taken to be mentally subpar. But individuals do the work of these systems, and individuals are thinking creatures, so choices are always also still being made.

SPEAKING TRUTH TO OURSELVES

Here we have to pause to admit a painful, curious twist in what makes speaking of such systemically normalized, but individually carried out, acts so difficult. It is not a matter of "speaking truth to power," or finding words eloquent enough to describe a true villain as, say, Shakespeare could. It is a matter—first and most difficult of all—of seeing, admitting, and thinking through the realization that there have been, and somewhere now are, times in which what "everyone is doing" is morally, politically, deadly wrong. Speaking that sort of truth is often more dangerous for the speaker than speaking truth to a few who are in power, because there is then nowhere to retreat, to hide, to be supported and protected.

This holds for critics of the past as well as the present. How could it be surprising that some people do not take kindly to the work of historians who point out, for example, that slavery would not have been possible if so very many people had not sustained and benefited from all the work it took to make the whole system function 'normally,' lucratively. But think of it: ships to design, finance, build, repair, buy and sell, and to hire sailors for, and cooks, and to buy and sell supplies for, and to stock with maps someone made and sold. There could have been no slaves without the slave markets either, and on both ends of the journey. No people enslaved in their own lands, no slaves to sell for profit before they are shipped. It is not, ever, just the visible, the Them, the singular agents who do extensive evils. Not possible, not at all.

Black civil rights workers sometimes said to white workers who went South, *Now it is time to go back and do this work in your own neighborhoods.* And isn't it interesting—and important for our topic now—that that was more rarely done, less appealing, more emotionally scary, and in some senses even more difficult than doing Good Work elsewhere and among others? The ordinary and widespread is essential to extensive evils, but it is hard to see, to name, and harder to stand against. It is sometimes dangerous, but recognized as courageous and right and noble, to stand up against intensive evils, to rush the house in which the Unabomber has holed up, to go after the drug dealer who has raped and murdered his child runners. But to stand up against extensive evils that shape "ordinary life"—your own, your community's—can lead others to say, *What's wrong with you? Trouble-maker. Malcontent. Idealist. Purist. Don't be so silly, so extreme, so negative.* And it may well simply lead to you, one person, being shunned, ignored, discredited, isolated, fired; unless or until there are others with whom you stand.

Irmgard Hunt has published a memoir of growing up among good, ordinary, struggling non-Jewish Germans as Hitler was coming to power. One day, she and her family joined a crowd hoping to see Hitler himself:

> Then it happened. Hitler came out and I ended up sitting on his lap and family history was made. . . . The applauding crowd disconcerted me . . . but I smiled bravely, checking every few seconds to make sure my family was close by . . . . At one moment I saw my grandfather turning away brusquely, striking the air angrily with his cane, trying to find an escape through the people. He had obviously had enough of the spectacle, feeling most likely that his granddaughter was being misused by the man for whom he had nothing but contempt . . . . The audience with the Fuhrer was over, and everyone would go home bragging about having seen him. Mutti [Mother] beamed at me, and Vati [Father] gave me a "well done" nudge on my shoulder.[11]

The grandfather is put up with, if barely, because "he was her [mother's] father." Irmgard's parents and their friends and other relatives try not to provoke his outbursts so they can get on with their normal lives. The little girl wishes the adults would not fuss at each other at all. Her grandfather's clarity is nothing but irritation to her, to her family, and neighbors. The smiling Fuhrer, squatting down to invite a small girl to sit on his knee, her proud parents beaming: it is the cane-brandishing grandfather who is out of order in that picture. (And always, there are those who will be out of order.)

Chapter Eight

The Ordinary for Good and Ill

The ordinary—a thick loam sedimented from a collective past of beliefs; knowledge; practices; acts and stories of leaders; visions of artists; pop figures; particular communities' versions and variations of these; our very own experiences; the geography of our place; the languages of word, tone, gesture we take most for granted; the paths in us laid by connections of our consciousness—is always the medium for our lives. To shift images, the ordinary for each of us is a set of glasses tinted a color we may never learn to see because we see everything already shaded by it as well as sharpened or dulled by the ways the lenses have been ground.

Here it is that the particular and the general can be so strongly associated, conjoined, that it is very difficult indeed to deal with differences, with change: it is this Christmas tree, this menorah, this wedding dish that *is* what Christmas, Hanukah, a wedding requires to be right. Here it is that we can, and must, practice the art of thinking that allows us to see and know and speak and do more and other than we are conventionally supposed, or enabled to, and here is where it can be most difficult to do so because the ordinary is usually what we stand on when we jump, return to after dreaming, rest in after traveling, after thinking. It is grounding, and pleasurable, to come back to where, without effort, things already make sense. Even if we do not like the sense that is made, I have to add: if there is a physical pull to entropy, to return to a resting state, there is also a mental pull to the ordinary, to a resting state, that can even override the desire to become happier.

But that is not all there is of the ordinary. The ordinary is not always the same. It not only changes over time, but it varies in any given time. On the most obvious level, it varies among peoples and cultures and eras. What was ordinary for the people in Darfur, Sudan, before the mass killings largely by the government-sponsored Janjaweed began is not what was ordinary for the

Serbs, Croats, Kosovo Albanians, Bosnians before the "ethnic cleansings" of
the early 1990s in that troubled region that also shocked the world. To speak,
as I have, of extensive evils being seeded in the ordinary that is not-evil does
not mean we can know the content, as it were, of all the "ordinaries" that can
go wrong, let alone that they are all alike.

It is not so much the content of the ordinariness of lives that can pervert
into the ordinary of extensive evildoers but, rather, the ways and extent to
which it has already sunk into banality, the desiccated husk of the loamy
ordinary. The bacillus of the plague is not the "furniture and linen-chests," the
"bedrooms, cellars, trunks, and bookcases" within which "it can lie dormant
for years and years," as Camus wrote. These shelter it, hide it from our view,
lull us into believing that keeping a proper household protects us. But the
bacillus itself works through our failing in attentiveness so that we become
no longer able to be startled back into thought and so, on autopilot, are ready
to go along when a neighboring group is declared an enemy of our independence, our very existence; this new careermaking chemicals for illicit use in
warfare by a leader against his own people is just another job; the job of a
mercenary fighting and killing for pay, anywhere, anytime, is just as acceptable as all others. These are not enabled by the ordinary that grounds us and
allows us to rest, but by the intellectual, moral, emotional stupor of autopilot
mode in which we are truly out of touch.

How else are we to make sense of the normalizing of lynchings as once
happened? What are we to make of these nonlegal executions, of some of
which, we now know, postcards were made, sold to folks who witnessed
these murders—some while picnicking—written on, sent through the US
mail without hindrance to friends and families?[1] These white people, the
ones who brought their families to picnic at a lynching and sent postcards
of it, were not possessed by hatred, were not under orders, did not fear for
their lives if they did not pack that basket and bring the tablecloth. They
were *habituated*; it was second nature *not* to connect with real people from
whom they had been raised to be out of touch. And they maintained that
distance in the face of daily invitations to be startled back into thought.
Their ordinary lives had deadened strands in them, distorted relations
about which they did not, dared not, think and so also could not feel
appropriately.

HABITUATION

Practice something long enough, and yes you become habituated: you can,
as a decent person, do all sorts of things, from good to horrid, that you could

not if you "thought about it too much," "brooded," had not learned to do it without "letting your imagination run away with you." You can commit the violence of surgery (as a surgeon put it to me years ago during a medical ethics project); offshore a company without compunction despite the people whose jobs and lives you ruin in order to hire desperate people for pennies; stick needles into peoples' arms and withdraw blood without flinching; try to knock someone out to win in the ring; walk past the too many homeless on your way to work. In ordinary life, we become habituated to the doing of difficult things in order to do things that help, that are needed, that our jobs require, that just get us through our days as ordinary people. This is usually okay and sometimes entirely praiseworthy. But there were doctors, surgeons and others, whose habituation allowed them also to work under the Nazi regime.

Habituation is part of ordinary life. We could not make it through life without it. In his *Nichomachean Ethics*, Aristotle advised us to practice virtues such as courage until they become a second nature, just how we are. But when systems go bad, if we have become too thoughtless about our own habits, we may be all too able to turn with the systems around us toward doing harm justified by rotten purposes just as we lived and did our work reliably for benign or admirable purposes before.

Habits, banality: each in its way is a kind of call us we grow not to be "too sensitive" to the daily frictions of realities in ordinary life. Need them or not, we know that, like layers of dead skin, they are both protective and risky: sensation, even pain, gives us information, tells us we should pay attention. We know this connection: *He is a callous man*, we say of someone who evidently does not feel with and for others.

COMMON SENSE

Any society, any system more or less formalized, has both ordinary and lowest common denominator dimensions of meanings. We could not share our worlds if we did not share a lot of meanings, and do so, in many cases, without thinking about it. It is exhausting, and finally paralyzing, to have to think about what is going on and what is asked of us all the time. That is one of the reasons it is so exciting at first, and then really wearing, to travel. Daily life abroad becomes a fresh, new challenge with startling results and sometimes neat rewards. Same for genuine education: it enlivens minds by loosening up, going more deeply into, questioning, sometimes replacing assumptions we did not even know we were making. But rest is nonetheless also necessary: there is only so much, we say, that we can take in and—more important—there is only so much we can think and rethink, perhaps in transformative ways. How much and how long it takes to benefit from such education can depend heavily on how practiced we are, not in learning but in thinking. (There are extremely learned people who are, I fear, not so good at thinking.)

In a healthy society in fairly normal times, among decent people, superficial phrase-trading, which stands in for in-touch common sense far too often, functions to keep communications among us going smoothly, and daily actions routinized enough so that we need not bother to analyze or brood about them. But the dangers of not thinking are always also there.

PROCESSING REALITY

The next time you find yourself in a waiting room with others who are being processed just as you are, say, for the renewal of your driving license, look around you. Very different, in truth, all those people. But those differences have been rendered almost irrelevant with regard to the renewing of a license. This kind of abstraction, stripping off all particularizing individuality, requires all sorts of control methods: we have to be given numbers, put in lines, be asked only the same questions, and be able to offer only the same kind of answers everyone else does, sit in the same sorts of chairs facing people across the same sorts of desks to take the same vision tests on the same kind of machines as everyone else. All of that is, on the face of it, neither good nor bad. It can simply be functional, and it is intended to be egalitarian. It can be effective. It is supposed to be efficient, certainly. Nonetheless, we do need to pay attention to how, in what has become part of an ordinary life, we can be rendered not equal, but all the same, and how that outrage to reality as well as human dignity is accepted as necessary, as efficient, as the only possible way to deal well with large numbers of individuals. The people whose actions affect us can come actually to experience us *only* as either the same or, if we deviate, stand out, become noticeable, *a problem, a risk,* and so also begin not only to avoid but to resent and more actively try to suppress whatever might distinguish us each from each and so—with our collusion (we *need* that license)—"we" become a "they" to them as those workers do to us.

Such processing and the ways it relates us to each other is an aspect of ordinary life that can turn it, and us, bad all too quickly. Genuinely equalizing systems do not grind us down into our very lowest common denominator: they empower us equally by calibrating to take account of differences that could disempower or over-advantage some of us. Treating everyone *the same*, as distinct from *equally*, violates our ordinary experiences of our real differences. We know to resent that, but as ordinary life becomes ever more processed in the name of efficiency and productivity and accountability not only by public offices but by corporate powers that touch and shape and drive our lives daily in ways government rarely does, we can also become less comfortable with equality that, as equality is meant to do, protects just those differences.

MORE MORALITY?

If the problem is that people can be moved into doing horrible things unthinkingly because they have become ordinarily thoughtless, then is the solution to establish stronger, more openly moralized systems? Precisely not: if people are able to be good because they are following systematized conventions, rules and practices, all you have to do to get them to do evil is to pervert the system on which they are dependent. Those who take their morals from outside sources, defining their own role as one of dutiful obedience, can find it far easier to reverse their "thou shalt not"s overnight if told to do so than, suddenly and without practice or support, to start thinking for themselves. In this sense too, the merely obedient can be unstable, unreliable.

Thinking is not unlike running: we are born capable of it, most of us; some of us continue to delight in it and to practice despite all those parental efforts to calm us down and make us behave; most of us pretty much lose the capacity and the delight except, now and then, when startled into action for a short burst, anyway. Ask us to think, ask us to run, when we are entirely unaccustomed and have internalized the feeling that it is more than a bit unseemly, that people will stare at you and worry if you suddenly burst into such action, and we are more likely to look around, to wait, to see if others might do it first to assure us that it is alright this time.

EDUCATION

Making use now of the crucial distinction between intensive and extensive evils, and reflecting in light of the question *What can we do?* that always and ever haunts and presses toward the difficult topic of goodness, the crucial importance of education re-emerges.

The thoughtlessness of banality enables violative injustices to become extensive evils, the work of many people over time. This is why formal education, itself a very widespread system that reaches most people very early, continues for years, and is concerned with developing minds, can and ought to become one of the most purposeful and effective provisions we could establish against extensive evil. However, schools at all levels would need to refocus. Some, of course, are not intended to promote thinking at all, but simply to "train" people, "equip them with skill-sets," and so on—to prepare them to fit right into things as they are. Others do not focus on thinking as purposefully and effectively as on acquisition of knowledge and methods. We can also suffer from pedagogies that stress "outcomes" rather than the process and practice of thinking throughout, and of course from the kind of tests for which any student who starts thinking for herself is at risk of failing. But that is anticipating another book while shortchanging a vibrant ongoing conversation among educators that has always also included those concerned with more than transfer of content and mere training.

Here the crucial point is that as long as our understanding of evildoing remains shaped primarily by intensive evil, another consequence is that we are not likely to focus as we should on widespread education in thinking. When a shooter has killed students, psychologists are called in, and guards. We do not sit down with teachers and work together on helping more people really learn to think, and enjoy it. Strictly in relation to such an intensive evil, we are not wrong to do so. The aberrant perpetrators of intensive evil do not need the rest of us thoughtlessly to do their work as do those of extensive evil.

MOVING ON THE CONTINUUM OF ATTENTIVENESS

The specific danger of banality—of the ordinary in its processed, sameness-enforcing, mind-stilling and so finally boring (mind-disengaging) forms—lies so close to its specific function of smoothing our lives so we can get on with them that it is no surprise at all we do not see the risk inherent in just that function, or do not catch it often enough in time. The banal, the conventional, the clichéd, after all, are doing their work when they carry us through the day without our having to choose, for example, whether or not to stop at the stoplight, whether or not to say, How are you? to our neighbor, or to puzzle over the meaning of "I'm flat broke," or "the blues," or "let's party," or "I can make a killing with this." The superficiality of such verbal or other gestures—which is mostly how we use them: as markers of prepackaged meanings we need only invoke—does not mean they are not densely interwoven with all the meanings of our lives. Not at all. Their function, I repeat, is continually adjusting us so we fit smoothly into prevailing material, interpersonal, social, economic, political orders that, unless we make an effort to assert ourselves against them, make a remarkable number of our moral decisions for us. So basic are these autopilot meanings that it is usually confusing, troubling, sometimes really infuriating to others when we disrupt them. It is hard, as an antiracist feminist slogan has it, to be the one who spoils the party. (That, of course, does not mean that ruining the party *per se* is always good, always needed, nor that we who did it were actually thinking, rather than just flailing about, perhaps grabbing for attention.) In some times and places, it gets people who try it killed. In some, the punishment is far less drastic but not inconsequential: refusing to inhabit and practice the same scripts as others can get one thrown out of the play, off the stage, sent home—fired, cast away, ostracized.

But accepting our freedoms and with them responsibilities requires the very kind of thinking that indeed can ruin the party—and, an intrinsic reward, return to us the ability to be astonished, rather than bored, by the ordinary. The connections between ordinary thoughtlessness and extensive evils ought not be forgotten, because we need to remain attentive, ready, and willing to wake up and think to have a good life even in the best of times.

With regard to extensive evil, what is lethal about most of us is nothing horrid: it is latent in the workings of minds making sense together over time, creating among other abstractions and generalizations some that turn into mind-numbing banalities about which we do not, and do not want to, stop and think, as Socrates long ago demonstrated. He was put to death. This is in every sense serious business. Our bodies want to grow call uses to protect us from physical friction; our minds—and all too often education designed only to inform and to train those minds—want to substitute banal clichés, insider and technical language, regulated logics (numeric, for example) for thinking to keep sharable intellectual, emotional lives on track, without friction.

It is hard, and it is a matter of moral as well as physical survival, nonetheless, to remain in touch with our worlds, ourselves, and others. Formally and informally, we can and ought to be schooled with that purpose very much in mind. Finally, after all, education, which we do understand to be "preparation for life," the best way of all to choose and change your life, is, as Socrates wanted to teach us, not only about how to succeed but how we ought to live.

What, then, not only disables thoughtlessness, mindlessness, but enables goodness?

We are about to explore that question. Here, too, we do need to recognize that it is not easy to connect thinking, attending, reflecting with the doing of good. Thinking seems too open-ended, sort of unanchored, the very opposite, indeed, of the sort of firmness in righteousness, the muscular will, the tough courage being good in distorted times is readily and usually thought to require.

Time to think a bit more about goodness, then, the ordinary kind that can become extensive, and the extraordinary intensive kind that, like intensive evil, seems to require something more dramatic than anything we could educate many for, ask of many, because it too always startles, breaks bounds, lifts us beyond ourselves but is not sustainable, not widely replicable. Intensive and extensive good relate to their opposite kinds of evil: the distinction between the former and the latter remains useful. It is not neat, though; complications also arise. (As always.)

Part II

GOODNESS: WHAT IS TO BE DONE?

Goodness is notoriously a difficult subject.

Chapter Nine

Philip Hallie

It Takes a Village

This much is certain: in the course of the two years of the Occupation, Le Chambon became the safest place for Jews in Europe. How did a life-and-death ethic become incarnate across the whole commune of Le Chambon?[1]

We started part I with Camus' *The Plague*, a fictional effort to depict truths about what I call extensive evil. Good was also at issue in Camus' book, but to explore *how goodness happened*,[2] it is more helpful, or perhaps just more convincing, to see what lessons we might derive from *Lest Innocent Blood Be Shed*, Phillip Hallie's historical study of the villagers of Le Chambon, in France. They actually were good, and were so over time, even as many Parisians (except for the Resistance fighters, Camus among them) fled or were either collaborating with the Nazis, propitiating them, cowering, or carrying on their ordinary lives insofar as possible. The villagers of Le Chambon are, then, very important when we turn to asking how to prepare to be good—in their case, also how to be nonviolent in defiance of extensive evil. There are other sources to be drawn on, but Hallie's is unusual in its focus on goodness happening among many in a detailed historical context.

The real story of Le Chambon is also particularly telling, I think, because in my terms it is a study of extensive rather than intensive good. That matters, because when we consider good as when we consider evil, we tend to focus on singular grand figures, exceptional, awe-inspiring people (and not infrequently, troubling ones: saints are difficult people). Romanticizing distorts here too: a few acts of extraordinary goodness that remain anomalous, astounding, individual, cannot help us if our real quest is to figure out how we might all be better, in time, over time. Hallie's is the story of a village of people who separately and together did over and over what needed to be

119

done, and did so without themselves becoming violent, without killing to stop
the killing.

Mine is a secular study, so I do have to note that religion plays an important
role in this story, appearing in negative historical light as the Catholicism that
historically oppressed France's Protestants, a group including the villagers of
Le Chambon, and positively through the leadership of Pastor Andre Trocmé,
Magda Trocmé, and the Pastor's assistant, Theis. These were leaders, but
the openness of the villagers to practicing independent, daily, on-the-ground
goodness in the name of their independent, protesting/Protestant faith was
crucial. Nonetheless, we will continue our secular focus, both because that
is always also relevant—even people who share a faith choose time and
again just what that means and asks of them, how far, and what, they will
and will not yield in which ways to its authorities—and because even the
Pastor, and assuredly his partner and sometime mentor in daily goodness,
Magda Trocmé, speak largely in secular terms. It is not an indication of lack
of faith—in the Pastor's case, quite the opposite—to say that they speak thus
out of profound conviction that whatever your religion, it is how you choose
to act with and for others daily, in ordinary life and when the ordinary has
been perverted, that matters.

MORAL THINKING

The author of the study of Le Chambon, Phillip Hallie, is a philosopher as is
Camus. It may actually be the case that Camus had Le Chambon in mind when
he wrote *The Plague:* any parallelism certainly fails to be exact between these
two books, but both tell the story of a small town or village attacked by extensive evil in which goodness persisted when there seemed no hope of stopping
monstrous harm, and amid much danger. Both Camus and Hallie, wary of
what the philosopher Hegel called "the fury of abstraction" (which allows us
to slaughter The Enemy, the Hun, the Infidel—abstractions, all such terms),
and wary, too, of the kinds of rationalism I discussed earlier, held their thinking about these matters as close as they could to experiences of actual people
in all-too-difficult situations. Arendt did so too, and further advised us to
"trace experiences rather than doctrines" if we want to understand "the thinking experience, the performance itself" by which, as we might say, consciousness can give rise to conscience as we practice thinking what we are doing.[3]

As Hallie put it, "[F]or me ethics, like the rest of philosophy, is not a
scientific, impersonal matter. It is by and about persons, much as it was for
Socrates."[4] Hallie does not say it, but we also know that, above all, Plato's
Socrates was a practitioner and teacher of thinking and not knowledge, of

which he claimed to have none. In "The Symposium," Socrates says that
he learned his method of question and answer, as distinct from [one-sided,
domineering] speech-making, from Diotima, a wise woman from Mantinea.
Diotima, he says, taught him to love knowledge as an admirer who yearns
for what cannot be possessed, which means, of course, as someone who
always returns to thought, a suitor for whom questioning, reflecting, considering never comes to a full stop. Thus, in the Platonic dialogues featuring the odd, brilliant figure of Socrates, the quest for greater clarity that he
pursues with his questioning engages him respectfully, intensely, with all
sorts of people he encounters out and about in Athens. As Hallie says of
this public thinking, "it is by and about persons,"[5] and most of all, it is by
and about how each one, differently, makes wiser or more foolish decisions
about how to lead a life depending not on what is known, but on how well,
how thoroughly s/he has thought about things. Socrates does not reject or
befriend people; as the best citizen Athens ever had (so he claimed when
the polis, the city-state, so famously condemned him to death), he rejected
or befriended ways of thinking that blocked or furthered a person's efforts
to act, to live, well.

Plato's Socrates, it is also important to note, could be a thinking friend of
Hallie's because both refused to devalue women and the homely works to
which their sex/gender was still largely restricted. Not only does Socrates
speak of learning his method—the famous Socratic Method, as history has
nonetheless called it—from Diotima, he also uses *midwife* as a trope for
himself and for that method.[6] Hallie struggles to learn similar lessons against
the gender-hierarchy grain and the romanticized narratives of singular heroes
that tend very strongly to go with that hierarchy to produce the Great Man
stories of both good and evil that skew our thinking in so many ways. Hallie
is perfectly clear that Magda Trocmé was in all ways both crucial and equally
central to the sustained good works of their whole village, as, each in her own
ways, were many other women who faced down police while also taking in,
providing for, protecting Jews of all ages.

Hallie also recognizes the "redoubtable [organization, the] Cimade . . .
[which] was originated and led by women alone." He tells us:

In 1939, when they began, the members of the Cimade helped care for dis-
placed Alsatians who had been evacuated by the French from their homes. . . .
But in 1940, after the defeat of France, they turned their attention to the most
endangered human beings in Europe: Jews fleeing from Central and Eastern
Europe. . . . [They] developed a web of *equipes* (teams) in the summer of
1942, when the intentions of the Nazis toward the Jews were plain, and with
these teams they took through the mountains of France to neutral Switzerland
the refugees.[7]

Philip Hallie knew that such allies, as well as all the women in the village, were crucial in every way to the slogging, desperate, dangerous, deadly struggle in Occupied France as elsewhere in Europe and this required him to keep switching off his yearning for a heroic male. Thus appear throughout his book variations of this direct recognition: "It is tempting," he writes, "to make the Trocmes all-important in the story of Le Chambon, but it is wrong to do so."[8] Not André alone, not André and Magda, not a small group but virtually all the villagers and allies beyond worked independently, and upheld their trust in each other. This was extensive good: it involved many, and it persisted over time because it was rooted in ordinary lives and their virtues:

> She shook her shoulders hard, raised her hands as if to push away the questioner, and said, "What do you mean? It had to be done, that's all." That simple yet perpetually mysterious answer is the fullest description she would ever give of how she helped to save thousands of refugee children. We had reached bedrock, and the spade had turned.[9]

CONVENTIONAL THOUGHTLESSNESS:
THE OPPOSITE OF EXTENSIVE GOOD

Hallie, in tune with Arendt and Camus, confronted, accepted, and set to work to think through what it may ask of us that, when it comes to the doing of extensive evil, our real enemies are not human devils, but our own dumbest, densest, out-of-touch, compartmentalized, autopilot, clichéd, conventional, inattentive, greedy, careerist, and, enabling all that, thoughtless selves.

Thus Hallie wrote of Pastor Trocmé's discovery when he was arrested and sent to an internment camp—a discovery reminiscent of Arendt's about "radical evil"—that evil indeed can be petty, banal, all too ordinary:

> He discovered people like the captain—patriotic, sincere, but above all, severely *limited*. These people were capable of repeating hate-ridden clichés without any concern for evidence or for the pain of others. Before he entered that police station in Limoges, he thought the world was a scene where two forces were struggling for power: God and the Devil. From then on, he knew that there was a third force seeking hegemony over this world: stupidity. God, the Devil, and halfwits of mind and heart were all struggling with each other to take over the reins.[10]

Later, like another philosopher, Martin Heidegger (who wrote scathingly about conventional submission to *Das Man*, or *The They*, as in, *I can't do that:* They *wouldn't approve)*, Trocmé's came to call the "halfwits" the

"Qu'en dira-t-on?" or the "What will they say?" people. Using a term that spread during the French Occupation, Hallie also calls them the "attentistes," the *Let's wait and see* people who let the Nazis consolidate power while they dithered, and who were "perhaps in the majority in France in those days": "Above all, they wanted to avoid personal discomfort, friction, and conspicuousness."[11] And so they went along with the would-be kindly but order-following police who sometimes bent the smaller rules, but carried out the deadly large ones. Occupied France, not at all unlike Germany, Nazified itself initially largely through such out-of-touch, self-protective passivity which, it has been noted, astonished the Germans who, for example, set a curfew immediately upon entering Paris, only to rescind it when it became evident that no one was planning to revolt.[12]

"STUPID," "DULL"—AND NOT

I think I need to pause here for a moment to observe that, while Hallie speaks of "stupidity," I do not believe that he meant a lack of intellectual ability. I believe he meant "denseness," "obtuseness," a willful refusal to take reality and others into account: a functional stupidity seen in those who are "really out of it"—who are, as we said earlier, *out of touch*. We all slip into using "stupid" that way: We say, *I did something really* stupid *today*, meaning not that I suddenly fell fifty IQ points but that I did something I know better than to do, something that, had I been thinking at all, had I not been *out of it*, I would never have done. And it is usual to write off a public policy, a way of doing things, a bunch of guys who get in trouble on Friday night as "sooooo stupid!" We mean, then, that obvious realities, if you would only stop and think for an instant, have been ignored and so harm has been done. "Stupid" and "thoughtless" are not the same, in short, although we confuse ourselves by blurring the differences. Very smart people can be very thoughtless just like the rest of us. We ought not forget that.

Camus wrote of the pre-plague city of Oran, if you recall, that it was ordinarily ugly. I think he meant something similar: not physically lacking but dull, without the light of life, of energy and thoughtful concern. Oran was, he says, caught up nonreflectively in commercial pursuits, peopled by citizens who could not even be bothered to develop vices, let alone virtues, but merely cultivated their habits and thought themselves happy. Recall also what we have said about *habituation*. Arendt wrote about "the banality of evil" and its capacity to spread with appalling speed when people choose to be thoughtless, to use conventions and clichés and procedures and regulations to replace their own consciences, to serve their own ambitions without qualm, to ignore realities that might derail them. In Camus' terms, when we thus habituate ourselves to do no more than go about our business, we turn our backs as the city of Oran did on the restless, changeable, beautiful and sometimes dangerous sea, a figure for all that offers respite, adventure, connection with other places and peoples, loss and new beginnings, renewal.

John Dewey, perhaps *the* philosopher of democracy, wrote about the moral ideal of democracy that it is the opposite and opponent of dullness, inattentiveness, and of conventional behavior. A democratic society, he wrote, "must see to it that its members are educated to personal initiative and adaptability. Otherwise, they will be overwhelmed by the changes in which they are caught and whose significance or connections they do not perceive. The result will be a confusion in which a few will appropriate to themselves the results of the blind and externally directed activities of others."[13]

And so it happened in France, where the *attentistes* failed to pay attention to the "significance and connections" of their encounters with the Nazi occupiers on the streets, in cafes, taking over their stores, goods, residences. Heroic voices did speak out, vividly portraying reality (Camus among them), but there was also a kind of jaunty humor used by those who observed extremely close-in how absurd it was to "wait and see" who the Nazis really were. In his "manual of dignity," a man named Texcier reminded Parisians, for example, that one really need not give accurate directions to a Nazi who was late and lost. They are not, he said, tourists, our guests, our friends. Texcier's advice[14] spread widely and quickly, persuading new people to join in resisting not because he invoked grand scale, intensive heroism but because he reminded people of something both profound and simple: there is a dignity in remaining honestly in touch with what is really going on and acting daily, in the moment, in ways that sustain your sense of yourself, your neighbors, your values. This simple dignity that carries us through our days with some grace counters the autopilot of conventionality and thoughtless cliché. It is small; it is common; it is literally a saving grace when systems turn bad.

The humor in Texcier's "manual of dignity" comes, of course, from the vast discrepancy between Nazis and tourists; that it makes us laugh as it did some aware Parisians tells us the degree to which not being "a risk taker" can be absurdly wrong and dangerous rather than, as it has seemed to many tragically faced with such choices, just a sensible way to be. A study of the rise of the French resistance notes that, "The first acts of resistance were small, spontaneous, and ill-coordinated, carried out by individuals acting out of personal feelings of rebellion and shame."[15] There is a start among the few; what then matters is whether and how others join in. Extensive good, like extensive evil, requires many people acting reliably together in time.

Chapter Ten

Preparing for Extensive Goodness

"Interest in learning from all the contacts of life is the essential moral interest.'

What, then, might be a few of the lessons that we can distill from Hallie's report and reflections on the village where goodness did not just happen but was indeed actively done?

A bit of background: Before the Trocmés arrived, Le Chambon was a village that could well have been a less prosperous version of Camus' Oran except—a not insignificant "except"—that it was Protestant in Catholic France, as we have noted, and so its people knew what it was to be oppressed and they knew also how to resist. But when André, Magda, and the Trocmé children went to Chambon-sur-Lignon, in south-central France, it was a depressed village living on the three months of tourist trade that barely enabled people with nothing much else to do for a living to make it through long, cold, dreary winters. Trocmé decided the village needed to be enlivened by some kind of "enterprise" and came up with the idea of a school that prepared students for the usual French advanced degree (the *baccalaureat*) while drawing them and others also into the study of nonviolence.

As Hallie says, "goodness happened there," and thinking happened there too. It came first looking as innocent as figuring out how to make life a bit better for the villagers, and the villagers themselves a bit better. Trocmé knew how much education matters, how formative, for good or ill, it is of community and the living of whole lives.

Another kind of context, too—a pause to gather some lessons concerning extensive good that have emerged as I have tried to disentangle as well as relate various threads throughout my quest. We will then return to the vivid instance of Hallie's antidote to Camus' vulnerable village of Oran.

- Extensive good needs to be distinguished from intensive good. Confusing them misleads and misdirects efforts to prepare to keep extensive evil from setting in and hampers working against it when it has become established.
- The work of extensive good is not singular, nor is it heroic in the superhuman mode. One can go it alone and do sustained good over time, but for the goodness I am calling extensive to develop, the abilities, commitments, and efforts needed to organize and to work well not only independently but with many differing others are crucial.Such good is not done only when people are possessed by an elevating passion of any kind. Throughout, it requires as it also practices and develops the arts and qualities enabled by thoughtfulness, those that allows us to take in what is really happening and engage with it well: attentiveness; informed imagination; inventiveness enabled by clear-eyed, in-touch realism; astute indeterminate judgment; and practical wisdom.
- The most evident virtues of the doers of extensive good are often the very basic, unromantic ones of hardiness, perseverance, and the reliability, the trustworthiness, these underwrite.
- Extensive good is empowered by long-term efforts to develop a good character (to be a good person; to lead a decent life; to be a responsible citizen, partner, ally, parent, friend). Such commitments express a deep need to go on respecting oneself that can override fear, and a congruent determination to respect others even in the face of the worst of circumstances.
- Acts of extensive good must be practiced, becoming a matter of experience and character as much as (perhaps more than) ideals, beliefs, theories so that when needed, we can be on time.
- Extensive good has a history—many histories, specific to times, places, peoples, circumstances—and knowledge of such histories strengthens self and community identities that can help us be ready and then sustain us in acting.
- It is likely that we cannot "produce" more "saints" through widespread education even of the right sort, but the qualities and abilities of extensive good can be practiced on a daily basis by most of us because they are the virtues of common decency and dignity, of good neighbors and effective, responsible citizens who think for themselves with others in mind.

That is a dense weave of complex strands, all of which do emerge from what we have been thinking through but surely do need to be further considered in the light of goodness.

OBSERVATIONS FROM CLOSE-IN

Hardiness, perseverance are sustained by a good character that has a stake in self-respect

> The word that best summarizes the life of the Trocmé family in the middle of the [Nazi] Occupation (and indeed from this time through the end of the Occupation) is not "'glory,'" and it is not even "tragedy." The best word is *surmenage*, the strain of too much work, too much tension—simply too much. There was danger, but the danger was quotidian, part of people's ordinary life; it was not the kind of danger that soldiers and their leaders experience in crucial moments of battle.[1]

> They resisted [despite the hard work, the tension, the sheer exhaustion] because it was, to them, a matter of ordinary self-respect to do so.[2]

As with extensive evil, extensive good takes time and many people doing it every day. Such goodness in the face of persistent terrible realities requires not a burst of heroic fervor, a kind of possession, but gritty determination, an ability to slog on through the muck, whatever comes. What helps people do that? *Faith*, I am told. *Principles*. But, while people who act because of their faith, and principled people with or without faith, can stand against wrongdoing at first, it takes more than that, and perhaps something other, to keep doing it against all odds, and, hardest of all, despite loss of hope that what one believes actually can and will prevail. Hallie found that among the Chambonnais, exhaustion and the retreat of hope did not, as evidently they could have, lead to despair, cynicism, passivity. Apparently, the villagers could keep going because doing the right thing was an end in itself, a way of life—"a matter of ordinary self-respect."

How many of us are so clear that self-respect is earned not by recognition, praise, status, net worth, power, influence or anything else externally conferred but by continuing to recognize ourselves as someone we can live with, and not be ashamed? This is ordinary, not heroic, but it is by no means common. It requires that we know ourselves as someone who simply could not do *that*. In terms of moral philosophy, this is an ethics, an *ethos*, in which virtue is both the means and the end of being good. That is, as Aristotle put it, we become good by practicing the virtues, becoming courageous by acting courageously, for instance, whether we are fearful or, on the contrary, rash. It is of course highly relevant that the Chambonnais had made their whole village, centered around the school André Trocmé started when he and Magda arrived, a thinking community for those who chose to practice being good as what "living well" means.

Realistic practice is needed in order to be organized and ready to act on time

> Long before [Trocmé's] came to Le Chambon, he had learned [when his pacifist choice to go unarmed in the middle of combat turned out to endanger the lives of others] that if we are to act on conscience, we have to do so *on time*—not "in due time," not languorously, but in time, *now*, when the hot chain of events had not yet hardened. . . . [N]onviolence, could, in fact, increase violence if it was not chosen in the right way at the right time.[3]

Edouard Theis, Trocmé's assistant pastor, also knew that, "[N]onviolence involves preparation and organization, methods patiently and unswervingly employed. . . . Nonviolence [without preparation] would have been suicide" [4] in a collaborating France that was not protecting its citizens against the occupiers.

Early on, in 1940–1941, André Trocmé, Theis, and those who worked with them at their newly established school in Le Chambon, "refused to sign an oath of unconditional loyalty to the venerable chief of the French State [Petain, head of Occupied France] . . . Vichy did not strike, and the people of Le Chambon found themselves discovering not only that the government of France was trying to steal their consciences under the mask of loyalty, but also that they themselves could prevent the theft without being smashed in reprisal."[5]

Being on time

I have mentioned *being on time* before, as I have the importance of practicing, of mutual trust earned over time, of organizing, all of which must be well started, at least, before extensive evil has entirely taken over or, if it has, before effective resistance emerges. The initial leaders in Le Chambon did not *start* by asking the villagers to risk their lives. They did not even start by asking them to refuse to sign that oath. On the contrary: they started simply by refusing to be silent about what was really happening all around them, thus refusing to collaborate in a redefinition on the ground of what it means to be a good person, a good neighbor, a good citizen. Speaking about immediate realities, they were reminding people that it is both necessary and possible to keep one's wits about one in order to be able to be good in a morally devolving world.

Trocmé and Theis preached against rising Nazi violence and called on people everywhere to resist (they were openly appalled at the US hesitation to join the fight, for instance, and said so). They preached neither vaguely nor grandly, though, nor did they issue immediate calls to specific actions. Refusing silence, they tried to keep people thinking against the grain of a suffocating reality setting in: "The sermons did not tell what those moves should be. . . . They were preaching an attitude of resistance and of canny, unsentimental watching for opportunities to do something in the spirit of that resistance."[6] This is the very opposite of romanticized good: it is practical, canny, attentive, and simply honest (similar in spirit and approach to the "manual of decency" distributed in Paris that reminded people that no, the Nazis were not tourists and treating them as if they were was indeed ludicrous).

Individuals were thus being practiced in making their own interpretations, their own choices, and doing so in a community of respect whose members they came to know they could trust through experience as smaller acts of resistance practiced people for larger ones. In addition to not signing a blanket loyalty oath, they and the villagers who freely so chose—some did not, and Trocmé did not blame them—refused to give the Nazi salute to the Occupied France flag. From unpublicized acts of conscience, to the taking in, caring for, refusal to give up all who came to them for help, the villagers each as well as together *practiced* what *they themselves* judged they should, and could, do. The horrors of Nazism when they came to Le Chambon itself did not therefore render them speechless, silent, isolated, and helpless before organized force. As individuals and as themselves an organized community, they knew who they were, who and what they could count on, how to act independently in concert. Among other things, their remarkable effectiveness over time grew from the fact that they knew how to be equal without being at all the same.

Identities of resistance can be created by connecting to histories of collective resistance

Hallie tells us about the situation of the Chambonnais that, "Solidarity and resistance not only in the face of persecution but against the national establishment of [Catholic] France, the law of the land, combined with devotion to the pastors who have maintained that solidarity and have led that resistance, are central to the spirit of Protestantism in France [thence also to the Chambonnais]."[7]

Such connections are personal and collective, not abstract: this is not the same as identifying with movements of which one has no past experience, with people to whom one has no long-term ties, in search of a greater, subsuming identity, an *ism* or *ology* within which to lose oneself and dwell as in a new world. The heroes and heroic actions important to the Chambonnais were historical, not mythical—which is also to say that they, too, were not abstract. Individual identities, choices, stories are not swamped but made more vivid by actual, unromanticized histories of resistance or other forms of extensive good.

This is a key reason an inclusive, transformed education is so important: there are many real histories of resistance, and it is disastrous for all of us to let them be or remain erased from the history (and other courses, including literature, sociology, law) taught in schools. If individuals as well as groups are truly aware that, *It is not just me; it is not just us; it is not just now that such things have been done to people—always there have been those who have resisted; this is how they have resisted*, such knowledge can become a part of a non-egotistic self-knowledge, identity, self-respect. Thus given connective, deep roots and perspective on present situations, people stand a better chance of resisting the isolation and alienation that can result even in otherwise good-enough times for individuals and groups devalued or overvalued by dominant social norms.

Refusing the choice between *pariah* and *parvenu*: Conscious *pariahs*/outsiders

People defined as outsiders, as were the Protestants in France, can find themselves faced with a forced choice between becoming a *pariah* or a *parvenu*.[8] That is, a choice between striving to become an insider where doors will not really open and so at best becoming a *parvenu (*an *arriviste*, a *nouveau riche*, a newcomer to privilege who tries too hard, who overdoes to the point of being, unknowingly, a laughingstock and not really an insider at all). Or, if not a striver, remaining a *pariah* (an "untouchable"; "beyond the pale"; an outsider who cannot ever hope to "rise" in the socio/religious order that nonetheless defines him or her).

Where those appear the only real choices our times offer us, there is nonetheless another possibility: if we are in touch with realities about which we refuse to lie, especially to ourselves, and if we know enough of our history and of ourselves to know that *they* do not finally define *us* unless we internalize it, we can choose to be *conscious pariahs*, people realistically within our specific situations but still able to think and make choices about who we are, what we can and what we need to do without yielding clarity or self-respect. The various "pride" movements in the United States thus turned alienating *pariah* identities into proud, shared, positive ones even while defying prescriptions for *parvenus*. For example, *We're gay, and we're proud*, the proclamations went: *Get used to it!*

Such resistant, realistic consciousness is surely enhanced by awareness of communities of resistance that extend one's own. Just so: the Protestant Chambonnais knew themselves to be and historically to have been both a devalued minority, and a protesting one. In the face of extensive evil, this gave them no small advantage in seeking still to be good when all around them others shifted themselves into the new, as they had lived by the former, conventions of the insiders—now, the Nazis.

In Occupied Paris, it was the *Parti Communist Francais*, the French communist party or PCF, that was notably ready to resist on time as it, among other groups but preeminently by itself, already had experience standing with and for exploited outsiders and, crucially in Europe then, had also been part of coalitions fighting against fascism in Spain. The PCF was, then, organized and connected beyond itself. [9] And it too involved youths and women purposefully and to very good effect: to be extensive, good cannot exclude categories of people. Equality can be a specific goal, but it is also its means and an end in itself.

Thinking friends: Solidarity and flexibility

André Trocmé had also had other experiences of finding himself as an individual within a challenging as well as supportive, traditional as well as contemporary, community. In his teens, living in a city occupied by the German Army in the early years of World War II, Trocmé "had become a member of the Union of Saint-Quentin. The union was a Protestant organization of young people, almost all of whom [except Trocmé] were the children of laborers. . . . They conducted their own services in the intimacy of their friendship,"[10] and shared in each other's struggles to be good, as they understood their religion both to ask and to help them to be. "Looking back as a sixty-year old man to those months in the union . . . [Trocmé] was sure that he believed more in the union than he did in the power of God. Here he learned to feel the power of human solidarity."[11]

Solidarity is, of course, the very opposite of the isolation, silence, powerlessness we feel before what we call evil, before terrorism of whatever kind, unpredictable or definitional of an order as in totalitarianism. The kind of solidarity Trocmé experienced can emerge freely, and so be felt as a gift rather than a requirement, from ongoing, above all honest, discussions that matter to the participants. When a group practices thinking together, its members can become simultaneously more distinctively themselves, and very closely bonded indeed. This is a kind of friendship in which flexibility, openness, individuality, independence of mind enhance rather than stressing union. Solidarity then emerges from inside, by choice, rather than being thoughtlessly accepted or forced on a yielding will from outside. This is not community or solidarity bound by obedience; it is the only apparently contradictory solidarity of the disobedient, of those who continue to *choose* to stand together.

Because of these early experiences, organizing groups to have ongoing, serious discussions, not as indoctrinating ideologues do but, rather, as educators and community organizers do, became basic to Trocme's work among the villagers:

> Every two weeks [Trocmé] met with thirteen people [in Le Chambon], and they all discussed a passage [from the Bible] they had been thinking about for those two weeks. Trocmé did not lay down an interpretation and ask them to carry it away with them; he helped stimulate their own interpretations and let them flower. Those thirteen leaders then went to thirteen different parts of the parish, and each tried to do with the people in his what Trocmé had tried to do with them: stimulate a *valuable* understanding of the chosen passage. . . . The local discussion groups doubled in size after a short time and attracted younger and younger people. . . . Above all, the ideas that came from each of these groups were . . . "fervent, practical, and concrete."[12]

The thirteen leaders came to be called the "responsables" (the *responsables*, not, you may note, the *disciples*). Hallie calls them, "the nervous system of Le Chambon."[13] It is more than likely, it is almost certain, that without this system of sustained individual and cooperative thinking about how to live decently, goodness might indeed have appeared in le Chambon, but intensively, not extensively. It would not have been sustainable, wide as well as deep and ongoing. As we shall see, Trocmé and Theis and the head of the local school organized such discussions even in the internment camp to which they were sent when arrested. They were not working for intensive, exceptional good: they wanted goodness to be ordinary—or, rather, they believed goodness to be ordinary, and worked hard to figure out how to help it remain so even under the Occupation, even when interned and at still more personal risk.

There is danger in intense union, of course: thinking cannot thrive where agreement is required, where coming into the certainties of knowing, of believing, of following a leader is the real goal and supposed reward. But Trocmé, a deeply religious man, a pastor, seems from early on to have held the tension between the transcendent and the immanent, between God and human, refusing above all to close off his care for other people regardless of faith, class, or any other boundary-setting categories of his times. Hallie writes of Quakers to elucidate this quality of Pastor Trocmé's thinking, evoking the light that is in everyone, asking to be seen. This reminds, too, of US Civil Rights workers linking arms and singing, "This little light of mine, I'm going to let it shine, let it shine, let it shine, let it shine." Faith can erase individuality, leaving us with the familiar love of humankind that is not manifest in love of any real individual, but such faith can also release thinking from even its own generalizations so that, each time, a real person, a real need, an actual situation can reawaken in many individuals the fresh thought required to act, there and then, effectively.

"Look. Look," said Madame Eyraud, whose husband fought in the French resistance, with the Maquis, and who took in and sheltered many refugees no matter the risks: "Who else would have taken care of them if we didn't? They needed our help, and they needed it *then*."[14] She did not say "I," she said "we": these are thinking friends, people who help each other remain attentive, in touch, ready to act well whether independently or together, but coherently with ordinary goodness through time.

When self-interest entails self-respect

> Their actions did not serve the self-interest of the little commune of Le Chambon-sur-Lignon in the department of Haute-Loire, southern France. On the contrary, those actions flew in the face of that self-interest: by resisting a power far greater than their own they put their village in grave danger of massacre, especially in the last few years of the Occupation, when the Germans were growing desperate.[15]

Conventional notions of self-interest vary, but usually they teach us that it is in our interest to seek our own personal economic and social advantage, just as "realism" in international politics generally means, and teaches, that nation-states will and should seek to enhance their own power, their wealth, their safety above all. Thinkers to whom self-respect is profoundly important may not always agree with such teachings. Interests are of many sorts. The Chambonnais did not believe that it was in their own interest to become complicit with murderers, torturers, oppressors, liars. From a distance, that may sound obvious, but in their situation then it would not have been so to many people. To have become so clear about what interested them above all, they had to have thought a lot about it, and they had. We remember: Trocmé and Theis had founded a school that taught nonviolence as well as the usual subjects; small groups of thirteen people had been meeting (as had Trocme's earlier "union") to discuss a religious text, mostly without the presence of the Pastor; the Pastor's sermons typically connected issues of what to do *now* with personal conscience, transcendent hopes, and real, grounded practicalities; and the Chambonnais all knew that their people too had been a persecuted minority that had nonetheless survived with pride and hope and clarity about what they lived for.

We can note here yet again that *being on time* remains a touchstone, along with self-interest in retaining self-respect, thoughtful realism, and the ability to work hard and long.

Extensive good has not the luxury of burning itself out in grand gestures: it takes preparation and practice and work among many independent-minded, thinking people who know that being good is transitive, relational: in many ways, it concerns others. Their self-respect comes to require that.

Organizing communities of thinking friends is not an exceptional practice

When Trocmé, Theis (assistant pastor), and Darcissac (village schoolmaster) were arrested and taken to an internment camp in France, they asked almost immediately for a room in which to hold Protestant services. The request was granted. The services became discussion groups in which resisters to the Nazis, largely again the Protestants and the Communists, tried to harmonize their beliefs about how to change everyday life for the better. Such a discussion between devout atheists and devout Christians was possible in part because Trocmé, challenged immediately by a Communist suspicious of the political commitment and skill of someone whose eyes might be fixed on eternity rather than this world, responded that, "For him, eternity was not as important as efficacy."[16] Ethics, he believed, is about how we act with actual people here and now.

To be free to continue thinking, this odd group figured out immediately that they could—as they then did—disguise their topic from the guard always there to listen to them by saying "Marshal Petain," who was then the collaborating French chief of state, when they meant Karl Marx. The guard was impressed with their discussions. Soon, for reasons other than those he reported to camp officials, the discussion groups became very popular indeed, with people listening and joining in the singing of hymns (real ones, familiar ones, with lines like, "Faith makes the strongest ramparts fall before our eyes . . .") through the open windows of the small room in an internment camp. Hallie tells us, "The camp was becoming an organized group of resisters against Vichy right under the eyes of Vichy. After the first week of meetings, many of the lank and grizzled inmates could be seen walking across the area to and from meals or to and from the latrine singing and whistling the melodies of Protestant hymns. Peacefully the camp had gotten completely out of hand, and the representatives of Petain's National Revolution never knew it."[17]

Theis and Trocmé, finally about to be released, refused (as they had before) to sign a loyalty oath to Petain and his orders. They were thrown back into the camp. The next morning, though, they were released, still without signing. Why, they never knew; perhaps they had become too dangerous to keep in there, these nonviolent discussion leaders. Perhaps they had secured rather than derailed their release when they continued to refuse to sign the oath because yet again there they were, giving others ideas. Resistance can be more practical than compliance sometimes.

Be leery of abstractions

The philosopher G. W. F. Hegel wrote of the dangers of abstractions, and, much later, a Hegelian scholar, J. Glenn Gray, thought about the ways we turn others into abstractions such as *The Enemy* and stop seeing real people, particularly and increasingly as wars drag on and those who declared them need to whip up flagging fighters, war-weary citizens, to keep the violence going.[18] Trocme and the villagers were practiced in being attentive, not abstract. Seeing a hideously wounded German toward the end of the Nazi Occupation, Trocme "found his hatred turning not against the enemy but against the war that had wounded that particular man so badly."[19] He also met a German soldier who had become a conscientious objector, a telegrapher for the army who refused even to carry a gun. On opposite sides, both saw real people, not *the enemy.*

Similarly, the Chambonnais, having thought about persecution, had come to believe that those who do harm and those harmed are both seriously damaged—which of course did not stop them for a moment in their efforts to save those about to be killed. You help a person who is wrongly acting as a killer if you refuse him/her a victim. The real enemies to which in times of extensive evil all people are subject, as Camus held in *The Plague*, are suffering, violence, death. It is they with which both Hallie and Camus say we must choose not to collaborate.

Here I might observe that *intensive* evil is not affected as is extensive evil when many of us make the choice not to collaborate. Why would it be? Intensive evils do not tempt us: they horrify us, and they do not depend on us at all. Extensive evil, however, cannot happen without many ordinary folks collaborating in the work of suffering, violence, death-dealing. It succeeds when it does tempt us, so extensive good has to tempt us on a similar scale. Perhaps now we might say that extensive good tempts us to maintain our dignity, to indulge in self-respect and common human decency, to remain friends with ourselves and so true also to our thinking friends.

Chapter Eleven

Looking for Good Beyond the Village

Even in the midst of massive infliction of harm, some individuals, less aware of themselves as resisters than the Chambonnais were, find—often enough, to their own surprise at first—that there is something others are doing, something they are expected to do, with which they just cannot go along:

> For a time, Americans [in the Green Zone, Baghdad] were ordered to wear body armor while outdoors; when Johnson found out that Iraqi staff members hadn't been provided with any, he couldn't bear to wear his own around them. "If you're still properly calibrated, it can be a shameful sort of existence there," [Kirk] Johnson said. "It takes a certain amount of self-delusion not to be brought down by it."[1]

It takes an achieved, "calibrated" self-awareness, we can now observe, *not* to move into the delusions that protect many other selves from paying attention daily to how as well as what they are doing, particularly when those delusions feel as if they make daily life easier for those sheltering behind them. Alleviating fear. Rationalizing injustices. Smoothing daily relations. Like secret handshakes, serving as signals that you are alright, that you are a team player, that you can be moved in, and up. But Mr. Johnson, as quoted by George Packer, feared being "brought down," "self-delusion," losing his own balance. He was not so much standing up for the good as he was just trying to keep his own feet under him. Few, in fact, manage to do that: we do not keep an eye on ourselves, thinking it not in and often even against our self-interest to do so. A drag on ambition, careerism, success, being quite so sensitively calibrated. Some people consider it self-indulgent, effete: *Shape up, toughen up, get real*, they say.

The haunting question is always, *How do we educate and prepare ourselves and as many others as possible to become—and, more and harder,*

137

to remain—thus sensitively, appropriately calibrated to other people, to the on-the-ground realities of actual situations in which moral issues need to be attended to? How do we act for even more than the intensive goodness which is always admirable but can flame out without much effect and sometimes even harm?

SELFISH INTEGRITY: MORAL INTROVERTS AND EXTROVERTS

Reflecting, we need to note this too: it can be a self-indulgent thing, good-ness. *"He couldn't bear to wear his own [protective vest] around them." I just couldn't do it. I didn't want to delude myself.* And its opposite? Doing bad things, making extensive evil possible, can be in its ways selfless: *I didn't hate them. It was my job. I was doing my duty. We served a higher cause. We knew people would not understand yet, but someday they would. It was necessary. I was part of something far bigger than myself. It is a crusade. It was hard on me, but I did it.*

Perhaps the difference is in where one is looking for oneself. Those who look inward and try to stay calibrated, in balance, on their own two feet, true to themselves in ways responsive to others and to real situations, are less likely to change their standards of what is acceptable to do when regimes change for the worse than those who habitually look outward, those who need to be rewarded with acceptability, praise, money, status, power in order to feel good about themselves. The former are more likely to reflect on what is happening, to calibrate it against their own sense of integrity and reality. The latter, looking outward, are more likely to think primarily about how to play whatever game is on offer successfully. To such people—moral extroverts, I might call them—a moral introvert is a poor sport, lousy team player, and really does think altogether too highly of her/his own importance.

A man called Aco, a Serb who saved many Croats from torture and death by his fellow Serbs, said, "I'm not defiant. My behavior has to do with the way in which I was raised. . . . They [his parents] taught me to respect others and myself. My father used to tell me every day that others would respect me only if I respected myself. That was his maxim."[2] In ordinary situations of the post-crisis sort, Aco often acted in ways sometimes considered rude and selfish by others. Goodness, whether intensive or extensive, is not merely being nice. Sometimes goodness is done by people we might not otherwise consider particularly nice at all.

Aco was, simply, a man who referred to his own conscience, not the conventional judgment of others. In good times, that often enough made him a boor; in a time of extensive evil, it led to intensive, but not extensive, good. Consulting ourselves, retaining our own integrity, is crucial; so too is the ability to act independently in concert with others if good is to be extensive. As with extensive and intensive evil, confusing one with the other misleads and can misdirect us as we keep asking, *And what might we do, how might we prepare?*

Another instance (in this case, tragically belated, but still admirable: we are not ranking, we are trying to comprehend a complex weave) of a "self-ish" need for self-respect, of a moral introvert: "An incident" in Vietnam was reported, its perpetrators brought to trial for justice by one member of a patrol that, "in November, 1966, had abducted, raped, and then deliber-ately murdered a Vietnamese girl." In an interview (by Daniel Lang), the one who broke ranks, violating the solidarity of the guilty, reflected: "We all figured we might be dead in the next minute, so what difference did it make what we did? But the longer I was over there, the more I became convinced that it was the other way around that counted—that because we might not be around much longer, we had to take extra care how we behaved. . . . We had to answer to something, to someone—maybe just to ourselves."[3]

COMPLEX RELATIONS BETWEEN INTENSIVE AND EXTENSIVE GOOD

To simply say, I cannot do that, or, What else was I to do when someone needed help? may seem too little to merit the label *goodness*, and indeed it may not often suffice even for intensive goodness. There is no simple answer here; so much depends upon the specifics of the situation. But think what would happen if the majority of basically decent folks, told, representatives that they should report what their neighbors say, what they read in the name of "national security," just shrugged and said, "I can't do that." This is not insignificant even when only one or a few do it. When we are ready, practiced, and act independently in concert, it is very significant indeed.

More people than is reported do usually act so. We should recognize that. We should praise it. From early on, we should teach for it: education that prepares us to make good independent judgments remains crucial for any would-be democracy and people anywhere who fear tyranny, totalitarianism. We can be proud that many individual librarians in the United States stood up to President George W. Bush's efforts via the Patriot Act (Section 215 of which was then often referred to as "the library provision") to get them to participate in tracking and reporting what people were reading: they simply refused. Others organized and refused noisily, publicly.[4] Think what it would take to *force* every librarian, every bookseller, every website, store, electronic device company, phone service, and everyone's neighbor to report if most of them just will not reliably do it. Extensive good, widespread and on time, is powerful precisely because extensive evils require many people, from the ground up, to do its contrary work.

This, I have to add in the age of digital data-mining, is one reason why governments but also other powerful organizations—there are global corporations now larger and more powerful than a majority of countries, and data mining is increasingly a resource in the seeking of huge profits—have always sought extensive spying capacities. The people, in our numbers, are a far greater threat to systems of control than any individual or particular group or even another country. Even a relatively few people can at least keep some things from happening. We would not need the singular, super-dramatic figures and acts with which the world became familiar in the first decades of the twenty-first century to reveal just how much data-gathering and mining is indeed going on if more people had been unwilling to take those jobs; to continue to do what was required to keep them; to remain silent as they realized and reflected on what was going on.

Sometimes, when the many fail to act, there are whistle blowers, and more: singular figures about whom, later and elsewhere, we make movies and TV shows, to whom we give awards (when they are safely not in our place of work, our community, our own area of comfort and self-interest and vulnerability). Interesting that we celebrate not the acts of many that can simply stop widespread harm from being done—because no one will stay quiet about it, no one will do the work that enables it—but lionize the few outstanding figures it is relatively easy for a perverted regime to counter. Those who do stand alone and fight back deserve all praise, and their example can lead to more resistance. But educating more of us to be prepared to martyr ourselves sadly means only that we will continue to need martyrs. It is not safe to confuse intensive with extensive good, and we have focused on the former as if it were the only or the best, the very model, of all morality for far too long.

We have learned, sometimes we have been taught, that goodness is extraordinary, superhuman, just like evil. We, along with the makers and purveyors of widespread culture, create abstractions that then contain, romanticize, and otherwise make evil and good seem very far indeed from practices of ordinary life, real people. It is true that singular isolated acts of intensive good bursting out in the middle of extensive evils can become heroic—but also genuinely dangerous. Foolishly dangerous. Worse: dangerous for others, as in Hallie's example it would be if pacifists laid down their arms in the middle of battle, leaving others suddenly unprotected. Furthermore, such acts by individuals when there is no prepared community of resistance, and when extensive evils have perverted simple neighborliness into shared fear and cultivated mistrust, can provide horrific opportunities for terrorizing, paralyzing, dividing people still further. Indeed, making moral heroics or, more important still, simple goodness terrifying rather than inspiring lest it spread—the greatest threat to extensive evil—by insuring that many others also suffer for the acts of intensively good individuals is a trademark of extensively evil systems.

Conversion to extensive evil is complete when simple, self-respecting decency has become hurtful, often deadly, even to its recipients. Intensive good can then be riven by contradiction:

> It happened so quickly.
> *[Her father's] hand that held firmly on to Liesel's let it drop to her side as the man came struggling by. She felt her palm slap her hip.*
> *Papa reached into his paint cart and pulled something out. He made his way through the people, onto the road.*
> *The Jew stood before him, expecting another handful of derision, but he watched with everyone else as Hans Hubermann held his hand out and presented a piece of bread, like magic.*
> *. . . The Jew was whipped six times. . . . Then it was Papa's turn. . . .*
> *A cart was turned over and paint flowed onto the street.*
> *They called him a Jew lover.*
> *Others were silent, helping him back to safety.*[5]

"Papa's" simple act actually led to the death of the man to whom he offered bread, and to the end of his ability to protect, even as much as he had, his own family and a Jewish man they were hiding. The Jew had to leave: Papa's house was now at risk. Papa had to regret that decency overwhelmed him even as he, and not he alone, knew just how deep was the need for it to appear sometimes, even then, when it was too late, too isolated. But by then, the simplest goodness had been turned by those who rightly feared it into something else that could turn even neighbor against neighbor, friend against friend, family members against each other. Those who understand extensive evils know full well that we in our numbers must be not only isolated but alienated from each other. It can be, or be turned into, a selfish thing, goodness, concerning self-regard which, when it leads to disregard for other realities, and even for others—as intensive good may—can not only fail to mitigate extensive evils but even work against extensive good.

Given its need for many people acting reliably over time as well as its far-reaching effects on others, extensive good in particular requires not only attentiveness, thoughtfulness, but a clear-eyed realism.

TIMING AND JUDGMENT

Just how hard, dangerous, even deadly the smallest unruly good acts unto major struggles to counter, to resist, to change systems going or gone wrong may be depends on many factors: Is the system just beginning to go wrong, or is it already entrenched in its perverted form? How completely does the center of power control instruments of violence, and is there still any hesitation to use them? Is it still dependent on uncontrolled public opinion to achieve or consolidate power? Are there enough conventional, ambitious people ready to turn against, to take essential jobs from, to step over their neighbors to align themselves with a rising power? Are there allies of those who will resist? How quickly, how effectively, do those who uphold the system move to silence those who invite others to think for themselves? Have the schools, the universities, the public culture institutions, the media, muted themselves? Have they gone so far as to become proponents of the perverting regime? How isolated, how alienated, have people become? Are there still organizations, formal or informal, within which people know, trust, and think with each other? Are there informal systems of communication, safe places to be with others?

Clear-eyed vision, analysis, honesty, others with whom to think and practice acting are necessary, but, as we know, it is difficult to judge when to do what in the middle of things. To put one of the most basic problems of being in touch, on time, for oneself with trusted others most simply: It often does not seem necessary—or, too many of us can avoid facing the necessity—to make a big fuss in the early days of a system being taken bad (remember the "attendistes," the French who chose to "wait and see" before acting against the Nazis as the Occupation began); it is hard to follow all that is happening a bit later as many more institutions and norms are adjusted; and then, when it is clear that something must be done, it seems to have become impossible (as goodness displayed is then met with excessive force, a classic technique of extensively evil regimes).

A very astute, honed kind of judgment is needed for goodness to have a chance. The magic moment when a big fuss seems called for and people feel safe enough to make it: ah, that is rare, and on the record must be fleeting since so often it is evidently missed. *This is too crazy; They're a tiny minority, however loud; people won't go along with it.* And then: *I'll lose my job if I'm not careful; I'm not a risk-taker; they questioned my neighbor.*

And then: *no one is safe anymore, so there is nothing to do but keep them from noticing you.*

And still, usually we could have known on time if we were paying attention, and we could have acted if we had allowed ourselves to recognize the very real reasons to do so. People have done so, even in the belly of the beast, and, if and when others have joined in, some such good acts have had significant effect even during extensive evils, even despite evident dangers.

"[I]n February 1943, as the Nazis sought to clear all Berlin of Jews, 2,000 intermarried Jewish men were rounded up and imprisoned." Their non-Jewish German wives heard they were detained in a building on Rosenstrasse, a street in the city's heart, and came from all over to glean any information they could. And then: "What began as a quest of each woman to find her husband soon turned into a chanting crowd that filled the street for more than a week. Loud demands that their spouses be released led SS officers to threaten to shoot. The Nazis let the men go home to their wives and families after eight straight days of protest. . . . [T]he women managed to save 2,000 Jews in the center of Hitler's empire."[6]

This seems extraordinary, but, courageous as it was, it was not extraordinary for each of the women whose husbands had been taken by the Nazis to choose to go looking for information about him. It became something other than a private, perhaps desperate, perhaps hopeful, certainly very anxious, perhaps outraged act by increments, by more peoples' choices, acts, meetings, in themselves small, as the wsomen discovered each other, literally together took a stand against the obviously overwhelming power of the men who were holding their husbands. The times, the situation, made their choices grand despite their directness, their simplicity. It can be a matter of timing, of plan, of luck that turns what might have been ordinary in not-so-bad times, or something deadly dangerous in horrific times, into something extraordinary: an experience of extensive good in the making.

As with extensive evil, the seeds of extensive good are always there, in the ordinary. For both, it is the spread to many that gives them their power.

MODESTLY CONSERVING VALUES

Camus' main character, Dr. Rieux, knows he cannot halt the plague once it has fully set in. He does not take that to be reason either to give up, or to indulge in frantic, finally useless grand gestures. Assessing realities, he says that what he can and therefore must do is try to provide possibilities for luck to have a chance. We could say that that is what the women who went to Rosenstrasse did.

Such times require judgment and choice and courage and clarity about who one is and must continue to be to have self-respect precisely because there is no certainty. What works, who survives, is then always also a matter of luck, but it is not luck alone that opens opportunities for its gifts. People have to sort out what is most important and, equally significant, what is most likely to have effect in situations in which, we have observed, even good acts can be used further to entrench a rotten order. The women protesting on the Rosenstrasse made it difficult for the Nazis to refuse them: women, good wives, themselves not Jewish, in public together in the very heart of the city. Mowing them down could well have outraged more people than the regime could risk—yes, even the Nazis. Dr. Rieux, unable to cure the sick, sets about trying to lessen the chance of infection: he sets up volunteer squads of people willing to risk their own lives by removing bodies that could still contaminate, and quarantining the living who have been exposed. Containing the spread of a deadly order takes a quiet, determined, persistent kind of heroism, not heroics, and it takes more than one or a few people who trust each other.

Other times, another situation, made heroes of the mothers and the grandmothers in Argentina who found themselves standing together against the *Junta* (a government established by force) that had "disappeared" their children and their children's children, some of them as yet unborn. Those women too were evidently powerless, but stood publicly in the Plaza de Mayo demanding justice day after day until the balance shifted. They did not initially mean to start a movement, to bring down a regime, finally to win international recognition for what they taught the world about the right to identity, about the necessity to refuse impunity to wrongdoers on a massive scale, which is what happened. They simply had to do *something* to help the people they loved most. *What was I to do? Go home and cook dinner after my pregnant daughter was taken? Forget that they killed her but saved her child? Where is my grandchild? I found out they gave my granddaughter to one of the killers of her mother to raise. I had to find her, of course I did. She, and we, have a right to reclaim her identity. The killers, the kidnappers, have no right to impunity for what they did.*

This is not grand saintliness, the mark of an otherworldly faith, an act of muscular will, an abnegation of self: it started small, within individuals but individuals who, acting out of their own feelings and values, found each other, created and then learned to build community, and it did turn into extensive good. It would be hard to say of the grandmothers, the *abuelas, but they were so brave, so saintly. I could never do that*, in part because that is what they would have said about others, not themselves. Here we are again, finding what is most important in the ordinary where even the poorest, least powerful women can each for herself and together in all modesty refuse to yield to perverting systems, refuse—as the *abuelas* so effectively did—to give their perpetrators impunity, the historic free pass of victors. Extensive good happens because people persist, work together, refuse to yield their self-respect even when all seems hopeless. We might even say that for most of the time, the doers of extensive good may not even manage to remain focused on their goals but, rather, on carrying on because to do otherwise would mean loss of their own identity, their self-respect, their sanity-preserving calibration of values to circumstances.

Moral heroes, whom we want to call something like saints, make us uncomfortable precisely because their goodness appears to be in such vivid contrast to what is ordinary for most of us. We cast the intensively evil entirely out of our communities as soon as we can, categorizing them as evil, as mad, so we will not be contaminated by them. We turn the intensively good into superhuman icons that our community can almost or literally worship so that we will not be revealed as the morally inert flops that, next to them, we have to judge ourselves to be. The stories we tell about such singular creatures display and celebrate what makes them different from us for good and for ill, and the more dramatically so, the better. This does not help us comprehend their goodness, nor the evil of others, but still more does it fail to help us understand what is going on when goodness has again, for a time in a particular situation, become undeniably ordinary, daily, just what one does, the only way of carrying on.

It is worth noting that the grandmothers of the Plaza de Mayo were initially largely traditional women. It was their ordinary virtues from better times that, when violated, turned out to be more than merely conventional. That they were mothers and would-be grandmothers might once have been roles more or less superficially inhabited but, violated by the Junta, revealed their deep roots. Authentic feelings emerged as protest and then, through experience of collective action, turned them into international campaigners against impunity, for a right to identity: they and their allies brought *impunity* and *a right to identity* into international legal concern, a very large circle indeed.

Simply put: Those who have a need to remain rightly grounded by values that intimately define who they are and so are startled into thought by the violation of those values are less likely to collude with their perversion than are those who held similar principles conventionally, just to fit in, to be "respectable." And then, when awakened thinking leads to the realization that *something must be done*, practical wisdom and good judgment make all the difference in whether their good actions have a chance to be effective, to build, to spread—to invite many more into thinking, judging, acting.

Paul Gruninger, a Swiss police captain and border guard who arranged falsified papers for Jews seeking sanctuary in his country, thereby dangerously defying policy announced by his superiors, was a conservative man who believed that Switzerland was as he had always been told, a good place for people to come for freedom. He held onto that belief as borders were closed, choosing to act to keep it true rather than let it become a lie. And he remained open to present realities. His daughter said, "He saw what condition the people were in when they arrived and he knew all too well what would happen if he sent them back. He would always say, 'I could do nothing else.'"[7] Gruninger remained attentive and thoughtful: he saw the contradiction between his traditional beliefs and present reality, and he saw that, to retain the former and, crucially, his own self-respect, he would have to act as if he were not the conventional man he had otherwise appeared to be. There are always some for whom the goodness of a prevailing system that is no more than a banality to most (like, the American Dream, perhaps) connects enough with a personal identity that its violation provokes thought, and so some kind of action.

It took Switzerland a long time to recognize Gruninger as anything other than a renegade border guard. That time, extensive good did not happen. Goodness remained intensive as Gruninger, rather than those perverting the Swiss heritage, was, in effect, quarantined, losing his job and social standing. His memory is now safely honored, but it took a long time. Had Gruninger known how to do more than act on his own, lone conscience, had he been practiced in thinking with others about the values that defined who he was as the villagers in Le Chambon were before the Nazis arrived, the effects as well as the story of this man's goodness might well have been very different, as might Switzerland's.

Conventional beliefs and values can lead us to fail in practical wisdom and judgment when situations change if they have become banalities that protect us from seeing what is real, here and now. Gruninger, or the *abuelas*, might have gone on being obedient, dutiful, proud of a modest, traditional role. That is (at best) what Gruninger's colleagues did, but doing so required not seeing what was really going on and that, it turned out, this dutiful and also thoughtful person found himself unable to do. Indubitably admirable as he is, it remains tragic that he was so isolated then, and may still be now as a singular Moral Hero.

There are individuals, there are systems, and there are also groups, organizations, movements. It does more than help, it is transformative when there is a civic or activist group to join and especially so when there are many, when public life is filled with such groups and, beyond them, there are movements to join or to launch so that there are many others with whom to think, speak, stand up, act. One person stepping out alone is easy to mow down, and perhaps more troubling still, easy for thoughtless others to turn against. *"Crabs in a barrel,"* as an organizer in the South said to me years ago after a very hard day: *Sometimes, you don't need to put a lid on the barrel. If one crawls up, the others pile on and pull it back down.*

GOOD LEARNING

What Gruninger lacked, despite having the crucial and profoundly admirable virtue of thoughtful integrity, was experience that developed the arts of free and collaborative action, of wisdom that is practical and judgment that is good in unpredictable situations. These are arts that can be learned (awakened, informed, practiced), but they run against the grain of highly traditional and/or top-down sociopolitical orders. I have then to observe that as I write, educational systems in the United States are under great pressure to become more like businesses, tightly managed by ends-oriented directors, run top-down, with radically disempowered faculty—adjunct, "contingent," nontenur-track professors who have no institutional power already make up 60 to 70 percent of US higher education's ranks—recast in mechanistic terms as "content deliverers" of standardized curricula, tests evaluations. I confess that it is not clear to me how all this management might enhance education for people who, among other things but crucially, need to be thoughtfully practiced in withstanding the banalities of all those conventionalized systems within which the germs of the plague are always still and again present. To live well in the real, changing world requires that we be independently, freely, collaboratively artful, not—and certainly not only—well trained.

Those who actually have acted well teach us this: To keep such actions up over time and make them effective, bursts of individual or small group moral outrage, of moral inspiration, of compassion and courage, while without doubt admirable, are not reliable enough. As we act, we should continue to explore together what can make goodness more reliable just as, history and our times painfully demonstrate, the doers of extensive evil can be.

This is among the most basic reasons why we need to educate for and practice together arts of thinking—attentiveness, reflection, indeterminate judgment, practical wisdom; along with arts and skills of action—communication, collaboration, community building, analysis and planning;

and characteristic attitudes—interest, openness, honesty, respect, hope, realism; and we need to have done so *before* we desperately need to act, not only alone, not only once.

ACTING WELL

All they are doing, some ordinarily good people say when asked, is what obviously ought to be done. People were hungry, hurt, ill, wounded, being exploited, killed: *What was I supposed to do? Walk away? How could I do that?* Such simple goodness is moving when we find it in individuals, but remember the degree to which Andre and Magda Trocmé and Edouard Theis had prepared to be and genuinely were not alone:

> Magda Trocmé was not the only citizen of Le Chambon who scoffed at words that express moral praise. In almost every interview I had with a Chambonnais or a Chanbonnaise there came a moment when he or she pulled back from me but looked firmly into my eyes and said, "How can you call us 'good'? We were doing what had to be done. Who else could help them? And what has all this to do with goodness? Things had to be done, that's all, and we happened to be there to do them. You must understand that it was the most natural thing in the world to help these people."[8]

It is important, I think, that we hear it when such people reject familiar singular as well as heroic terms for what they did. There is something wrong with our moral systems, and/or our thinking about them, if those who have actually participated in extensive good, that most crucial kind of acting well, cannot recognize themselves, their allies, their experiences in what we say about them.

It is then a problem, as I keep insisting, that intensive forms dominate our imaginations—Jack the Ripper, Mother Theresa—leading us to expect, to want, to explain how "goodness happens" by adducing supra-personal agency that is as big as the effects of the deeds, as big as the historical as well as the moral reality facing us when such extremes become actual. It is not enough to say that the first president of a newly liberated country was a "good person"; we want stories of founders much better than we could ever be who somehow magically wrought wonders by the sheer strength of their character. Pure Good alone will suffice for such amazing achievements as those of Nelson Mandela as we have created him, for example. But then we forget about the tens, hundreds, thousands and more of others without whom nothing at all could have been done, let alone succeeded. And we forget also the sustained hard work it takes for all those many people to try to change a perverted system even when leaders have been overthrown.

For the many doers of sustained good as for sustained evil, doing the daily work of deadly systems or resistance to them is moment by moment, day by day—which is where and how we act, always—and so not such a big thing, even as it can be exhausting, "too much." It is each time and most times simply the thing to do to get through this task, this day. Those we want to lionize as great leaders actually, in person, get bored, exhausted, testy, angry, unreasonable, lonely, and, also like all of us, they are good at some things, terrible at others. They can strategize and maneuver, say, more often than they craft a vision, or vice versa. And if others of whom we do not often hear did not cover for them, perhaps do basic work they cannot or will not do, criticize and love them while taking care of their own crucial daily tasks, the *surmenage*—the too-much, the slog—could sink the ones we want to think heroic. They are doing the on-the-ground work of goodness against the grain of their real situation and doing it well enough to keep going: not glamorous, not singular, and as deeply admirable as anything human.

We remember then that no one on any level of responsibility can long sustain over-the-top moral passion for good any more than we can do so for ill. We know this: people "burn out" doing good works. When I was working with a team developing an ethics curriculum for a teaching hospital, I heard frequent references to "compassion fatigue." How, we then wondered, might we help fledgling health care providers do good and do it well on a daily basis precisely without having to be moved to do so by compassion adequate to the suffering they faced each and every time, day after day? I found myself adding "justice fatigue" to our concerns: what wore out the doctors' compassion was as much helplessness to fix situations that were grinding their patients down, breaking them in differing way, as it was a surfeit of empathy and care. How are we to educate doctors and nurses (always much more than "health care providers," as teachers are more than "content providers") in ways that prepare them to go on doing what good they can despite far too intimate, repeated experiences of the persistent injustices that are related to what is wrong with many of their patients (poverty, racism, sexism, poor diet, unhealthy living environments, dangerous neighbors, no insurance, and on from there) that undercut their best efforts to be healers. Passionately held ideals and intense compassion do not suffice for the long haul, and if they are relied on without acknowledging that, they not only burn us out, they can turn us cynical, coldly dispassionate, until we are living a dangerously compartmentalized life. Realizing that compassion in unjust systems can indeed lead to intensive good but undercut the persistence needed for extensive good can be very important.

Those who participate in the ongoing acts of extensive good know very well that their motivations must be basic and daily, ordinary, and realistic enough to sustain them. Alexander Werth, we remember, said of others who refused actively to go along with the Nazis in France in the 1940s, "Resistance in the early days of Vichy and of the Occupation was totally disinterested. They resisted because it was, to them, a matter of ordinary self-respect to do so." Their resistance was not, then, actually "disinterested" as we also observed earlier. We each and all have some interest, at least, in maintaining our self-respect. Werth seems to be struggling even as Hallie (and most of us) have when confronted with goodness that is precisely not extraordinary in its ongoing motivation. A regular old daily desire to maintain some self-respect seems not to be enough, to need to be glamorized, exaggerated, and in that, falsified. People have resisted, have acted well in the face of grave dangers and temptations, persisted in very frustrating healing efforts, simply in order to be able to recognize themselves in their actions, to feel good enough about themselves to get on with life. As Socrates knew, we must be able to be our own friend if we wish to go on thinking rather than lying to ourselves, hiding from ourselves, and so looking to others (from whom we also hide our secrets) to tell us who we are, and what to do. "Lost souls" is a telling phrase.

There is a saying among some activists that captures something of this: *He's the sort of revolutionary*, they say, *that you hope won't make it back from the barricades.* And they mean: He's over-the-top, an extremist, a self-dramatizer, unstable in his passionate intensity. He may be good, people may think he is a hero, but he cannot be ordinarily so, and it is ordinarily that we lead our lives.

I fear that we will fail to learn what we can about extensive evil and its counter, extensive good, as long as we continue to think either of these is alien to our ordinary lives.

Chapter Twelve

The Banality of Goodness?

Purposefully "doing good" can itself become unthinking, mindless, no more than a sop to conscience, a prop for conventionally defined self-esteem, a way of passing boring time or earning points for some other purpose we have in mind (getting into college; preparing to run for the school board; being thought to be good by our neighbors; seeking compliments from our coreligionists; getting out of the house when retired). Certainly, admirable things may be done as a result of all sorts of motivations, but that is no protection against banal conventionality, mindlessness. Even dramatic intensive goodness can be motivated by a kind of reflex notion of heroism that is entirely conventional. It is then a matter of luck—for the recipients of such acts as for the one acting—whether what is thus thoughtlessly done turns out to help, or hurt.

Unthinking obedience to or use of good conventions in decent-enough times is evidently less frightening than when mindless conventionality enables massive evils, but thoughtlessness—any mindlessness, taking us through life on autopilot—puts us at serious risk of colluding, and perhaps worse, with the larger systems that shape our worlds if, as, when, they once again go wrong. The mystery really is not how so many good Germans could have become Nazis, nor how so many good Christians could have been slaveholders, or good Arabs, slave-traders, or how many good parents could send their businesses overseas to profit from the virtually, sometimes actually, enslaved labor of other peoples' children. The mystery, I fear, is how so many of us so often, without even thinking about it, no more do good than we do wrong, or evil, but simply behave ourselves, or absent ourselves, or try to do well whatever the terms of the game. We do not even choose; we simply reach into our grab-bag of conventions, of processed concepts, and follow the one that seems most familiar, most likely to seem apt to the people whose approval we generally glide along on. Or not: often enough, we just keep walking, pay no attention, do not remember, do not feel, as is rightly said, called upon to do something. Realities call out to us; we do not hear. This can be the case even when we are doing something because we think it good: anything can be done thoughtlessly.

Extensive good, on the contrary–a genuinely lived goodness that becomes a bedrock of lives, and for many lives, over time–takes account of realities in our changing, contradictory, complicated, plural world. While awareness of "the claim on our attention that everything that is makes on us simply by existing,"[1] as invoked by Arendt, cannot be recognized every day, all the time, lest we drop from exhaustion, it can be a call on us remain open to experience. This is a commitment of respect, of relation, and makes it possible to respond in morally appropriate, rather than mindlessly banal, ways. Thus the Chambonnais villagers could be equally good while acting differently, on their own, as needed. Such action can be sustained effectively through time too, precisely because, being thoughtful, it keeps us learning and so able to adjust, get better, act differently as situations change.

Much more interesting, too, this way of being in the world, and that is more important than it may seem. John Dewey, the great educator and philosopher of democracy, teaches us that "Interest in learning from all the contacts of life is the essential moral interest."[2] We are then practicing being with, learning from, acting together with other people with whom we can be genuinely engaged.

These are all qualities that can keep us going, enlivening as they are, but it is important also not to forget that extensive good can require the sheer, stubborn persistence that can awaken when we are worn down to our core. It is to be hoped then that we find there the values and commitments that we have through time made definitive of who we are. Extensive good requires, but also develops, very deep roots.

Those roots go deeper than our individual core: they connect to our human being as conscious, thinking, judging, free, and therefore morally responsive and responsible creatures. This is the opposite, as it is the opponent, of the determinedly superficial banality that enables great evils, including all too central banalities that salve and can substitute for consciences.

GOOD STORIES MAY MISLEAD

Here too, on the healing side of our inquiry, we can confuse the extraordinary with the most important. It is not surprising that when we think of goodness, we can make mistakes similar to those we make when we think of evil. As with intensive evil, the startling singularity of a person, a group, an act that evokes moral praise captures the imagination, holds it, and—perhaps most tempting—promises to make a good story. That the heroes of such stories simultaneously seem to be holding themselves to higher standards than most and to judge themselves more harshly is part of what fascinates us. They do make for good press, admiring fans, another kind of Superstar.

But goodness itself, as its practitioners—and those who know them well—experience it, remains difficult to think and to speak about, particularly when it is extensive. We can recall Camus saying that the great duration of a plague makes it, finally, monotonous, and Hallie telling us that the villagers had to keep going despite the *surmenage*, the too-muchness of the struggle. Lasting good, like lasting evil, does not make for great stories featuring superstars. It is, for good as for evil in their extensive forms, the reliable workers that matter. Not very titillating or inspirational, the reliable. This is, however, precisely why we do need to think and speak about something other than the good stories that can turn out not to illuminate but to recast, to re-form, to substitute for realities and the restless questioning of thinking, the patient attentiveness of mindfulness.

IS "GREAT" TO "GOOD" AS "EVIL" IS TO "BAD"?

In settled, ordinary times, there are always a few people who stand out as profoundly good. Whatever they think of themselves—characteristically, they quite genuinely judge themselves to be worse than many others—these are the people we take to be what Aristotle called *moral exemplars*. We can think of them, think with them even in their absence, when we need to make a difficult moral choice. In hard times, under rotten systems, not only such uncommon goodness but even simple decency practiced here and there by a few people can seem not just good but great, downright miraculous, beyond the humanly exemplary. "Saints," we may call such a remarkable few in either case, meaning, as we do when we say someone is not "bad" but "evil," *this* is over the top, breaks the bounds. Still, it is interesting that we do not have, for goodness, a trembling, awe-full parallel for *evil*. "Saint" comes closest, which is why I have sometimes used it in this inquiry, but it is rarely used as unambiguously, with as much intensity, as *evil*; it is more closely tied to specific religions; and it is less often used not for one but for many people doing good things over time. "A saintly people": I would bet you have not heard that as often as you have, "Those people are *evil*," "the axis of evil," and "an evil time." "Saintly" also admits of degree: someone can be said to be more or less saintly. Not so with evil: Rarely heard, "He is sort of evil." "A touch of evil," perhaps, but that "touch" we understand to be pure, just not spread throughout.

I have been drawing parallels, but they are not exact. There remains much to say about differences in ways we think and speak about *goods* and *evils*. For one thing, "good" is the opposite of "bad" as well as "evil," and that is a problem. "Bad," as I noted earlier, is just not adequate to, is downright ludicrous if used for, some actions. The guy who stole my car may be bad, but he really is not evil. The man who stalked, raped, tortured, killed, dismembered forty-five women before he was caught is so far beyond *bad* that we reach for the term *evil*, as we do when the government of a whole nation takes up murder as legal work. But, much as we want Pure Good, it is not clear what term we might reach for when "good" would be ludicrous: *Rescuing thousands of refugees from death is a good thing to do* seems more than a bit wan, does it not? To stand alone, or to be among the many who persist in standing, against repression is, we feel, surely more than being "good."

Is "great," "greatness," the opposite of evil, then? Quite evidently not, although the need for something extraordinary may tempt us to use it. *Great* simply is not the same thing as and evidently does not mean just an extreme expression of *good*. Alexander the Great is not remembered and thus titled because he was so very benign. In saying something is "great," we mean something is huge, impressive, has far-reaching effects whether for good or ill: *The great flood of 2008; the great warrior; the great Depression; the Great Awakening; the Great Spirit; the greatness of Greece*. I have heard people say, "Hitler was awful, of course, but he was also a great leader." I really have. Greatness we can associate even with evil (I would do so carefully, but my experience is that I am in a minority).

A difficulty here is that although linguistically we mark a chasm between *bad* and *evil*, it is not so clear that we do so similarly between regular old good and either over-the-top, intensive good, or the ordinary doing-right of many over time of extensive good. It seems we are not as impressed by the power of extreme goodness as we are stunned by extreme badness. Or perhaps the problem is that it is more difficult to romanticize great goodness even when we are thinking of the unusual outbursts of intensive good. To convince us of the goodness of a god or gods, we are often told stories of a deity's great power for the good that, like those told about evil, turn out to be really scary: a flaming sword of righteousness; a devastating flood to cleanse a sinful world; a many-armed god dancing on the bodies of demons; a voice that speaks like thunder; a warrior charioteer advised by a god in the midst of the carnage of battle; deities, ancestors, that test faith by demanding, oddly enough, that adherents do arguably bad things (sacrificing living creatures, for instance, including humans, even their own children). It is as if we need to borrow something of the awfulness of evil to inflate goodness. Maybe we are tempted by evil as we are not by good and so need to attribute more power to it.

PURPOSES, PROBLEMS OF RELIGION

Perhaps, then, we need to think a bit about religion in these contexts. From a thinking perspective, a purpose of religions, their stories, images, rituals, creeds, and the conundrums they often pose is to take us beyond the limits of our usual kinds of thinking into speculative realms that stretch our capacities for abstraction, for imagination, for poetry—for faith that does not submit to empirical or logical requirements for acceptance. No wonder we turn to religious speech, whether we are religious or not, when faced with extremes of good, of evil. The—or *a*—problem is, though, that we have then left behind the actual, real world in which we need to deal with good, bad, evil actually happening. And if we take up residence in realms of faith that, precisely because they do concern belief as distinguishable from both perception and reason, have no necessary relation to empirical reality, we may misjudge badly what needs to be done just as we do whenever we get lost in cliches, conventions, technical terms and other abstractions and banalities. For example, if all bad things are dealt with as *a test of our faith*, what we think about is likely to be just that—ourselves, our very own faith. That need not help us become attentive to what really happened this time; who really did it and why; how that differs from what happened last year; what in fact ought here and now be done.

I am afraid it also has to be said that, while religions sometimes give us potent conceptualizations and terms and images that enrich our conceptual and emotional vocabularies, they also come with long histories of various kinds of complicity in the doing of great harm. Lord knows, religions have a large share of responsibility for purposefully inflicted suffering, killing, and rupturing of peoples' relations with each other of all sorts. Harm can be done when some are full of righteous certainty that they and they alone are in possession of Truth—and when such claims are made and spread by humans with their own potent brew of greed, careerism, and power lust masked by religion.

So, it is not a metaphysical or theological or any other dualism that I am wondering about when I reflect on this Good/Bad-Evil question. It is something more like common usages, the work that we want done by these moral terms as we go about our real and daily lives, that interests me here.

OVERREACHING GOOD

Back to where we started, then: I know we sometimes need the extreme term "evil" when something overtops "bad," but, as noted, it is less clear what we do when something overtops "good," whether as an individual, short-term act or as an extensive, longer-term set of actions by many people.

We do, though, react not dissimilarly to extremes. When a Jeffrey Dahmer turns out to live next door, the general response seems always to contain something like this: *But this is such a good, decent neighborhood, and he was just another quiet man, a good neighbor, kept to himself, but still, you know, just one of us. Things like this just don't happen here!* Not really so different from finding out that a Mother Theresa came from your neighborhood: *Well, amazing, you know? I mean, we all grew up here, and we go to church/mosque/synagogue/temple and all that, but we don't, what shall I say, take it all so seriously? People like that just don't seem like they'd have been in your sixth grade class, now do they?*

Such extreme people: they might do anything, whether it really shook up their neighbors or not. Perhaps this is why we often call over-the-top goodness "saintly." That does not take it entirely out of the realm of the human, but it does remove the doers from the category of ordinary, if not as extremely so as calling someone a "monster," a "devil," "evil incarnate" does: we have not, after all, called them "god." I guess we want to remain in touch with the extremely good, just not close enough to make us actually sit down and try to learn something with, about, from them singly or in extensive numbers. But those who have acted well, whether intensively or extensively, are nonetheless characteristically uncomfortable being called "good," let alone "a saint." It seems they precisely do not want to be other than human, that that is, indeed, their moral calling: *What else could I do, and remain who and what I am?* We want them to be saintly. They are just trying to remain what being human means to them.

Despite our romanticizing and desire to mark off the saints among us, we have also had an understanding of goodness that links it to the humble (which is not really the ordinary, but is often confused with it) since well before we had notions such as *the banality of evil*, of "ordinary people doing evil things." It is not shocking to think of goodness of any kind as humble, as simple, if not ordinary or normal: such a view can be found among Shakers and Buddhists, for instance, as well as Christians focusing on "a humble carpenter" with the common name, Jesus. Good people, from the saintly to the more ordinary, are readily pictured as quiet, unpretentious, probably not stylish folks whom we may fail to recognize as especially moral until later, until we need them, until around them many turn bad so, despite themselves, they do stand out.

But when actually faced with such goodness, we can get twisted up in efforts to see it as extraordinary after all. The humble Jesus becomes the Christ, which I, and I assume you, certainly am not. There are often tales of super-asceticism, astounding self-sacrifice, repression, self-abnegation—all admirable, perhaps, but, you know, really too extreme. *I couldn't do it*, we think of Martin Luther King, now safely if secularly sanctified (to the ongoing, if ever more rarely publicly expressed, irritation of people who knew the real human being, and know, too, how many others were crucial to a movement, to this extensive good). The people in Le Chambon and some of the others we have met would also dispute such sanctification: *But we didn't do anything so special. We just did what had to be done.* And we, determined to revere them, may then take their apparent humility (I think they would call it honesty) to be another indicator of their saintliness, their extraordinariness. This is a far cry from Le Chambon, and from Camus' good characters. As Tarrou, the disillusioned ideologue who is the good doctor's nearest and most helpful friend, puts it, "The good man, the man who infects hardly anyone, is the man who has the fewest lapses of attention."[3]

SUPEREROGATION AGAIN

Actually, there is a term for overreaching good that violates the norms of ordinary or even impressive good. Interestingly, today it is used mostly among moral theorists and philosophers of ethics. Perhaps *supererogatory* is just too hard to say (although it is gratifying when you get it right). Moral philosophers use the term, the concept, as we think about human actions, but those whose focus is on regulating our daily behavior (public officials, jurists, religious officials) or explaining it (social scientists, sages, elders) do not often refer to "supererogatory acts."

The term originated among Roman Catholics to name a surfeit of good deeds by an individual, deeds that were, in effect, overpayment and could therefore be 'banked' toward salvation. As a now philosophical term, "supererogatory" means more than, beyond, outside of any reasonable obligations. It is not a supererogatory act to reach out a hand to stop a child from falling off a dock, or to swim into deep water to save her. Plunging into a shark feeding frenzy to decoy them away from devouring someone else's child: that is supererogatory. That is beyond *good*: we are aware of not expecting it of ourselves (even if it is morally profoundly wrenching to picture that child's situation and know that we will not jump in), and we do not morally require it of others. Almost as with a bad act, people will more typically try to stop you from a supererogatory act—*Don't let her run back into that burning building, that rip tide, that eye of the hurricane to try to save the child; she'll only die herself.*

The distinction between *good* and *supererogatory* is useful for intensive good, even though it is in some tension with traditions allying modesty (if not self-abnegation) over heroics, as we have seen, but it does not help us think about extensive good. In times of extensive evil, of massively violative harm-doing, the simply good thing to do becomes rare, odd, very special. It could then be supererogatory to do no more than give a crust of bread to a man being starved by his captors when doing so could get him and you killed and endanger your family. Such an act in that actual situation is simultaneously shockingly dangerous and obviously good (again: here, our minds want to stop). It is intensive good because it stands out, is not joined by others, is not replicated, and so does not spread. It leaves the doer both admired, and—if she lives—ever more isolated as well as at risk. It is supererogatory—a good act no one, we believe, can morally be required to do (and, in reality, perhaps ought not do, either). It turns into extensive good when, like extensive evil, it is experienced by those doing it as ordinary, simple, just the thing to do but is also done among and with others who can and will keep it up. Extensive good, however, also requires that we remain attentive, thoughtful, in touch, on time. Such an act among others that spreads and persists surely ought also to add to our salvation bank account, but the doers of such acts feel strongly that they are not only not supererogatory, saintly, but, because *good* does get inflated through its association with the astounding qualities of intensively moral acts, not even "good."

Yet there is credit here, and of the most serious if not familiar sort: there is a lifetime that prepares for such moments, few or many, of against-the-grain action. Such a life is by no means necessarily shaped by adherence to any set of ethical or religious principles. Even on the contrary: moral dogmas, ethical principles, public laws can be of little use when, in any real, particular situation, I must figure out what is actually going on in order to choose what I ought to and can do. Dogma, ideology, authorized knowledge, and principles can also, we should admit, prepare us to be obedient, to submit to their authority, when, as sometimes does happen, systems have gone bad and *obedient* is precisely what we must no longer be. What we need is to see directly, clearly, in their particular forms then and there the first signs of things going bad, the openings for collective action, and then the ways we actually can resist.

MAKING A REAL DIFFERENCE

Paul Farmer, a doctor who is an expert in infectious diseases, set out to cure the poorest of the poor whom others had effectively written off as *hopelessly mired in poverty* and so doomed to be prey to disease, injury, illness. This abstraction—*poverty*—can be and often is used to explain myriad things, more or less usefully, but poverty, of course, is not an agent. It cannot do or cause or cure anything: it is a condition, variously defined, variously experienced, variously itself caused. Farmer calls poverty and its differing causes and sustaining institutions to our attention in many ways, including in its malign use as banal simplistic explanation, thence excuse, with particular efficacy: he shows what can really be done when we stop making excuses. He has set up clinics in Haiti in which he demonstrates that it is not their poverty that makes some people's condition untreatable. It is actually quite simple: poor people's diseases can be cured if there is a cure available for their specific illness, if they are diagnosed in time, if they are administered the cure, if there is adequate follow-up and supportive care. Just as for anyone else. Farmer's biographer thus tells us that the doctor, "described giving antibiotics to an impoverished TB patient, then wrote: 'When she received them, she soon began to respond—almost,'" Farmer observes ironically—*"as if she had a treatable infectious disease."*[4]

Here, what could look like intensive goodness—Farmer is picked out as extraordinary, spoken of as a kind of saint, considered unique—has been turned into extensive goodness. Many people work in the clinics; many are served; the clinics providing health care (and education, community, hope, trust even when miracles cannot be done) have persisted over time. Farmer refuses the misuse of conventional and appropriated social science categories as well as prejudices that stand in the way of seeing simply and simply acting as needed. He remembers basic medicine: a person, rich or poor, contracts tuberculosis if exposed to the bacillus, not otherwise, and can be cured if properly treated, and if not, not. But yes, conditions and circumstances do also come into play: weakened, malnourished, overworked people living in crowded, unsanitary conditions are more vulnerable. Nonetheless, we do know the proximate causes and cures of many now treatable illnesses. That they are enabled by injustice, shall we say, does not change what needs to and can be done directly for the infected. We ought not doom people to die of curable diseases because their situation makes them more likely to contract those diseases.

While he combats real illness in the real people who need immediate help, Farmer also works against injustices: human systems, human choices create poverty. We should take it on too. His biographer writes: "He had sent me a copy of his latest book, *Infections and Inequalities*, a prodigiously foot-noted discourse with case studies of individual patients to illustrate its main themes—the connections between poverty and disease, the mal-distribution of medical technologies in the world, and 'the immodest claims of causality' that scholars and health bureaucrats had offered for those phenomena."[5]

NOT TO KNOW BUT TO DO THE GOOD

Nothing is without contexts that also call for our attention and action, and we remain responsible. I am afraid that always, yes, we need to continue to think, to rethink, to watch ourselves thinking, and to do it afresh tomorrow before, during, and after we act. This is why Gandhi called his political actions "experiments in truth," as we have seen, and it is why the second-wave feminist movement developed "consciousness raising" groups in which women explored connections between and among their most personal, private, common experiences and large-scale political inequalities. To be and to do good is more work than to be bad, even evil: you have to stay awake, and you have to practice both independence of mind and cooperative action, both open attentiveness and active reflection, direct simplicity and understanding of complex, changing contexts. Dr. Paul Farmer cures people; sets up clinics where others have not; secures funding; tells individual stories and provides scholarly works with "prodigious" footnotes. "Doctors Without Borders" work around the world and in the least-served, most devastated areas. Like the resistance movements we talked about earlier, these extensive goods also cannot be done without ongoing thinking, recalibrating, redirecting, adjusting to what is possible here and now, what was learned last week, what others know and contribute even from far away, and sheer dogged persistence. There are are further horizons even for extensive goods too, as there always were: how might we provide health care for all as an ordinary thing? Extensive good, like extensive evil, can indeed become just ordinary—but not banal, or, it too can become oppressive.

As Aristotle put it, if you are inquiring into ethics in order to do the good rather than only to know it, you will find that good character—a disposition to act well for the happiness of doing so, because it is simply an enactment of who you are—requires practice to develop and to inform choices over time. Those who thereby develop the practical wisdom needed to make good judgments in always particular circumstances also develop a *second nature* and sense of self founded in it. If they act on their own in unfortunate times, they may well become known for intensive goodness; if they also act with others, practicing together, they are preparing for ongoing extensive goodness—a good life, a good order, for all. Aristotle, I should note, arguably does have both kinds of goodness in mind (if not the terms I suggest). He recognizes that acting together in public for the good—being political—is higher than private goodness. Without going further into this classical Greek view, we might say that in terms of our inquiry, the public, political practice of the proper goodness for human beings is crucial to keeping whole systems from being taken bad by a rotten few. Public life is about providing the contexts for basic decency to be practiced by many who are, in democratic discussions, supposed to be free, equal, and rational (as Social Contract theorists put it).[6]

Work with others to discover and enact provisions for the public good can be an effort to realize extensive good. Systems can go very wrong indeed; they can also go further than we might imagine toward the good. In most ordinary times, as I fear that history and our own times tell us, most of us are more likely being prepared for extensive evil than for extensive good, even while we learn to admire the few saintly sorts and to fear the few monstrous ones. Like the people of Oran, we turn our backs on the connecting, challenging, equalizing sea and cultivate not character but pleasurable private habits we can satisfy if only we make enough money, if only we play the game by its rules and "succeed." Then it is only a matter of luck when and where the plague again sends its rats into the streets to die before us even in our most 'respectable' neighborhoods. Then, if we, where we live, are not the afflicted, we can cluck our tongues in shock at what *those people* are capable of doing, and get on with our own lives as if we were immune—for the time being. As the poet Paul Eluard both warns and promises,

"There is another world, but it is in this one."[7]

*****

With goodness, its arts, and its real possibilities now in mind, it is time to explore still more closely why and how people who would otherwise have been decent folks can become perpetrators of extensive evils. The more carefully we think about how we become vulnerable to horrific conversion, the more we may be able to think of what we are doing in time to resist it, to refuse our collaboration, to be and do the good simply because that is who and how we are in this world. This work, too, is individual and systemic, and never finished.

Part III

FERTILE GROUNDS FOR EXTENSIVE EVIL

In a novel titled *The Reader*, a young man hitchhikes to the site of a now and finally empty concentration camp after the defeat of Nazi Germany. He makes this trip because he "wanted reality to drive out the clichés." He is picked up by an anonymous middle-aged man. When the driver hears where his passenger is going, he asks, "What is it you want to understand? That people murder out of passion, or love, or hate, or for honor or revenge, that you understand?" The younger man nods.

The driver: "You also understand that people murder for money or power? That people murder in wars and revolutions?" The younger man nods again.

The driver: "But the people who were murdered in the camps hadn't done anything. . . . You're right, there was no war, and no reason for hatred. But executioners don't hate the people they execute, and they execute them all the same. . . . And you think that I'm talking about orders and obedience. . . . No. . . . An executioner is not under orders. He's doing his work, he doesn't hate the people he executes, he's not taking revenge on them, he's not killing them because they're in his way or threatening him or attacking him. They're a matter of such indifference to him that he can kill them as easily as not."[1]

We have been asking how this "he," this indifferent executioner, can do what he does, and how some cannot, will not. By now we can say that he can do his job in a fully perverted system when the potential for him to do so was already there, cultivated quietly in the many ways we are rewarded for *not* thinking with full attentiveness about what we are actually doing. And I fear those ways really are many. Our inquiry needs to turn the soil to find them, these indulgences of thoughtlessness that grow into habits, into call uses of the soul that protect us from life's roughness at the price of losing sensitivity to the startle of nerves that should warn us when the ground is shifting under us.

Chapter Thirteen

Seeding Prepared Ground

We know now that contexts will always also matter. From a distance, what happens can look like this:

In a time in which things are harder than usual for many of us, when we are off-balance, anxious, angry, a new group appears, seeking power. Those who speak of and for it appeal to us by using a language that we recognize, connect with, and are animated by. They are vivid, forceful, emotional, and promise to better our lot in life, to make us less economically and socially insecure, less vulnerable. This new order, if we go with it, will open doors for us to money, power, status. We listen. Our minds begin to change, both consciously and on the pre-conscious level on which we sort out what we want to make of what we experience. We hear differing uses of familiar language but soon also new terms that catch on and circulate widely, thereby marking who is now "in" and making us feel more like winners if we, too, speak that way. Regulations, manners and mores, styles, some laws also change: we are confirmed. This is real: something is happening, and one can choose to improve oneself along with it. Soon the new order convinces us that it is unavoidable, even triumphant. Even before it has consolidated power, it convinces us that it is a done deal. We determine again not to be left behind, to be with it, to benefit, even as increasingly we also recognize that some people will lose out, and some must be cut out. That is clearly their misfortune, we decide, and we distance ourselves from them as the new regime gives us categories and terms for such as they, the losers, the brakes on progress, the threats to a new or retrieved golden-age, world order. We wear the markers of our new status more of the time (looking the part matters, being evidently insiders, cool, powerful, the winners). Even when we have qualms as we see signs of danger, we decide again to go along. After all, we are not risk-takers, and we have careers to forward, lives to live and people to take care of, significance to be achieved.

That is a sketch of the transition points, remarkably similar across instances of extensive evils. Behind it, closer in, there is a denser weave of ordinary life and lives that can prepare us all unwittingly to collaborate with the plague. I trust I do not need to say that I do not mean "the usual suspects": poverty, alienation, isolation, hopelessness. These can indeed be conditions for the breeding of ability to cross over to serving extensive evils, but they are so little the only ones that it is not very helpful to keep repeating them. Again: those with a lot of education, social status, success in professions have always been significant actors, and numbers, among the perpetrators, the enablers, the "*attentistes.*" Let us, then, move below, behind the banal explanations to this denser fabric.

EXPLORING INDIFFERENCE

Elie Wiesel, survivor and writer of the Holocaust, has said that it is indifference we have to fear. We have also heard that all that is needed for evil to prevail is for good people to do nothing; that turning our heads lets the murderers march on. I agree, but wish also to fold in the realization that good people doing nothing is indeed a necessary condition but does not suffice for extensive evil to get its difficult, sustained work done. Extensive evils must be supported by shared social conventions, clichés—banalities—that keep its many, many workers actively engaged by their work, trying to do well at it, to earn its pay and its perks and its status. And yes, those many workers must also manage to remain indifferent—I would say, first, *inattentive,* a choice to be out of touch that makes indifference possible—to what they are actually doing. A question: *How do executioners become and remain able to be indifferent?*

Our ordinary lives in less perverted times can prepare us to achieve such indifference. Many, probably most, of us do the jobs we must have—I say this with both pain and anxiety, but I think realistically—not for their intrinsic interest, our belief in their redeeming social value, our admiration for our bosses, but for the money. Good job = good pay. Some seek and do their jobs also to have colleagues, a kind of community, and status, and as work takes up ever more hours of our lives, to avoid being isolated. The American Dream, we say, is to make more money than our parents did, to own a house and a car, to go shopping just for fun, to send our children to good schools so they will "do even better." There is no mention of what we are doing to earn that money, what our employers are doing with their profits, whether that product or service is good, indifferent, bad or in collusion with evils in its ways of doing business, in its effects on employees, neighbors, health, the environment.

We can, and of course some do, instead pay attention, be engaged, take responsibility of many sorts and make the best we can of our work life as we do of our public and private lives. The difference does have to do with luck, but it also lies in whether we are mindless or mindful, attentive or closed in by clichés and other banalities, by the games required to keep or advance in our jobs, whatever they are. We can also be either *conscious* or collaborating *parvenus*, if you recall that earlier discussion: even if we must keep our job to survive despite not finding it in many senses worthwhile, we can remain aware rather than more comfortably self-deluding.

What is of concern is the very real possibility—I am afraid I believe it— that most societies, economies, and their educational systems prepare reliable workers who do not think what they are doing. That society and education mostly do prepare us to go along and if possible succeed within prevailing norms and systems is hardly itself extraordinary; neither is it always necessarily wrong, or bad. Cultures not only have established, conventionalized ways that characterize them and help us know how to fit in, but even have ways to make possible the doing of things most people are taught are wrong, taboo, even horrible. They outlaw murder, but they also prepare ordinary folks to become fighters who kill, and executioners. They discourage the use of force to settle arguments, but they prepare some of us to be armed police officers who can and do use strength, weapons, forcible restraint. They also often enough generously support practitioners of violent sports, spies, interrogators who can hurt, lie to, betray people. Societies can preach respect and kindness to others, and they can reward bosses who fire people knowing what it will do to them, to communities, and makers of public policy who can choose categories of people to be denied as well as given benefits, health care, highways, a new dam. Social orders virtually by definition shape and can limit what we think about, how we think, what we find acceptable and unacceptable to do, and because societies are complex and not rationalized, they do also prepare us to live with some pretty wild contradictions.

I mentioned this earlier; now let me say a bit more. It was a surgeon, when he joined a "medicine and morals project" of which I was a part years ago, who said to me that he is *trained to do violence to bodies*. This man was pursuing a further degree in philosophy, in ethics: he needed to keep thinking about what he was doing. Many health care providers, however, told us during this project that they were repeatedly advised, by professionals as by friends and intimates, that they should not "take their work home," should not "dwell on it"—that they ought not think about it. Even talking about it, which is today considered helpful, can turn out to be a way to avoid thinking. Formulaic phrases abound in many group therapy and support groups, so one can speak one's own truth but in terms prepared by others, never having to pause, to reflect, to experience the truth in order to find ways to communicate it afresh, as it really is to you. Rejoining a community in which you can speak about your experiences in the same terms others do, and so feel understood and understanding, is healing unto itself. It may not, however, actually involve *thinking* about those experiences, so it may close wounds but leave their site scarred, no longer responsive.

All of this can turn out to have prepared and habituated us to be indifferent rather than attentive. Scientists have worked on germ warfare simply because they were offered a good lab and funding. Why not? They were taught science absent its political, social contexts, for the most part. Doctors have experimented on inmates who had no real choice. The doctors were neither good nor bad on purpose: they were playing within their game, indifferent to its collateral damage because it remained, within their professional norms and rewards, irrelevant. We are still working to change this in many fields.

As cultures, polities, professionals, workers, citizens, we are to varying degrees (that do matter) practiced in indifference that allows us to focus on what we are doing by the rules and not on their meanings, implications, effects. We are also, in usually less direct ways, practiced in political rather than personal indifference. As citizens, we are implicated in the killings and interrogations and incarcerations and intrusions of wars, of imprisonments and executions, of violative experiments, of violence and violation in the service of what we choose to see as some societally valued good, often enough without a whole lot of thought (which need not mean without a whole lot of chatter).

Again: there is nothing essentially wrong here. This is how societies, cultures, nations work with and through us. They need reliable workers and carriers of their values and purposes, just as we need some stability, widely shared meanings. But then there is also this: these moral opt-outs are also what extensive evil requires and provides those who do its work. This, of course, is why it is here, close-in, that we most need to avoid prolonged lapses of attention if we would remain rightly calibrated.

"GROUPTHINK"

Most important is that we are taught not to think "too much" (as if that were a problem in this world of ours) to prepare in all sorts of ways to get the work of our society, polity, and economy done, from work that we can recognize as involving harm to that which has no connection to harming others at all. There are a lot of more specific ways we may allow ourselves to be, and be rewarded for being, thoughtless. That these ways are most often conventionalized and heavy on insider jargon is a significant aspect of what gives them potency and reach. Many of us want to be up on what is happening, to be insiders, to use the latest technical term—to speak and think in concert. Just watch what happens when a new psychological diagnosis (*ADHD*, for instance), or term for social change (*tipping point*), or political phrase (*the world is flat*) is written about in a jazzy bestseller. Media-spread analyses of intelligence failures before 9/11 also gave us a term that spread until, ironically enough, it too became yet another banality: *groupthink.* All of a sudden, there was a lot of groupthink about *groupthink.* And so we are practiced in not thinking freshly for ourselves, unless we manage to develop a thinker's allergic reaction to any overused, insider-marking concepts and phrases. Such an allergy works well with, but is not the same as, the famous bullshit detector for which we do admire people. Bullshit, like and with lies, is indeed to be alarmed about, but more subtle and more deadly are the conventions and clichés we barely notice.)

CAREERISM

Giving us a job that rewards hard work with pay, perks, status, that makes us feel like "winners," goes a long way toward turning our minds off with regard to anything but playing that game well. In good times, that only makes us less alive, less interesting, less humane, and more dependent on the employers and systems that keep the bounty coming than we ought to be. When systems go bad, it can turn us into the hard workers that a different game, an extensive evil, requires:

> Eichmann was not Iago and not Macbeth, and nothing would have been further from his mind than to determine with Richard III "to prove a villain." Except for an extraordinary diligence in looking out for his personal advancement, he had no motives at all. And this diligence in itself was in no way criminal; he certainly would never have murdered his superior in order to inherit his post. He *merely,* to put the matter colloquially, never realized what he was doing. It was precisely this lack of imagination which enabled him to sit for months on end facing a German Jew who was conducting the police interrogation, pouring out his heart to the man and explaining again and again how it was that he reached only the rank of lieutenant colonel in the S.S. and that it had not been his fault that he was not promoted.[1]

Careerism is, I am sure, rarely so enduringly absorbing: Eichmann is not just like you and me. But careerism is nonetheless often captivating to a degree we should notice, and take far, far more seriously. I now believe careerism to be prime among the preparations for extensive evil: it practices and rewards us for playing a game well and in its own terms, absorbing us to such an extent that attentiveness and free thinking can yield entirely to a calculating, analytical intelligence that moves only within the bounds of the game.

Christopher Browning, in his study of Police Battalion 101 that was turned by the Nazis into a mobile killing unit, tells us that, "The two men who explained their refusal to take part in the greatest detail both emphasized the fact that they were freer to act as they did because they had no career ambitions."[2] Note that they actually could refuse and do so without physical fear, just considerations of "career ambitions." One of these two men then explained that he "was not a career policeman and also did not want to become one, but rather an independent skilled craftsman, and I had my business back home . . . thus it was of no consequence that my police career would not prosper."[3] Had he not had his "business back home," there seems little reason to doubt that, career in mind, this gentleman would have murdered as he was told, but not forced, to. It is also striking that he seems to be so out of touch that he does not realize what he is revealing about what mattered to him. Another officer, Lieutenant Buchmann, mentioned "an ethical stance" among his reasons for refusing to murder men, women, and children (especially women and children) close up as he was ordered to, but continued to say that, "I was somewhat older then and moreover a reserve officer, so it was not particularly important to me to be promoted or otherwise to advance. . . . The company chiefs . . . on the other hand, were young men and career policemen who wanted to become something."[4]

To become something, to advance in their careers, they murdered close-in many, many people.

> *Those who said No, or simply avoided doing such work, tended to be older men. What difference did that make? Were they wiser, less swayed by Nazi rhetoric, less prone to passionate causes or murderous fury? No, they simply did not care as much about advancing in their careers. In truth, this was the single most startling thing I found through my years of inquiry into the crucial question of how the reliable workers of extensive evil could have done it.*

I found this astonishing careerism in Europe, in the United States, in Africa, in Eastern Europe, and more: people in very different places and times can, and do, kill as part of a job when there are such jobs available for those with an eye on "bettering themselves." Being determined to play the game well, being a careerist, sets people up, prepares us, to do our jobs well—what can I say? No matter what: *we will do no matter what* for status, pay, advancement, "success" in prevailing terms. This has been so hard for me to process, yet so impossible to avoid, that I will return to it yet again: if it took me awhile to get how deadly serious a matter this is, perhaps it will be hard for you too.

CATCHY SUPERFICIALITY

A Manson cult, or a larger cult such as the community founded in 1974 in Guyana that came to be called "Jonestown" and led to mass suicide, has to close itself off from others, from normalcy broadly understood, in order to develop its own entrancing meanings. By contrast with such intensive evils, thoughtlessness that allows us to be moved as desired by others into extensive evil cannot be isolated. Extensive evil is conceptually a dustbowl evil, cutting minds off from anchoring, feeding roots so they can be moved quickly, massively, at will, right out there on the broad plane of the public.

We are prepared to become political, moral tumbleweeds to the degree that we have moved ourselves onto the surface of our lives, minds, relationships, and become indifferent to thoughts and experiences that might challenge them. We may make it through a long and even a good life that way if we are fortunate and live within reasonably stable, sensible, decent systems. But those who are preparing, extending, defending a horrific system can use such thoughtlessness. They can become very good at selling us what they want to, working with the illusion that we are actually in touch with our real needs, our wants, our purposes, and making our own choices: "In his diary a German writer described the ease with which people 'shifted themselves into gear' without being asked—self-Nazification (Selbstgleichschaltung), in the phrase of the day."[5] Evidently, they were used to going along, ready to keep doing it. But still, they did not do so without assistance: "[T]he most powerful dictatorship in Western Europe [Hitler's] was directed by men who scrutinized their subjects' opinions as carefully as politicians in a democracy worried about their approval ratings."[6] One of the reasons Nazism remains a force in today's world—as a real political program, however smaller its organizations and weaker its adherents, but also strikingly as a set of images with which to conjure—is precisely that its planners, and then legions of professionals, early worked very hard to make it appeal to an initially mixed, not yet broad public. This does not mean, as is usually thought, that all the meaning shifts by which people "self-Nazified" were affected by dramatic propaganda and hyper-dramatic rallies, although there certainly were some. I might even suggest that such drama is ineffective for extensive evils early on (later, they do consolidate power), because there are so many people, and such different people, who must collaborate, and, as in Germany, there may well be important groups and individuals who are repelled by gross mass spectacle. They know its dangers.

The more dangerous changes are the very small ones, the kind of slight shifts in meanings that Klemperer, the linguist, noticed as behavior, again on a small, close-in scale, changed in ways that ought to have alarmed everyone. Remember this? "Jews sadly noted . . . the silence of a store clerk who refused to answer an inquiry, the politely worded requests to drop their memberships in leisure and civic associations, or the embarrassed silence that greeted them as they walked into a favorite café."[7] The attentiveness required to be good must be fine-grained, able to see wrongdoing well before the perpetrators feel safe enough to use their own versions of "shock and awe," of spectacle as well as terror, to ratchet up their power.

The broad reach and easy, fast spread of such bounded, conventionalized nonthinking—of what we call "superficiality" or, more seriously, "mindlessness"—is common. It is what enables fads, "common wisdom," social conventions of many sorts to be passed along as no more than social gestures. It takes no effort for others to pick up, to use and spread clichés, and doing so makes the purveyors of such "in" phrases comfortably attuned with a remarkable range of groups. People as different as urban sophisticates and rural social pillars, when spreading catch-phrases among themselves, feel connected, proper, hip, and—odd though this truly is—clever. And there is nothing secret about ads and slogans, and so on: the more we encounter them, the more likely we too will absorb them.

To prepare to stop extensive evils, we are well advised to pay at least as much attention to the latest big thing in pop and commercial culture as we do to seeking early clues that someone, some small group, is breeding monsters in the dark. Have we become overdependent on pop culture for shareable meanings, for status markers? "Paying attention" does not mean establishing thought police or censorship, I hasten to add. It means just that: stop and think now, and again.

"A DONE DEAL"

Alphonse, a *genocidaire* who was successful enough to have been an organizer of others and particularly well rewarded, tells us how open planning was beforehand:

> The platform of all the Hutu political parties had been proposing Tutsi killings since 1992. Those agendas were descriptive and meticulous. They were read aloud at meetings and warmly applauded. . . . We wanted the ideas of the president and the majority of Hutus to prevail. We wanted to end up winners in every situation. . . . We found ourselves faced with a done deal we had to get done, if I may put it that way. When the genocide came from Kigali, taking us

by surprise, I never flinched. I thought, If the authorities opted for this choice, there's no reason to sidestep the issue.[8]

What would otherwise be categorized as, and felt to be, horrific deeds can evidently be turned into an "agenda" one can support if it is repeatedly spoken right out loud as part of public discourse by recognized leaders whose likely-to-be-successful side you want to be sure to be on. The very light of the public—today invoked by the buzz-word, "transparency"—that ought to illuminate what is really going on so it is subject to evaluation and judgment, can be used to dazzle, to befuddle, to "spin" reality, as we say knowingly, with far too little horror about such willful distortion of a shareable, real world. Sunlight, as it is said, can disinfect, but some things ought to remain evidently contaminated. Displaying them can serve as inoculation against horror, outrage. We can then find ourselves ready to go with "a done deal" that just needs us to do our part to be a winner in the new public order in which impunity as well as rewards for perpetrators is implicitly promised. It is worth remembering that intensive evils do burst from invisibility, deep secrecy, out into the light, astonishing us and immediately producing flurries of activity, but extensive evils cannot hide. Certainly they can and do use lies, all sorts of distortions and even more distractions, but these serve to take over rather than hide from the light of the public.

Extensive evil and extensive good require individual choice, as do all acts, but both are also inherently and necessarily public, political: they concern the ordinary world and what manner of people we can will.

OCCUPIED MINDS, ON TRACK

It helps if recastings of realities (neighbors becoming *losers*, *leeches*, cast as threats; looting and rape regularized as *reward*, not crime; sweatshops as *economic opportunity*) continue so that people get used to them, so that newer phrases do not catch their attention. If you are perverting a whole set of systems, you do not want anyone's attention caught. You want their minds to move right on with you, on the tracks you are laying down. Be careful here, though. You actually do want their minds to be functioning: "descriptive and meticulous" discussions are fine. They occupy the mind, keeping attention on your platform, on work to be done, struggles to be taken up, goals to reach, rewards to strive for, all of which will take some instrumental figuring out, some shrewdness, some narrow-gauge, means-ends assessments, and a genuine interest in self-advancement—just as careerism in other times and places does. I used the image of tumbleweeds for minds moved by sweeping, broadscale, publicity. The image here is perhaps of game players as they approach being gamblers, from chess fanatics to games on electronic devices, to poker: our minds then can be intensely active, but they are also *occupied*. We are precisely not thinking around, about, outside of the rules of the game. We are just trying to win by the rules of the occupation. *Focus* in rewarded, not reflection. There is no time for that.

What purveyors of extensive evils do not want to do is startle people into reflexive, reflective, interpretive, narrative, evaluative thinking. You do not want them mentally, imaginatively, emotionally to move back into their own independent minds, although you do want them to be that get-the-job-done sort who is *tough-minded*, able to develop a *thick skin* and plow ahead toward the goal, the outcome, the reward. *What the hell is* this? is precisely what you do not want them asking, nor, most of all, do you want them thinking, *This is something I can't do even if everyone else does it; even if my leaders ask it of me; even if I will keep my job, make more money if I do it; even if I end up on the winning side because I did it.* You want to keep a whole lot of people busily thinking about the details of the agenda and the work to be done to realize it rather than what they are really about to do. Anything to avoid, *This is something I cannot do*, let alone, *and nobody else should.*

Extensive evils, let us then say, can move from agendas, plans, visions of a few into systemic, sustaining, public forms when it is clear and widely observed that jobs and extra goodies are available—from loot to sex (for males, sexual access—without consent—as reward for, expression of, and in the service of dominance is horrifically familiar), to status, community, a career, political power. Such jobs should also be explicable and legitimated by an insider's logic authoritatively taught that helps careerists and political wannabes play effectively.

It is not only thoughtlessly held moral dogma that can be turned inside-out far more quickly and easily than people can learn to think for themselves. It is also competitive, rewarded gamesmanship.

People can switch games very easily if winning within career-defined bounds is what they know best how to do, and where they have anchored their identities.

REFRAMINGS: "MISFORTUNE," "FATE," "THE WORKINGS OF HISTORY"

"In 1940, when Alfons watched the Gestapo take away his best friend, Heinz, and all Jews in his village, he did not say to himself, 'How terrible they are arresting Jews.' Having absorbed knowledge about the 'Jewish menace,' he said, 'What a misfortune Heinz is Jewish.'"[9] Think for a minute: Alfons had not written off his friend Heinz as inhuman, or subhuman, nor did he see his best friend as "other," and certainly not as a stranger. He knew and liked his friend, and already knew him to be Jewish. "Jewish" had been marked as wrong for him, one can imagine, but Heinz, his friend, was not wrong: what Alfons failed to do was to be startled into thought by the moral, existential discrepancy between what those in power were teaching, and what his own immediate experience gave him to know. When that discrepancy was made manifest—when his good friend was taken away as a Jew—he went to "misfortune" to explain it, and no further. That is, despite the horror of seeing such a thing happening to his well-known and loved best friend, he reframed an outrage of love and justice as "misfortune."

"What a misfortune" for "them" and for me: no one is at fault, in this reframing, for this dire thing that has happened, only the working out of implications of what a boy has been taught are natural, undeniable, scientifically validated categorical differences among humans. As he had been prepared to do, Alfons had simply, devastatingly, stopped thinking—of his friend, who has been absorbed into "Jewish"; of Jews, who have been transmuted into a race and a "menace"; of whatever he has been taught about who should and who should not be arrested, and what for; of the proper role of officers of the state. Nothing of all those translations catches his attention even when something awful is happening to his friend before his very eyes, so well have the adults around him conveyed to him that this, he must not think about, nor ponder, nor question. They have taught him not to look for human agency, choice, and so also moral responsibility wherever doing so might get him into trouble, and they have also given him *fate* and *fortune* as substitutes for real causes and conditions.

For others, there need not even be religiously or scientisticly legitimated "fates" and "misfortunes"—such as, by the "science" created from Marxism, class warfare whose losers are fated to wind up on the trash heap of history (interpreted too readily as another "done deal" that adherents just have to "get done," with no personal responsibility for what History hath wrought). Social conventions of no more substance than propriety have sufficed for people to take into their minds recategorizations that can change friendship to indifference, love to rejection, protection to punishment, sympathy to scorn, respect to diminishment. And so have parents punished a son who lost a schoolyard fight for being "weak," "a sissy," and taught him thus to scorn, even hate, victims lest he be one; and so have employers refused to hire people who use wheelchairs because a socially shaped disability is taken to be their personal identity: they *are* "disabled." And some Jewish men give thanks to god that they were not born a woman. And "honor" in some other patriarchal faiths is defined in ways that justify the killing of a woman who has been raped for shaming her family, changing your little sister into someone you can personally murder.

And daily, people maintaining proper behavior let others know where their place is in all sorts of ways that seem trivial and also practice us in adjusting: why not? These may be nasty but also not deadly, until or unless they become used to convert us smoothly into something that really is.

Many people go along with such perverting conversions not because they are all and equally true believers; secretly prejudiced; reverting to the monster that is in us all. Some people always fall into those patterns, but not many.[10] No: many people go along because of something else very basic to human societies we have already touched on but that surfaces again in all these instances. *We are meaning-making, meaning-seeking creatures who depend on categories to sort out our experiences, our very sensations*: Am I hurt or angry? Is that an oasis or a mirage? Is it desire I feel for other men? Would a good person do that? We are therefore vulnerable when those categories are shifted, and with them, how we make sense of realities within which we just do have to keep making meaningful choices. This is how evildoing becomes ordinary, and that is what extensive evils require. In order to resist, we have to be more aware of and reflective about habits of the mind than most of us are most of the time.

Here too, I think of education: surely it ought to help us not only develop, refine, inform our habits and learned categories of mind, but practice us in being reflectively aware of them; thoughtful about the work they do in shaping realities for us; capable of judging their adequacy, and their effects.

CHANGING MEMORIES, AND LOYALTIES

Clearly, ways that we are primed to go along with perverting systems are of the gravest concern, but still we are in the realm of the ordinary, of the ways we negotiate who we are and what we will and will not do. Not in the forefront, on the side where we can keep from thinking much about it, a friend, a neighbor, a colleague, even a lover, a spouse is recategorized, as an *inferior*, say, a *half-breed*—someone who is not quite right. Such recategorizing makes us vulnerable to more. No such conceptualizations stand free; they are interwoven with other things we think, with memories, with feelings, with sense of self. If my neighbor is not what I took her to be, what happens to my warm feelings about her, my memories of what we did together, my sense of identity? If I was so wrong and—now that I think about it with my reframed category in mind—if I was so badly misled, how am I to make sense of a whole lot of things I thought I knew, and felt? Memories have to be reinterpreted: I am off-balance, less rooted and sure of who I am. My usual, barely reflected-on but anchoring loyalties are being uprooted. I become more vulnerable to the shifting winds.

In such a state, what "they," the authorities, the in-people, the group, the bosses say "those people" are and how "we" must treat them, can be not only accepted, but finally welcomed to settle the confusion. I can be told that I am still alright; that if I was betrayed, I was neither a fool nor complicit, because "they" are really clever. I can be told that this just proves what a good-hearted person I am, a virtue that now I will have to learn to guard against, good as it is, because "they" will only use it to prey on me. Confused, I may turn to authorities sooner, more dependently.

This whole business of branding others in simultaneously conceptual and emotive ways entangled with self-defining memories and loyalties is also quite common. It is one of the things we practice as children as we form and reform in-groups, out-groups, creating *nerds, freaks, cool kids, jerks*—pick your terms, and feel scorn for those who do not know and use them correctly. And so we learn to classify and reclassify, promote and demote, accept and reject individuals, groups, jobs, clothes, dances, music, and on and on. Marketers also play to this complex social sorting, and are paid very well for doing so: *Buy this to be cool.* We experience it at work: there are jobs others look down on, or up to; there are the cool folks and the mere strivers, and the losers. Societies of many sorts run on who knows whom, shows up where, can get in which club, is or is not invited, is or is not quoted. Seeking to find or maintain balance, we are not unused to changing our loyalties. Societies just do have insiders and outsiders within differentiated strata, and ways to fall, ways to rise across them. At base, neutrally, we come to know what and how things are by comparison. Which does not mean that that cannot go very wrong, like everything else human.

Once one has turned on a family member, a teacher, a friend, recategorized him or her radically, one may need to do so to more and more people in order to justify that first, most difficult, reversal—that betrayal. Once one has lied to protect one's organization, one belongs to it more firmly; once one has overlooked a harm done by one's colleagues, one is more likely to join them next time. There are moments of clarity that halt these reframing conversations for a while, just as there are times of more dramatic change, but the process itself is more or less part of most lives. It is similar with resistance: once one has refused to change loyalties, to recalibrate memories to suit a new story, to write off a friend, one has learned that it is possible, experienced its effects, become better able to do so in future should one choose to. Far from Paris, the villagers in Le Chambon-sur-Ligne *could* refuse to sign an oath of loyalty to the leader of Occupied France; did so; nothing happened—and on they went (not that that alone sufficed, of course, but it could mark a turning point).

These are all usually small-scale re-creations of ourselves in relation to others, but they can be turned to the doing of good or bad things, or, initially and perhaps until it is too late, just as readily to evil. They can also practice us in maintaining self-respect when we are awake, aware, thoughtful enough to recognize when it is crucial this time *not* to recalibrate our sensitivities.

INSULTS, PEER PRESSURE, SEX/GENDER IDENTITIES

It is hardly only teenagers who are unduly subject to peer pressure. So are virtually all professionals, for good and for ill. The Polish police example we used earlier surfaces in raw fashion dimensions of some socialization processes we usually gloss over, allow to remain hidden. If I ever doubted some of the most popularized uses of Freudian, as of feminist, analyses of males violating the bodies of others as proof of how hard, dominant, forceful—how virile, how masculine, what a man—they are, testimonies of males who have been pressured by peers to join in group violence would dissolve that doubt. As are so many aspects of study of extensive evils, this too can be downright humiliating: Are so many males really so malleable, so little-boyishly tough-guy, so childishly excrement attracted/repelled, so adolescent gender-scared as to be pressured into horrific behavior, even murder, by being called things like "shithead" and "weakling"? To avoid being called a "sissy," "girly," "cunt," "queer," or other homophobic, misogynist, childish epithets, a man will kill? Yes. Rape? Yes. Torture? Yes. (But not all men will; never all.)

CLEANLINESS, PURITY

Need I then observe also that there are notions of strength, and of purity and cleanliness, that are in desperate need of redefinition? If you doubt that, consider "ethnic cleansing," as genocidal killings and removals were called in the Yugoslav wars in the late twentieth century, or read records of early Nazi speeches in which virulent anti-Semitism is muted in favor of calls to purify, to cleanse, the *volk*, the German people, in order to return it to its proper, pure, clean, hard strength. The historian Claudia Koonz suggests the term "ethnic fundamentalism,"[11] noting that Hitler, always attuned to which emotive generalizations would sell masses of people on his still-rising regime, learned that crass anti-Semitism drove too many people away and so turned to something less direct, less overtly negative and threatening but open to being directed back to murderous racism: calls to purify the *volk*. Some people are then not thought of as "people," or as "folk," but as impurities, as germs, scum, pollutants, cancers. And what is the logic of that depiction masquerading as an analysis? The good, clean, pure, healthy must join together to protect themselves from being sickened unto death, and this organic, health/ illness, life/death framing is readily scientized. It was used to move many more into complicity, at the very least, by the Nazi leaders invoking eugenics, but its basis was already there in germ in those common little boy, sexualized "filthy" epithets used as part of male peer pressure as we saw it among the Polish police. "Shithead," they called a man, however quietly he broke ranks because he did not want to murder. A familiar insult already there, readily converted to deadly purpose.

"EDIFYING PHRASES"

Heinrich Himmler, Reichsfuhrer-SS, head of the Gestapo and of the Waffen-SS and, from 1943 through 1945, Minister of the Interior, is reported to have said to a physician named Kersten that the Final Solution "would mean much suffering for the Jews. . . . 'It is the curse of greatness that it must step over dead bodies to create new life. Yet we must . . . cleanse the soil or it will never bear fruit. It will be a great burden for me to bear.'" The philosopher Russ Shafer-Landau, author of textbooks on ethics, says, "This, I submit, is the language of morality."[12]

Himmler also speaks of the heroic call on the killers to "remain decent fellows" bizarrely enough by becoming "hard" enough to participate in genocide:

> I also want to talk to you quite frankly on a very grave matter . . . I mean . . . the extermination of the Jewish race. . . . Most of you must know what it means when 100 corpses are lying side by side, or 500, or 1,000. To have stuck it out and at the same time—apart from exceptions caused by human weakness—to have remained decent fellows, that is what has made us hard. This is a page of glory in our history which has never been written and is never to be written.[13]

It is strikingly clear that Himmler knew he had to have reliable killers who could keep it up, neither folding nor becoming rabid, going out of control. He was being realistic also in his realization that the deeds could and needed to be moralized for the doers.

While we are exploring seedings of extensive evil, I then have to note that the idea that it is *difficult* to do what we ought to do, that it requires that we grid ourselves against temptations of mind, heart, and body is not uncommon in conventional moralities. To be moral, we must be able to do what is right even if it goes against the grain, troubles our feelings, is *hard*. But this of course can also become dangerous. In perverted times, it has been the ones who could not kill who were called moral weaklings and cowards, and shunned as moral failures, too soft for the real world: upside down and backwards, but the logic of what it means to be *moral* remained familiar enough to help people transition.

> *Put most simply, one of the best ways to move and keep people on the unre-flective, out of touch end of the continuum of attentiveness is to keep them off balance by shifting the grounds on which they stand so they look outward and elsewhere to find something firm by which to orient themselves—and then giving them just that: something cast in edifying phrases that, often redolent of sex/ gendering processes in male-dominant societies, call for firmness, hardness, getting on with what needs to be done witout going soft.*

Reflection, emotional responsiveness, being in touch: these then become temptations to be avoided, whereas when things are good enough, they are usually admired ways of being, if—let us be honest—generally understood to be a bit risky because they can make someone who indulges "too much" less able to just get on with the demanding business of life.

In sum, whatever formations of identities, whatever recategorizations are historically significant in differing times and situations, extensive evils find us prepared from childhood on to stick with our peers, be "team play-ers," "get on the bandwagon," switch loyalties rather than stand up even for friends, let alone for the "losers," and to think of morality as hard in many senses. As perverted systems spread, ordinary virtues already often rede-fined, recategorized as we have moved through life, age groups, schools, jobs are shifted again, and again, until the most familiar virtues are disabled from any role in keeping us from going along—or, terrifyingly if "we" are among the to-be-victims, from seeing, opposing, fleeing instead of continuing to try to "fit in."

BLURRED GENERALIZATIONS, SLIDING OVER DIFFERENCES, CONTRADICTIONS

Externally defined meanings that can become a distorted sort of common sense to an extreme extent must be accessible to many people, and be readily useable without the sort of bumps that cause people, even if mostly unac-customed to doing so, to stop and think. They must, that is, be on a level of generality that allows us not to encounter discrepancies unto stark differences. As we know, marketing and advertising, which historically developed in tandem with propaganda, provide us with examples. If you are marketing a product, a candidate, a corporate reputation, you want an image and a slogan that come together as a "brand" that speaks emotively to a great many people. It ought not invite inquiries concerning its precision or accuracy. An effective brand must be capaciously general and emotive at once, capable of moving us to fill it in for ourselves with the particular meanings that speak to us. And so phrases move among us: "Where's the beef?" was once heard all over the place, spread from an advertisement into sermons, political rhetoric, and scholarly exchanges as "the beef" managed to stand for any kind of substance as opposed to triviality.

A more complicated example: "I support our troops" became a clichéd phrase in the United States in 2007, as the US occupation of Iraq dragged on. It did not start out as a mental bromide; relatively few clichés do. Its purpose was most of all to make it clear that the speaker was not like the protestors of the Vietnam War era, that s/he was respectful of the warriors if not of the war. The phrase served, then, to express everything from intensely personal feelings (such as a soldier's parents' pride and anxiety) to efforts to criticize the war without immediately offending supporters of the warriors. Very quickly, such a broadly useful gesture became a cliché, and the only apparently genuine, "I support our troops" blurred with authentic care to become part of the mystification, the obfuscation, of the whole tragic mess. So did *Thank you for your service*. The real soldiers, some of whom were motivated by movingly held principles of duty and sacrifice for their country, were both praised by all sides and treated shabbily in too many instances when they returned. And the very large number of "warriors" who were in Iraq not as drafted citizens nor as an "all-volunteer military" but, rather, as what have always been called "mercenaries"—renamed with the spin term, "contractors"—along with the huge private military corporations that profited from those contracts were barely mentioned, let alone made subject of public concern. We were *supporting the troops* with such mindless if often well-meaning determination that we shut down inquiry into who else was actually fighting, who and what was making the fighting possible, who was even doing some of the "interrogations" that involved torture, who was being paid very little and who was profiting hugely, as well as the necessity of the war in the first place.

Leaders talking people into accepting the use of violence yet again also reach for historical terms, phrases, names that have been smoothed by overuse until people no longer really hear them but simply react as expected. President George W. Bush and others in his administration spoke of "Pearl Harbor," of "appeasement" and otherwise used historical terms from World War II that can still stir Americans to outrage and to action, despite the fact that Saddam Hussein's Iraq had not sent the men who crashed planes into the World Trade Center, did not have the means, nuclear or otherwise, to threaten the United States, and had in fact been supported during the Iraq-Iran conflict (1986–1988) by some of the very Bush people now calling other people "appeasers" for not supporting a war *against* their ally, Iraq. Ludicrous all around, but it worked well enough. Never underestimate the power of familiar, emotive clichés that might have had some relevance in the past but have become reflex triggers now.

I fear there are lots of ways to get us humans to externalize our minds, or, what comes to the same thing, to let them be occupied by others. At some points and various ways, we all hand over the activities of thinking for ourselves to other people in exchange for the coin of certainties, of acceptability, for the rewards of money, for social standing. But no: no one can make us choose to slide from decent to evil. We make that choice, sometimes even determinedly. Life is smoother on the surface. Until it is not.

But now I have to underscore that the cure for all these ways our minds can be occupied and changed is not unthinkingly to refuse to change our ways of thinking, our concepts. Becoming an immoveable block is not better than being a moral political tumbleweed. Both are extreme; both might sometimes, nonetheless temporarily, be called for; and in any case, there is a lot of thinking to be done about, as well as between, any extremes. *Here it may be most important to remember that being able to recategorize is also almost coextensive with being able to learn: it, too, is a given of our humanity, preparing us for good as for ill just as and because it prepares us to continue trying to make sense of our world, being attentive to and interested in it.*

Extraordinary forms of good and evil I call "intensive." Extensive evil and extensive good are rooted in what it means to be human in our plurality and differences, and so in ordinary forms and formations of our living together. Simply, that means that we cannot escape moral responsibility. It goes all the way down into the givens of our consciousness, to our specific human freedom that is actualized when we think, act, and, as both creatures and creators of meanings, participate with others past and present, near and far, in making, changing, failing, saving ourselves and our worlds in small ways, and sometimes in great.

The seeds of extensive evil in the ordinary cannot be removed. They are basic functions of conscious, meaning-making, social creatures, and they are also capable of flowering into extensive good if carefully tended.

Chapter Fourteen

Large-Scale Enclosures

Meaning Systems

We have been exploring the many ways ordinary lives and institutions can prepare us to fail to be on time in realizing that a system is going radically wrong, ways that also prepare us to do perverted work reliably. There is a great deal that allows us to avoid being attentive, being startled back into thought. Our minds can be externalized, occupied, preoccupied with the superficial, clichéd, blurry. As a common thread, I have noted earlier and in relation to these the dangers of being out of touch, on that far end of the continuum of attentiveness. I think, then, that we should now focus on some more extreme examples of what being out of touch can mean. There are abstract identities, kinds of knowledge, institutions and organizations that provide enclosures for minds and in some cases also for actual people in which we can see being out of touch writ large.

SCIENTIZING

Here is the powerful Nazi Heinrich Himmler again: "What happens to a Russian, to a Czech, does not interest me in the slightest. What the nations can offer in the way of good blood of our type, we will take, if necessary by kidnapping their children and raising them here with us."[1] Himmler was speaking to SS officers who were at least loosely familiar with Social Darwinism and eugenics (the science of "good breeding") that was adopted by the Nazis as well as the British and the American scientific establishment of the times. By the logic of eugenics, Himmler's pronouncement was entirely rational.

Unfortunately, we do know that scientists, also being human, can indeed hold prejudices that may then be masked and simultaneously legitimated by the authority of their degrees and institutions. Like the rest of us, they can also have lousy political and moral judgment. When prejudice, lousy judgment, and influence coincide, other prestigious, authoritative, and powerful institutions may pick up and then inject scientized—masked as legitimate—prejudices, with all their failures of moral imagination and empathy, into public discussions and policy as fact, as knowledge. The history of science in relation to *race*, to *sex/gender*, thence social policy and law is highly instructive in this regard. Consider that, "The Nazi sterilization program developed within a broad context of eugenic programs in 28 American states as well as several European nations." And this:

> The framers of the Nazi sterilization program looked to other precedents, such as a 1927 U.S. Supreme Court ruling, written by Justice Oliver Wendell Holmes to justify sterilizations. In the wake of world war, when "the best of a generation of young men risked their lives for the nation," Holmes wrote, "it would be strange if it could not call upon those who already sap the strength of the state for these lesser sacrifices [sterilization: being rendered unable to have children] . . . in order to prevent our being swamped with incompetence. . . . Three generations of imbeciles," one of our great Supreme Court justices wrote in an infamous line, "are enough."[2]

Then as now, it was not easy to question, let alone to refute, concepts that developed and became common among experts. *Imbecile*, along with *moron*, for example, now openly nasty epithets, were then medical terms used among some of the most prestigious scientists at Harvard, Stanford, Yale, as of distinguished jurists discussing the writing of Oliver Wendell Holmes. But eugenics evidently has a deadly logic. First, you must decide which human traits are best. Who is to do that? By whose criteria? And just how free of prevailing social hierarchies are those criteria likely to be? And then someone must decide how to go about having more of those traits in the population.

Those planning eugenics policies are not thinking of education and equal opportunity to improve people: they are thinking of traits that (the science of the times tells them) can be bred for. On that track, it makes sense to keep the "less desirable" from breeding: how to do that? Well, persuasion is not likely to succeed: *they* will continue to breed, messing up the human stock. So, sterilization suggests itself. *They* are not likely to consent to that (and even if *they* did, they are hardly reliable). So, law backed by force must be used. The Nazis followed that logic where it led. To rid humankind of all people and peoples their science defines as inferior, those who plan to breed a super race—or even just a "better" one—must remove all carriers of bad genes from the pool. There is practically only one way to do that, a way for which new terms were created: *eugenics*, *thence*, to *The Final Solution*.

Whatever other motivations there may be, a program for appalling extensive evil is right there, in the logic of a science animated by new understandings of genes, taken up by good faith, "enlightened," social, legal, political leaders committed to working for the improvement of humankind. Thus the enthusiasms of authorities can also be thoughtlessly deadly, and since they have power, the perversion of systems that takes us from ordinarily good and bad to evil on a grand scale ratchets up in speed and spread when they make what in retrospect are so clearly egregious even if authoritative errors. And still: "Research shows," we say sagely, and, "scientists agree. . . ." And the word spreads. Very early on, we noted that being thoughtless is not a matter of intelligence, and that education can spread rather than impede it. Here we see that writ large: the "findings" of science can be received and acted on with virtually no understanding or critique as if they were issued by modern oracles.

CLOSED SYSTEMS, ALTERNATIVE REALITIES

Using categorical systems—systematized, high-level abstractions we use to do our diagnostic, analytical, interpretive, explanatory work as, for instance, surgeons discuss bodies, or football fanatics discuss games—is always, in fact, a potentially risky business. Of course, in our professional and intellectual lives we use such systems or at least some of their abstractions, just as, of course, we use generalizations (lower level, less systematized abstractions) in our daily lives. These are among the achievements of humankind that, importantly, allow us to formalize and pass on our knowledge, arts, sports—anything that people have done seriously together for some time. Someone who is knowledgeable about dental hygiene uses systematized abstractions; so does a skilled carpenter, a software developer, a gang member, an art historian, a physicist, a veterinarian, a beautician, a bar tender. Very important, helpful, interesting, these systems, as long as they do not lose touch in a radical way with messy realities, as long as we do not move inside them and close the door against the uncouth, uncool speech of outsiders.

Consider the highly abstract mathematical models beloved of defense strategists, and some social scientists (particularly, it seems, economists, although political scientists cannot be far behind, nor other scholars who envy and may emulate them). Consider highly honed, long-debated, powerfully explanatory political ideologies such as libertarianism, liberalism, conservatism, and (somewhat distinguishable) economic ideologies such as capitalism, socialism, fascism. Consider conceptually sophisticated, absolutized religious worldviews, theologies. Consider psychological theories that define what is wrong with people categorized by those systems. Consider philosophies such as Confucianism, Marxism, Pragmatism, the lasting effects in the West of the Enlightenment, of Islam, Buddhism, and Hinduism elsewhere.

Each of these, all of these, can be held open to questions that can renew their insights, refresh their wisdom (some more readily than others, of course), and each and all can also come to seem in their most stable abstract formulations gratifyingly elegant and even beautiful, as physicists, mathematicians, philosophers, jurists like to say about a good proof, argument, solution, theory. These highly honed complex conceptual edifices can seem to offer glimpses of the good, the true, the beautiful all together which is, for some of us at least, far more appealing, salvific, inspiring than the sloppy, plural, changing, often alternately too dull and too frightening world we share with all those roiling, random, confusing other people who keep saying things that would never have occurred to us and cannot readily even be heard as coherent from where we stand. I am a philosopher; I know the temptation of an elegant simplicity rich in implication but itself stable. For love of the world, I hope work that is thus appealing can be a healthy, illuminating quest, and unending.

It is, however, possible to begin to think such a system, or at least some of its more elegant abstractions, is actually what reality is—or should be. Reflecting on his field, the international economist Andrew Kamarck wrote:

> With considerable hubris, there is a trend among some economists to believe that economics is competent to analyze practically the whole of human activity, both inside and outside the economy . . . .[One] has blithely argued that economic theory explains the whole of human society, that political, legal, and social institutions can be explained as the efficient outcome of rational individuals pursuing their preferences.

"Poor, uncomprehending Henry James, in contrast," Kamarck then observes, "admonished us to 'Never believe that you know the last thing about any human heart.'"[3]

The very real danger is that, in some or even most situations, precision comes to be confused with accuracy, a logic known by a few experts with practical wisdom, and decisions that affect lives are made with dangerously undemocratic, unrealistic certainty. For example, the familiar phrase, "All things being equal" preceding a precise formulation cast as a prediction: All things are not, or let us say are very rarely, "equal" in the real world. They can sometimes be equalized, though, so there can be—if I continue to use this as my example—a temptation to make the world correspond to one's theories. We might say that a strictly behaviorist view of human action that takes us to be predictable when one knows the system of rewards and punishments of the time will become more accurate in situations of less freedom. Less freedom, more predictability, more chance of making your neat plans for everyone's betterment work. Such logics, if nothing else, are evidently pitted against the unique, the anomalous, the free, the nonsensical as well as the simply messy, unstable, changing.

There may be, then, not only political ideologues—people so caught up in their belief in the rightness of their own political theory that they set out to impose it on all of us—but scientific, theological, mathematical, philosophical, sociological, psychological, economic (this is not a complete list) ideologues too. It is one thing to have great respect for such magnificent human achievements as these fields—I do mean that—and to consult them for all the help we may get from their knowledge. It is quite another to overlook all that history teaches us about the limitations, and sometimes glaring errors and so also potential dangers of *applying* (as distinct from *consulting, considering*) any such systems. It is not safe to hand our lives over to experts. As Aristotle noted long ago and rightly, philosophic wisdom (in a general sense) just is not the same as practical wisdom, which arises, when it does, with experience. This of course is why, as we observed earlier, Aristotle opens his famous *Ethics* by saying that with it, we are inquiring not in order to know but in order to do the good—or, more aptly still, in order to do well at practicing to be good. The point is not that all systems of thought must also be practical— which would reduce what we can know, dream, admire, comprehend terribly, and anyhow, who can ever know just what actually is practical?—but that we need to know the difference, and honor it, so we know, think, act, and judge appropriately.

In short: People caught up in a highly rationalized, abstract system of explanation as of categorization may not be open enough to the startles and shocks of realities to avoid causing harm regardless of their good intentions. An individual human is always more and other than a category, a type, a measurement on which a diagnostician of whatever stripe has focused: we are never nothing but female or male, nothing but poor or wealthy, nothing but smart or dumb, neurotic or sane, nothing but sick, nothing but healthy, nothing but Indian/Polish/Jewish/Catholic/Irish/Chinese, old, young, a consumer, rational or irrational—name it. *Nothing but* is a very dangerous thing to be because it is never accurate, even if it is useful in quests for precision. And public policy based on the findings of experts unleavened by the practical wisdom of those seasoned by experience, the ways of knowing of artists, of elders, can give us planned cities, or neighborhoods, or parks, or schools, that at best do not work out as planned. Examples, I fear, are legion.

Divisions both literal and figurative are not in reality absolute. People come and go, physically, online, among jobs and faiths and causes, and people have memories, languages, and imaginations. Transitions between and among worlds of meaning, between and among subworlds and their meanings, are made daily. So, for most ongoing extensive evils, the meanings and provisions its workers encounter as they move through their days must be *made* to be coherent enough to allow those who need justification (the balanced-enough workers the extensive project requires) to feel some continuity among aspects of themselves, their lives, their values, their actions at and away from their jobs (more on this soon).

A warning here, though: Learning that abstract systems and ideologies can become dangerous, we cannot then simply decide to be "realistic," to trust only "the practical sort," rejecting all "ideologues," "fanatics," "extremists," or those "elitist" "egg heads" and "academic snobs." Those may well be prejudices themselves, and too often mask an anti-intellectualism that protects other sorts of dangerous thoughtlessness. As observed earlier, emotion, for example, can be as abstract as reason can be. Consider the sentiments given voice on July 4, not to mention Valentine's Day. Sentimentality is no more reliable a way to be in touch with actual people, history, actions than a "cold" logic.

"REALISM" VERSUS RESPONSIVENESS

Higher up in social orders as well as chains of command than, say, the Polish police officers who did close-in, daily killing of the "unfit," we encounter some other ways of being on the out-of-touch end of the continuum of attentiveness. Pierre Laval was a major player in France's collaboration with the Nazis. The historian Raul Hilberg tells us that Laval was not a fanatic of any sort, but, rather, a "pragmatic politician," neither a "modernizer nor an ideologist." He had twice been Premier of France in the 1930s. In the spring of 1942, he became the collaborating government's premier and, being such a practical type, he made deals with powerful Germany. This, political analysts might call being a "realist." Among other things, "he sought the release of French prisoners of war in exchange for an increase in the number of French laborers going to the Reich," a deal that probably strengthened him with the more privileged among his political supporters while getting rid of those from whom he expected no help and perhaps even trouble. Then, in the summer, still in 1942, he accepted the German demand that twenty thousand stateless Jews be deported from unoccupied France: "Among the victims were several thousand children who had not been expected by the SS and Police. In a gesture of largess, Laval declared that the children did not interest him."[4]

I want to say that in this, Laval is like Eichmann and Saddam and, at a significant remove, he is like Oliver Wendell Holmes when he was being "realistic" about the threat of "imbeciles" to a healthy people and nation. Laval, in his political, professional deal-making, was also bizarrely out of touch with the realities of what he was doing, but at the very same time, he too was operating successfully in his sphere, in his time and place. We cannot then use explanations or even interpretations that allow us to say, in whatever discipline's technical language, that such leaders are crazy, out of control, possessed, coerced, stupid—or even necessarily animated (and so also blinded) by prejudices. Any or all of those, and more, could be in play, of course, but still what we have when we look closely at the doers of the work of mass evil on many differing levels of command is a picture of functional people doing as if it were ordinary what we want to think any sane and/or moral person would see immediately is extraordinary, and dead wrong.

By familiar conventions, they can be admired as realistic as well as rational in their deal-making based solely on seeking advantage, profit, greater security for their country or corporation, but in disordered times, what they do as "realists," as "practical" people is all too significant in establishing massive harm as the order of the day. Becoming used to disabling our moral awareness in order to be "realistic" can thus be a dangerous, if very common, practice and not obviously the remedy for "idealism" of any sort. To be a realist actually requires that we be able to think about the situation, not only within it, and not only in its game-defining terms.

NATIONALISMS, RACIALISMS: ABSTRACT IDENTITIES WRIT IN BLOOD

Related to scientizing and other large-scale epistemological systems are modern mass identity concepts that make use of *blood, ethnicity, race, class, sex/gender/sexualities.* These, which all have complex histories of being understood to be *by nature, natural*, are therefore particularly prone to scientistic misuse. They are variously in play in nationalisms, where they can serve to anchor a polity and its people in some supposed certainty about who they are and are not: *We are Americans, but those people who snuck in are not.*

A meta-source of legitimacy can be invoked to underwrite even an apparently startlingly different system as it emerges. So, for instance, where nationalism took over from monarchies, from empire, "cultural community of shared language, religion, and/or other characteristics" was invoked as if it already existed even as such communities were more and less violently created by expelling those now defined as outsiders, or worse. With the purposeful creation of nationalist narratives that taught people to value and to find identity within "a durable, antique past, shared kinship, common origins, and . . . progress through time," *both* "new claims to rights, *and* patriotisms that could deny those rights to those not of the blood, faith, soil became potent."[5]

Thus, for instance, historians remind us that Europe in 1848, following uprisings and revolutions for liberation, and for rights for individuals such as freedom of speech, was also "awash in conflicting ethnic claims":

> In Frankfurt, radicals demanded a unified German state. But what about non-Germans living in that future Germany, like Danes and Poles, and what about Germans living outside a unified Germany? One German politician chillingly noted "the preponderance of the German race over most Slav races . . . is a fact." . . . Smaller nations weren't much kinder.[6]

Tragically, just as prejudices can linger in and deform science, definitions of individual rights can still sometimes reveal a birth in nationalistic, more or less racialized/sexualized divisions. Consider the "rights of an Englishman," of "a *real* American," a citizen versus a "guest worker" ineligible by "blood" for citizenship that would entail rights.

Despite the emotively pitched physicality of terms of "nature" such as "blood" and "race," such narratively constructed "imagined communities"[7] with their extended identities are highly abstract. Nationalism binds strangers *as if* they, who in their real, daily lives have nothing whatsoever to do with each other and never will, were blood kin. Such identities can, for that very reason, become particularly intensely held. Being entirely abstract, they are not readily contradicted by anything, or anyone, real, material, immediate. *Who* someone is can then be trumped by her/his "blood" or nation, by *what* in those abstract terms she/he is defined as being: not this person, but a representative of some *kind* of person (an Indian, a Chechen, Irish, etc., where nationalisms are at issue, even when people have defined themselves as *a nation* without having a state).

Racialisms (a term used to indicate where notions about *race* have been used to create, describe, analyze, invoke supposedly socially significant "kinds" of people, divided rather than simply differentiated and more or less hierarchical) and their related racisms (active stereotypes, prejudices, hatreds "explained" with concepts of such divisions by "kind") can flourish within nationalisms as an informing logic, admitted or not, scientized or not, religiously inscribed or not. The problem with being "of a people," a "race," a "blood"-defined nonpersonal identity is that these are not characteristics anyone can change, so if one's "kind" is turned by a perverted social, economic, political order into "a problem" requiring "a solution," there are, horrifically, very few options other than separation, expulsion, or, as the "final solution," genocide. States more or less rooted still in racialized nationalisms need not carry that deadly logic as far as the Nazis, but in their differing ways, they all teach us something crucial about imagined identities and how they can be reframed such that abstractions—*blood, race, nation, my people*—come to seem undeniably, forcefully, real—more real than the actual people with whom we daily live, love, work, play, and face our individual mortality.

Belief, created by such racializations, that people really do come in politically, morally, and socially significant natural "kinds,"[8] can take on deep roots while also spreading over the surface, stifling minds with its sheer conventionality so that, even faced with startling harm to individuals we know and love, we stay on the old tracks. Remember Alfons' acceptance of his friend Heinz's "misfortune" in being Jewish?

For extensive evils, such pre-categorizings of *what* people and peoples are, from the individual to the abstractly inclusive level, serves to underwrite beliefs of those who are indeed necessary to do the daily devastating work. That is, while racialization, a very familiar abstract identity category, can prepare for extensive evils, flat-out racism is not necessary. We remember: Arab and Euro-American enslavement of African people was certainly facilitated by racializations that fed and were fed by racism, but the ancient Greeks enslaved people they conquered without notable racism. There is slavery, or active complicity in it, of Africans by other Africans still today. Arab slave traders had differing relations to Africans they enslaved than did, say, the British. Girls and women and boys around the world are sold, tricked, and kidnapped into highly profitable (no, not for them) sexual slavery. Ancient Romans enslaved Greeks too, and it was hardly unknown for Greek slaves to be the teachers and most decidedly not defined as the "inferiors" of their "owners." Lines blur. Nonetheless, significant numbers of human beings sorts have violently taken over the lives of other human beings of many in order to use them as they will, as no more than tools, means for the ends of others, and the differences among these vicious forms strongly suggest that while racializations can help the doers of horrific harms do their work, racism is not required, nor alone does it suffice. A common thread of money and profit-seeking is far more evident in the history of slavery of all kinds.

I think we can say, though, that, like careerism and competitions for political power, nationalistic, racialized categories of identity—which are always and throughout mutually constructed with sex, issues of "breeding," enactments of gendered hierarchies—can be used to prepare ordinary people to do massively deadly work when the high level of abstraction that gives them their usefulness and reach is taken over by those who are converting large systems of meaning, business, belief, law, governance to their own purposes and profit.

Here too, what can be fine and even good in basically decent times—identification with many rather than just a very few, awareness of differences (when not frozen into divisions), loyalty to community, patriotism, identification with universals that make it possible to think substantively of human and not only individual rights—can also prepare us to do terrible things in different times if we are not practiced in thinking about as well as within those definitions.

ALWAYS AGAIN: SEX, SEXUALITY, GENDER

In *Generation Kill*, we read that male marines cheer each other on with "Get some!"[9] and generally, daily, casually as well as in times of tension and crisis, speak a hypersexualized, hyper-heterosexual, hypermasculinized, violent language. Of course, there is no surprise here; who does not know it? It is ordinary, and that is the point. In the violent, violative, misogynist realms of common profanity, many "games" and "comics," pornography, "shop talk" among men, some blockbuster movies, "art" films, and novels, the ordinary seeds of extensive evils are more than usually evident (not necessarily more active, more dangerous: just less veiled).

These sometimes also racialized sex/gender hierarchies are available to be turned into tools of real violation when already denigrated, disempowered people are turned into spoils of war for the victor; symbols of the manhood of an enemy, and so to be defiled; possessions to be used at will, discarded, even murdered; vehicles for male bonding and status-establishing; no more than a means of relief, escape, entertainment. In Darfur, rape has once again been used (and as I write, still is being used) as a central tool of a genocidal program of dominance. To a remarkable extent, dominance, from the intimate to the global, is sexualized and gendered.[10]

These all-pervasive systems can be startlingly similar in entirely unsubtle ways from pop culture to "high" art, from online behavior to boardrooms, pool hall to country club to barracks. That there is now in some countries a growing awareness that an equation of masculinity with superiority, dominance, and the violations and violence these can require and breed has not yet broken those too-close ties. Where feminist and other questioning scholarship and movements have taken hold, however, we are becoming used to objecting, and acting, in concert. Education matters; practicing thinking matters; working with many others in public matters.

Systemic racializations, nationalisms, sex/genderings, ethnicities, class and caste hierarchies require ongoing, finely tuned critique also because, from among other thoughtlessly held generalizations, clichés, conventions, these are very likely to be encoded in legitimated knowledge, religions, laws, ethics. They are, then, very difficult to think about, to reconsider, not because they seem almost trivial, as clichés do, but because they are setting the terms of a culture about sex, sexualities, reproduction: what it means to be female or male, to be "a good woman," "a good man," prescribing who may and may not be educated, own property, inherit, vote, and more.

Such reach and depth mean that these are arguably the systems that provide the most direct translation route from a decent enough society to a perverted, deadly one. For a vivid example, we can turn to "Freedom Fighter: An Abolitionist's Crusade," published in *The New Yorker* in 2014.[11] In Mauritania, where slavery was not outlawed until 1981 (making it the last country in the world to do so), provision for police and legal action against slaveholders remains weak and sporadic enough that, out of 3.8 million people in the country, some one hundred and forty thousand are enslaved (Global Slavery Index estimate). Racialized class that still marks darker-skinned Africans as inferior to the lighter Beydanes—an Arab-Berber minority that largely controls the levers of power—and a sex/gender hierarchy that, among other things, legally treats all adult women as minors and denies them secular education in this "avowedly Muslim country," mix in the brew of hierarchies there (including those between other Africans and descendants of the originally enslaved people). What is simply assumed to be right, ordinary, proper, the way things have been and ought to be, rarely yields to public policy even when the leaders really want it to. Enslavement continues elsewhere as well, illegal as it is, but, while "people endure slave-like conditions in other countries in the region, . . . the problem in Mauritania is unusually severe: 'Some proximate form of slavery has continued to be a foundation of the social structure and the division of labor within households, so there are many more people who are willing to support it as an institution.'" The extensive evil is already present, not just seeded but widely as well as deeply rooted in common ways of life and belief. Secular education is limited. Religious authority is invoked. Free thinking is socially unacceptable.

And still, we note, there are several sorts of abolition movements in Mauritania, largely varying, it seems, along a strategic scale from efforts to persuade authorities to make real change, to civil disobedience. Biram Dah Abeid, the leader of one of the more activist and risk-taking movements and himself born a *haratin*, a slave descended from the Africans originally enslaved by Berbers and Arabs, sought out a secular as well as a religious education. He was the first in his family to do so. It "allowed him to question more than his father had. 'I freed myself,' he said." Abeid studied Mohammad's teachings to figure out if it was correct that Islam supports slavery, then continued to study the issue through Western philosophy as well. He also knows about Gandhi and King, and has made himself a student of the history of slavery in his own country.

As we saw in Occupied France and elsewhere, there are always some whose minds keep working, who prepare, who find thinking friends and a sense of identity with others near and far who have struggled for the good. What leads me to mention Abeid here, in particular, is that the extensive evil of slavery in Mauritania so evidently requires people to free their own minds before escape, let alone resistance coordinated into a movement, is possible because there, it is said, the persistence of slavery is far less a matter of whip and lash and chains than it is of deeply enculturated beliefs, daily racialized, gendered sexual, domestic, economic realities that by now seem to slaves as to masters just the way things are and ought to be. (To some; never all.)

*****

So, now we turn to considering institutional enclosures smaller than empires, nations, countries and their cultures, focusing in on examples that support but can also contradict systems of dominance woven into daily lives.

Chapter Fifteen

Physical Enclosures of Bodies, Minds

The Krome detention center of the U.S. Immigration and Naturalization Service is a sprawling complex at the edge of the Everglades, about thirty miles west of downtown Miami. . . . Krome was attracting local and national media attention for allegations that detention officers were mistreating detainees. The officers who ran the camp were immune to the effects of bad publicity, one of them told me later. "We knew about the criticisms, but it wasn't something we really paid attention to. To tell you the truth, everybody in there felt untouchable. It was our world."[1]

Krome was an enclosed subworld in which ordinary people worked by the norms within its walls, regardless of how out of synch those norms were with the mores, morals, laws by which they were raised and that continued to prevail outside. There is nothing trivial about doing your job within organizational conventions that actually are radically different from those you could remember do still exist if you would stop and think, reflect, picture to yourself what it is that you are actually doing. You could, after all, imagine your other selves, your "outside"' self—a spouse, a mother's child, a democratic citizen, a friend, a parent, a neighbor, a church/mosque/synagogue/temple goer. But when we work in such places—and many of us do, even if few are as glaringly discrepant from the rest of our lives as places of incarceration—the choice, the desire, the temptation not to think about what we are doing from anything but the inside-these-walls perspective is evidently very strong.

INSTITUTIONALIZING CORRUPTING RELATIONS

Krome detention center was a world in which "sexual favors" were "coerced" from "young female detainees" "in exchange for promises of

195

release"[2]—or were, simply, coerced from females with no one to report it to who gave a damn or would do anything anyhow, women who would likely eventually be sent to another country from which repercussions were highly unlikely:

> Sexual abuse of prisoners is a common practice, and INS detainees are especially vulnerable for the simple reason that they can be deported. As a 1993 Justice Department investigation "concluded" in another Krome case, "[Detainee's] version of rape and forced oral sex is corroborated only by her subsequent statements to public health service personnel. There are no witnesses nor any physical evidence. . . . Moreover, [the woman] has been deported to Haiti. Under these circumstances, this matter lacks prosecutive merit."[3]

This is enclosure in several ways, obviously: among them we do have to observe a tragically familiar sex/gender power imbalance.

Treating the objects of one's job as no more than sources of either trouble or gratification for oneself extends to other kinds of violation and exploitation too: "INS officials reported that the detainees' property was not always returned to them when they were deported or released."[4] So what is going on here? Do such enclosures—of their employees as of those subject to them—bring out the worst that is always latent in us? Should we learn from Krome no more than the age-old preachment that humans are greedy, lustful, violent creatures when not controlled by institutionalizations of morality and law? And might that be the real lesson to be learned from extensive evils? It is human nature, as Thomas Hobbes, not to mention many preachers and prophets said long ago and last week from many pulpits.

"BASE INSTINCTS" CONVENTIONALIZED

There are obviously what proper society likes to call "base instincts" in play here, particularly desires to have what one wants, here, now, and regardless of effect on others. But the doers, the workers, of extensive evils are typically jobholders (from office workers, guards, supervisors, engineers, etc., to paid killing squads). They are, to themselves and to those in related roles around them, people with institutionally defined tasks to do. Those whose own careers and status depend on getting the overall job done are likely to fire anyone *really* in the grip of "base instincts" more than now and then when colleagues are not there, or are willing to turn their heads—or join in. We know that has been, and is, the case if only because, if it were not, extensive evils would be impossible. They would break down into erratic orgies, spasmodic attacks, exhausting sprees. Consider: The "best" slaveholders kept their overseers under control so that the enslaved people they worked would be healthy and calm enough to do their work well. The overseers did need to be able and willing to whip, to maim, to brand, to kill, but those who did so for their own monstrous pleasures unnecessarily damaged the goods in their charge: not at all ideal workers, those who cannot control their base desires.

The workers, the perpetrators—legions of them—must then be assisted in encapsulating their worlds so that they can do their jobs reasonably effectively, and then return to a radically different sort of experience "outside"—in modest homes; or in the Big House far from the slave quarters; or, perhaps, at classy addresses in Greenwich, Connecticut, and Silicon Valley, removed from lower level workers fueling profits directly and indirectly—that helps them carry on, day after day after day. The Krome workers were not well enough managed in negotiating the transition from inside to outside; they lost balance; this enclosed institution got in trouble (too late for far too many detainees, but eventually).

CHAMELEONS: IN AND OUT, OFF AND ON DUTY

This is all evidence for something else crucial to think through. We are also capable of moving into and out of moral, amoral, immoral worlds that radically contradict each other and doing so over time in ways that make us able to get along, to fit in as "ordinary" in several ways alternately. We can do so for remarkable lengths of time, even for years. Nazi concentration camp workers did their jobs, participating actively in starving, beating, murdering staggering numbers of individual human beings during working hours, and then returned home, often to families, to children, to friends with whom they proved to themselves that they really were still all right, still normal, still good people. They had lighthearted parties. They took vacations. They sang songs and picked fruit and scratched their dog's ears. So did the executives and non-enslaved workers at companies to which concentration camp inmates were marched to work.

And so do government-paid torturers do their work, and profit-seekers in the forests and mines of the Amazon who wiped out whole villages, and keepers of brothels offering girls sold by their parents and bought for use by US citizens who love and care for their own children, and profiteers who know that their policies require the use of women's labor in another country at wages that will not feed one person, let alone a family. Whether or not you judge each of these—we could expand the list—to be instances of extensive evil, they are examples of systemic injustices and the harm they are enabled to continue doing because the necessary work is encapsulated, enclosed, so people can get it done, go home to play other roles, return refreshed and con-firmed in their sense of themselves as decent people.

We do not need base instincts, which I am quite sure we have along with their opposites, to switch codes like that. We just need to have practiced doing so in all the ways we have touched on thus far, and more. We start learning how when we learn to behave one way at home, another at school, another with friends, another with colleagues, another in a different job or profession. In effect, we can all code switch—move in and out of two or more languages, or, here, subworlds, cultures, defined groups. In and of itself, this is just another expression of our performative selves, and it can certainly also be good as it prepares us to join and be with people quite different from us. Still, extreme instances can require more: performative selves with almost no core of integrity, little coherence, just multiple ways of behaving. Because we can adjust our behavior and attitudes quite smoothly if we have practiced—and ordinarily, we have, although to quite differing degrees—we know already that a man with a job that pays him for it can change from a father to a killer and back every morning and evening. The difference is whether we know what we are doing and continue to reflect about it, to question, to judge its worth and its effects on self and others or, instead, go on autopilot when we enter the enclosure of the work world so we can play its game without the awkward disruption of a mind that says, *What are you doing? How can you do that?*

STATUS

Having returned to reflective thought, a former guard in a brutal detention center says of his then colleagues and himself:

> You know what it is? . . . All those guys are cop wanna-bes. That's what it is.
> All those guys out there want to be cops, and there's no way they can be cops.
> They got a badge, you know? They got a badge. People that can't get into real law enforcement—because that's not law enforcement—but they go around say-ing, "Oh, we're officers," and "We're this and that." They're nothing. But they have that complex, you know? And I tell you this because when I first got there and got my badge, I felt the same thing. I tell you from experience. I was going, "Wow. I got a badge and a gun now." They gave me a gun, and I hadn't had any training. I had never shot a gun, and they gave me a gun.[5]

"They're nothing," I was nothing: "I felt the same thing." Then: "They gave me a gun." "Wow." And then the author of this book puts in a parenthesis: "In one recent year, five INS officers committed suicide with their weapons."

No matter what, the daily hard work of harming, dominating others takes a toll because it is *not* done out of raw hatred, bursts of irrationality, pure evil, utterly flawed characters. It is done by ordinary people whose usual flaws and weaknesses and personal hurts have been hooked into systems—insider systems, where harm is normalized as part of the job, and outside systems, where provisions have been made to keep the work of harming from breaking those who do it (if not always entirely successfully). The INS guards were not in a society in which what they could do to other people had been normalized, made legal outside as well as in (not that there was not anti-immigrant feeling, but raping, stealing, beating can still get you in trouble).

Is there a connection here among people ranging from those who feel they are "nothing" and so are vulnerable to doing any kind of work that allows them to—is designed to—make them feel like "something," and people convinced by their social placement that they are "something" and take that to be an entitlement to use power for whatever ends even an utterly distorted system allows? A desire for status that confers power over others surely does suggest itself as another of the enabling factors potent enough to allow the privileged as well as the underprivileged to convert to doing truly ugly work. There is here no evident, primal, causal "fear of the Other," or "base instincts," or "passionate prejudice," though. We may ordinarily have a taste, a desire, even a lust for power and status, but this is a drive that can be thoughtfully modulated, even redirected, transformed into effective leadership for the good. I think we all know, and can comprehend, people who are "driven to succeed," to be loved, admired and find that troubling only when it swamps good judgment, authentic values. How we think about and within and against our actual situations goes on mattering.

BOREDOM

The guard in the quote above also said:

> I had a totally different frame of mind. I hated going to work there. I really did. Because I was locked up—they made us work twelve-, thirteen-hour shifts. It wasn't eight-hour shifts. You worked twelve-, thirteen-hour shifts locked up in that environment with a bunch of people wanting to get out. . . . A lot of things we did in there weren't right. I mean, we made guys stand in line—they just stand there, just to stand there. "Don't move," you know. And we'd make them stand there all day long.[6]

Such actions may be another, if extracurricular, indulgence in dominance by those whose job requires them to remain in control of others, but it is important to notice, too, that in truly enclosed systems, and perhaps most others, we cannot write off boredom as a factor enabling the doing of harm. Boredom, too, is ordinary, and it, too, prepares us to do things of which we might not otherwise be capable. Nothing like it to turn the mind off, to turn it away from our immediate situation, to lead us to want to do anything, anything at all, to feel awake and alive again. Somewhere between such dangerous mind shut downs and the frantic, all-absorbing and so also antireflective busyness of other peoples' work lives there is work that animates our minds, engages and practices us in being thoughtful. A society that has too little of that kind of work may well be at risk.

In some of those enclosed systems, the harm being done is quite obviously manifold: the detainees and the guards are all being violated, if unequally and differently. For systems that are so harmful to people in all roles within them to keep going, rewards and punishments must be effective indeed, and they must work within a larger social order that sustains them, crucially by making some kind of sense, giving some meaning, to what people do.

WORKING FREE

The man I quoted above came to and realized what he was doing, and he reflects on what he did with an apparently nondefensive directness. Experience can get through to us. We can start thinking again. We can remember reflectively. We can act. And we can live with the guilt of knowing what we did because we do know that we came to understand, to judge, and to stop doing it. In that, we come to know that we are also able to choose to be better than we were, and to live with the greater vividness and interest that renewed attentiveness returns to us. If we will.

Durwood Myers administered a detention center, an "INS-contracted jail," in Oklahoma. As "a former cop who helped integrate the Jackson, Mississippi, police force in the late sixties and early seventies, Myers also makes a point of integrating the dormitories and sports teams at his jail."[7] Having had the experience of the Civil Rights movement himself, he persists in working against some of the oldest, most pernicious categorizations of people, and he does so—as he did in Mississippi—from within some of the very institutions that have been used to enforce those categorizations. We do choose; we can change; and we can change systems too.

Remember the former INS officers we encountered earlier? By contrast, Myers says, "My staff is not an authoritarian staff. They're not on a power trip. . . . Most of my officers are gray-headed." Myers was sixty-five when he said this. "Since they are no longer 'out to make a mark in the world,' they tend to avoid 'the authoritarian complex.'"[8] And they no longer have the excuse that they "have to do it" for the sake of their jobs, present and future promotions, and status. Here it is again: careerism constitutes an alternative kind of reality for a remarkable number of people, allowing us to avoid reflecting on the actual content and effects of our work. Myers was not hiring older people for their experience and wisdom, at least not alone. He was hiring people who were no longer careerists, a lesson we learned earlier, listening to the older men in the more horrific situation of Police Battalion 101 when it was turned into a Nazi mobile killing unit. We remember that, "They were young, with 60% of them under the age of thirty-six," the men of the SS and SD under Hitler—the men we met earlier who pushed beyond Hitler's orders to do even more murderous things to prove their competency, to position themselves for promotion.[9]

Myers also adheres to three strict hiring rules: no ex-cops, no ex-Marines, no ex-correctional officers. He himself is all of those. He prefers to hire people who "built fences or cowboyed or farmed."[10] Instead of the usual self-justifications and rationalizations (we are all very creative when we feel the sharp stabs of guilt), Myers seems to have analyzed himself and those around him and recognized just how powerful are the norms that make it possible for people to do violence, including that which is fully legitimated by a prevailing social order and political system and so prepares us to continue. Mr. Myers—someone who has kept thinking and learning about tightly closed-in, closed-off, institutions where reality itself can be reset to normalize the unacceptable—would not be a good candidate for work within a system that has gone as far bad as those of extensive evil. He learns from experience, and he thinks about what he has learned in order to do better (in both senses). These are such small, sensible virtues, and they are those that turn out to keep us from doing small but also very great harm, to do small but also very great good, and to keep it up.

BEING CONSCIENTIOUS

Mr. Myers is probably not as rare as we might like to think (best to think he *is* rare if we want to hold on to explanations such as, *They made me do it; everyone was doing it; it was just my job*). Nonetheless, it is painful to observe how little it takes to keep most of us doing our jobs even in extremely distorted systems. I find it moving, sometimes admirable, sometimes horrifying that when people have a job to do, given a chance, we will do it. We will do it conscientiously. We will adjust ourselves to it, taking on its logic, and find identity and pride in doing so well. It is a fine thing in us, this conscientiousness, as is our ability to take pride in doing most kinds of work well. And: conscientiousness can replace conscience.

TRANSPORTING CATEGORIES: MEDICALIZING

In tightly enclosed systems, sometimes categorizations are kidnapped from other systems to cover up the harms we are actually doing in a subworld quite other than those from which we borrow our masking terms. For example, in an interview, "Russell Bergeron, INS chief press officer" is asked about the use of sedation. He responds: "INS does not sedate detainees. . . . We have no jurisdiction and no authority to sedate anyone, and we do not. We cannot administer sedation to people, and we simply don't do it. If an individual is sedated, it's because a medical decision has been made by competent and qualified medical doctors that an individual needs to be sedated because of a psychological or physical medical problem." [11]

Clear, definitional jurisdictional lines there. Detainers cannot sedate people; medical and psychological professionals are the only ones who can. But look what happens: "One day, [Mr.] Ebibillo resisted deportation; the next day, the PHS [Public Health Services] physician determined him to have 'passive/aggressive personality disorder . . . and [to be] potentially aggressive and capable of hurting others or himself.' On the basis of that 'diagnosis' he was tranquilized."[12]

This is what I mean by "kidnapped meanings": A man named Ebibillo is in fact sedated. He is "tranquilized." Why? He refused to go along with INS's orders, which I think we can assume violated his independence and his dignity along with his life choices by picking him up and "detaining" him and then deporting him. The issue here is between Ebibillo and INS in their fully defined, oppositional roles. INS would find it easier to manage an outraged, perhaps desperate man if they could sedate him—but INS cannot do that. So, "resisting deportation" becomes "aggressive" as in "passive/ aggressive personality disorder," a categorization that has meaning not when we are thinking about why someone might resist being deported, but only as a "psychological or physical medical problem." From what, from whose, perspective is there a "problem" here? Whose is the aggression? Does not matter: Ebibillo's actions have been recategorized as medical/psychological.

Expertise actually plays that translational function in all sorts of ways, and is usually accepted, perhaps useful. This is not "obedience to authority" but it is common enough that we can become inappropriately obedient simply because we are used to having doctors diagnose us, preachers characterize us, teachers correct us, security officials care only about our papers. All this can be for our own good, until it is misused, inappropriate, and so becomes violative.

As with unthinking use of social or scientized categorizations, the use of one profession's terms across enclosed institutional boundaries can be merely inappropriate, but it can also enable serious, institutionally enforced, legitimated harm. Thus "sedating" people who stop "being compliant" is also justified as necessary to protect other people, as it might be in a hospital for mental patients with histories of violence. It would then "be negligent of that medical facility not to issue that medication to the people, because they have a responsibility to protect their employees and the other patients at the hospital."[13] Those in charge are precisely not allowing themselves, nor wanting us, to remember the obvious: that a detainment facility in which people are held against their will by decision of political authorities is most assuredly not a hospital, not a healing facility.

By that logic, citizens outraged at a new law who organize a march to protest it are being noncompliant and the government should call in psychiatrists to diagnose them as displaying "passive/aggressive personality disorder" so they can be sedated. Psychological categories may always be dangerous when used politically, we might note, because they turn character and actions of people who are acting as individuals, as free citizens with rights, into pathologizing diagnoses. If your job requires you to treat adults in ways that limit their freedom, violate their wishes, frighten and harm them, it can help to be told by an expert, *It's okay. That guy is mentally ill. He must be restrained.* And sometimes, perhaps he really must be. There is always a need for judgment to temper our choices concerning the appropriateness of expertise in *this* situation, here and now.

A graduate student who worked in a scientific laboratory once told me that it helped her kill the occasional lab rat when her advisor instructed her to "sacrifice" it. For what? For the greater good. For the advancement of science. To further the lead scientist's research agenda. To be a good assistant. To earn her PhD. All potentially valid and legitimate; all also preparation for "sacrificing" other people under a genuinely perverted regime. *Sacrifice:* to make an offering to a deity. All the better, perhaps, if something difficult is done to prove devotion. (Ah, yes. Morality is *hard.* It can ask us to do what we really would rather not.)

ESCAPISM, VACATIONS, R AND R

Genocide "is an exercise in community building," the scholar Philip Gourevitch has observed—it "brought people together." One perpetrator likened hunting down Tutsis to "communal work duty," and admitted that he'd enjoyed it. "The genocide was like a festival. At day's end, or any time there was an occasion, we took a cow from the Tutsis, and slaughtered it and grilled it and drank beer. . . . It was a festival. We celebrated."[14]

In the extreme instances that, later or from safely outside, appall anyone who is thinking, decision-makers know that there is an ongoing need to help people avoid being fully attentive to what they are doing, to erase, overlay, reinterpret, substitute not only concepts and categorizations, but memory. This can be done, we find out when we look closer- in at the operations of these enclosed systems, whether fully extensive or more limited, by providing perpetrators with alcohol and/or drugs, "partying" with plenty of sexual intensity, dramatic settings for "r & r—rest and recreation," so the whole job becomes "community building," with the hard parts smoothed by the anticipated rewards, the stimulants, the fun with others. You are not alone; you are in supportive company, and you need not—even cannot for a bit, while intoxicated in various ways—stop and think. The intensities of such indulgences shared with others against whom you do not need to protect yourself as you do around "outsiders" to the work you are doing—all of these are purposefully used. Arguably we see this not only in provisions for the doers of harm on an institutionalized level, but for similar reasons in some of the parties thrown by the contemporary robber barons in the United States and elsewhere. Among other functions, such over-the-top parties proclaim not just wealth but exemption from the norms of the little people. They allow the doers to think of themselves as different and much better than others, a very common belief indeed among those who do not want to realize what they are really doing and what it is or could be doing to others, to a shareable world. These counter-experiences should, then, have sensuous, sensual, emotional, and conceptual intensity, so that feelings of shame, guilt, disgust, fear, self-doubt, even self-loathing that can result from regularly violating balanced feelings of moral implication with others are overmatched by experiences of being rewarded, indulged, respected, included in higher caste worlds.

In 2006, I came across an article covering the possibility that the huge aviation corporation Boeing would be added to a lawsuit being brought against "the former C.I.A. director George Tenet and private aviation companies," "if Boeing can be proved to have played a role in Masri's rendition." With the ACLU, the man bringing this suit was Khaled el-Masri, "a German car salesman who was apparently mistaken for an Al Qaeda suspect with a similar name, in January of 2004." Masri was arrested, flown to Baghdad, and then to Kabul. On board, he was "chained to the floor," Masri has said, and then "spent the next four months . . . under interrogation." He was "released in May, 2004, on the orders of Condoleezza Rice . . . after she learned that he had mistakenly been identified as a terrorism suspect."[15]

Okay: all problematic—why did the people who worked for the airline go along with it? There was big money, obviously; the bosses, who do not actually do what needs to be done themselves, chose as so often to seek profits, as excessive as possible (as always, some differ: one executive quit). But my focus is now on the people who did the morally, physically ugly work on the planes. Why did they do it? Why, having done it, did they not then feel guilty, reflect, find a way to object? Imagine having put chains on a frightened, even desperate, perhaps angry, perhaps crying person who is being abducted by a power as big as the United States, and watched him throughout the flight. Imagine afterwards going home to your more usual life. Reading the newspapers. Listening to your neighbors, your children, perhaps some of whom are deeply troubled by reports leaking out of such behavior on the part of their, of your, country. How might you be helped *not* to keep brooding about what you have done, been part of?

The *New Yorker* report tells us, "The American flight crew fared better than their passenger. Documents show that after the 737 delivered Masri to the Afghan prison it flew to the resort island of Majorca, where, for two nights, crew members stayed at a luxury hotel, at taxpayers' expense."[16] On a much more expansive, expensive, continuing scale this is also, of course, how the executives of corporations colluding in the doing of such things keep themselves going with calm-enough consciences despite knowing what they are really doing. They indulge in sense-pleasing, and numbing, luxuries, living within bubbles of wealth that can effectively attenuate the sense of mutual implication with the lives of all those grubby, miserable, no doubt envious others against whom gates of privileged communities can be literally and symbolically locked.

Those who plan to get this work done do know—or soon learn—that there will probably be an effect, a kind of powerful emotional kickback, particularly among the not-so-wealthy, actual doers of the deeds. People new to the doing of willful harm on orders may remember what they did with the kind of somatic vividness the removed decision-makers can easily avoid, dealing only in words and numbers, in abstractions, as they can do. This is risky for the decision-makers, this vulnerability to vivid memories among the doers. It could lead them to talk too much, and to the wrong people, or, less dramatically but no less problematically, it could lead to their refusing to do such a thing again, and perhaps telling others who will then also refuse. So, they will splurge to reward the doers, thus both numbing and implicating them in enjoying the spoils of wrong-doing. And again: thus being rewarded is not unusual. We are used to the idea that special effort and work can be recognized that way. We are accustomed to doing things for the sake of rewards, not for their own sake, from a very young age: work hard for a grade, even if you dislike the subject, are mistreated by the teacher; work at something you do not like doing to make money to buy a car; do what it takes to get hired, to get promoted. Nothing necessarily wrong with letting rewards alone justify our work, until there is.

Chapter Sixteen

Laying Out the Strands

In February of 2006, *The New York Review of Books* carried an article by Nicholas D. Kristof about events in Darfur titled, "Genocide in Slow Motion."[1] In slow motion, we can pull out in some detail what is going on in order to bring it together with key strands of this query, the quest to comprehend, thus far. Because comprehension does require moving very close in even as we also compare, contrast, reflect, I will draw heavily on Kristof to begin.

Drawing on his own investigative reporting as well as two books under review, Kristof writes that the Sudanese government responded to acts of rebellion by long-disempowered and oppressed tribal members in Darfur by deciding "to launch a scorched-earth counterinsurgency campaign, involving the slaughter of large numbers of people in Darfur."[2] As always, such a decision meant that the leaders had to find many people who were willing and able to kill and keep killing over time, reliably. Kristof observes, "It was difficult to use the army for this, though, partly because many soldiers in the regular army were members of African tribes from Darfur—and so it wasn't clear that they would be willing to wipe out civilians from their own tribes." The government thus turned to "irregular militias" to do the slaughtering. That these militia members were not from Darfur would not ensure that they would murder masses of people, though. Contrary to blithe statements about how we "fear the Other," let alone the basically racist notion that tribal peoples are always ready to slaughter each other—which was invoked by the Sudanese government itself when it wanted to "pretend that the killings were the result of tribal conflicts and banditry" so they could "deny that they had any control over the Janjaweed," the killers they hired—people who are quite different from each other can and do live peacefully and to mutual benefit and pleasure quite often. In the case of Darfur, it is also noteworthy that people on both sides were Muslim (as, we remember, the Hutu and Tutsi in Rwanda were Christian, with a majority Catholic). Something has to happen for some differences to be used as reasons for sustained, programmatic murder, and something else also then has to be done to sustain those who do that killing.

Even so, we can breathe again here, too: not everyone went along. Kristof cites a "telling account of the chief of the Baggara Rizeigat Arabs, a seventy-year-old hereditary leader who has kept his huge tribe out of the war and who is quietly advocating peace—as well as protecting non-Arabs in his territory."

In stark contrast, needing workers to pursue its agenda, "Sudan's government released Arab criminals from prison and turned them over to the custody of Musa Hilal ["chief of an Arab nomadic tribe" with a long history of "hostility to non-Arabs"] so that they could join the Janjaweed [the irregular militias, themselves Arabs from nomadic tribes]." The government "set up training camps for the Janjaweed, gave them assault rifles, truck-mounted machine guns, and artillery. Recruits received $79 a month if they were on foot, or $117 if they had a horse or camel. They also received Sudanese army uniforms with a special badge depicting an armed horseman." Like guards, I have to remember, in detention centers in the United States whose badges made them feel like "someone."

The Janjaweed were also, according to survivors, "accompanied by soldiers," which would make them feel legitimated as well as backed-up, and would have raised their sense of status too, most likely. Again, not unlike the INS prison guards and on from there: give people status, tools, legitimacy, pay, and some sense that what they are doing is regarded by the system in power as serving a cause that they can support, and there may well be enough people to do the hard work of violative and deadly harm to many other people, day after day after day.

A distilled statement of what these murderous "militias" were about comes from a survivor, who said, "They attacked the people, saying, 'You are opponents of the regime, we must crush you. As you are Black, you are like slaves. Then the entire Darfur region will be in the hands of the Arabs. The government is on our side. The government plane is on our side. It gives us food and ammunition.'" The killers have adopted a supposedly justifying purpose—crushing opponents of a regime to which, as Arabs, they apparently have claims to belong. Those are claims to be "winners," to be on the side of power and, as always, largesse—status, money, loot, and we have to say rape, sexualized dominance in the extreme. Still, the Janjaweed doers of harm are not outlaws: the government's planes are "on our side," giving the favored killers, the rapists, "food and ammunition" and the promise of more land once the "Black" people are erased. The terrifying, horrific Janjaweed are doing jobs that give them sustenance and status, confirm their identities and solidarity as significant people. We have seen this before.

Justification for killing is also given in the too familiar form of racism, abstract categorizations of people by "kinds": the people in Darfur, who belong mostly to three different tribes, have in common that they are "Black" and so are, in the Arab view (not all; never all), "like slaves." There is a history here, as there so often is. Among Arabs (hardly alone), some have been slave traders, so a rationale for doing horrible things to other people is available and obviously still potent. Note, however, that this racism is not stand-alone potent. The Janjaweed are not just released to kill those they have learned to scorn as inferior racially to them. They are paid, given status, provided with a more nationalistic rationale and, even then, are "accompanied by soldiers." Unleashed passions, as we have now seen many times, simply are not sufficient to, and can even disrupt, getting the job done. Extensive evil requires that even if those vulnerable to extremes of such passions are among those enrolled, such actors must be directed by those not in thrall to emotion, by "cooler heads," as Americans, anyway, are prone to say. Where there is a big job to be done, there will be bosses of some sort trying to manage the work and the workers, encouraging "team work," rewarding job-specific achievement, doling out status and, as necessary, the memory-erasing "rest and recreation," details of which even legitimate armies of democracies do not like to dwell on and do indeed know to use.

THE TRIFECTA: GREED, CAREERISM, STATUS

We have mentioned greed and status before, and careerism: these are separable if related, and although they do not seem on the face of it adequate as prime enablers of extensive evil, each and especially all, as it turns out, can be just that.

But surely greed is not what drives much less needy people, sophisticated people far in every sense from the Janjaweed—boards, bosses, employees, stockholders, for instance, who could not so readily be bought? Surely they do not approve of doing *anything* to make money? Well, it does have to be something they *can* do, but then, when the money is big enough, so all too often is the temptation.

Consider our earlier example of the treatment of Mr. Masri on a Boeing plane. Jane Mayer[3] discussed the involvement of Boeing, "the world's largest aerospace company," through its "subsidiary called Jeppesen International Trip Planning," in "'extraordinary rendition' flights" used by the CIA for terrorism suspects. "It is not widely known," she writes, "that the agency has turned to a division of Boeing, the publicly traded blue-chip behemoth, to

handle many of the logistical and navigational details for these trips, including flight plans, clearance to fly over other countries, hotel reservations, and
ground-crew arrangements."

As always: not everyone went along. An employee who found out about
these flights "said that another executive told him, 'We do the spook flights.'
He was told that two of the company's trip planners were specially designated
to handle renditions. He was deeply troubled by the rendition program, he
said, and eventually quit his job."

But was the motivation of those who stayed and did the work *greed?*
This employee recalled the managing director of Jeppesen International
Trip Planning, Mr. Overby, saying, "It certainly pays well. They"—the
CIA—"spare no expense. They have absolutely no worry about costs. What
they have to get done, they get done." An ideal client for a profit-making
concern, in short: one that can be overcharged with no fuss or bother
because what they want is an eager contractor that will not want, no matter what, to lose this fount of money. How, then, can we not observe that
greed is a major motivator for participation in horrific work also among
those who are already well-off, and is a driver at the highest levels of
decision-making where most of the money, and credit for bringing it in,
goes, and stays.

Companies, and individuals, can be doing just fine economically and still
drive themselves to make more, ever more, pay and profit, status along with
career advancement. Others will go along with changes in their jobs—as
Police Battalion 101 did, as some employees at Abu Ghraib did, as arms
manufacturers have when the highly lucrative international arms market
beckoned. Call it whatever else you will, this is at ground level a willingness
to submit other values to the primacy of a desire for the trifecta of career,
status, money.

There are people for whom keeping a job means the difference between
eating and starving, but it is not people at that level of desperation who carry
the burden of work of extensive evil. There are more stabilized people who
will do what is asked of them in order not to lose their jobs because they fear
being unable to pay the mortgage on an expensive house and car, say, and that
is morally quite different. And there are those who are extremely wealthy and
still want more and ever more: morally startling, and all too evident.

We have also found the prevalence of ordinary greed in Germany, and in
Rwanda:

> We began the day by killing, we ended the day by looting. It was the rule to kill
> going out and to loot coming back. We killed in teams, but we looted every man
> for himself or in small groups of friends. Except for drinks and cows, which we
> enjoyed sharing. And the plots of land, of course, they were discussed with the

organizers. As district leader, I had gotten a huge fertile plot, which I counted on planting when it was all over.[4]

Another Rwandan told his interviewer after the slaughter that he and the others whose job—that is what he called it—consisted of the "simple" task of slaughtering any and all Tutsis, "had tasted comfort and overflowing plenty" and "cast off obedience and the inconveniences of poverty. Greed had corrupted us."[5]

STILLING CONSCIOUSNESS FROM WHICH CONSCIENCE CAN ARISE

It keeps turning out that what you actually need for the work of sustained, massive harm over time is functionally smart, hardworking, ambitious folks who do not think or speak much about, let alone reflect on and judge, what they are doing in their jobs and/or social roles. What you want is people who brood about how they are doing in their jobs not in terms of what they are actually doing, its meaning, its effects on people, but, rather, on their career advancement, their pay or profits, the status conferred by their position (uniforms, badges, titles, company cars, corner offices are important). You want people who like to "have a good time," who can use drink and drugs and sex and the thrills and glamour of partying happily, so that they can return to their work ready for more. You want people who will turn their whole attention to concerns about whether they are being recognized, paid well enough, moved up the ladder, getting that bonus or not.

Remember Eichmann: "Except for an extraordinary diligence in looking out for his personal advancement, he had no motives at all. . . . It was precisely this . . . which enabled him to sit for months on end facing a German Jew who was conducting the police interrogation, pouring out his heart to the man and explaining again and again how it was that he reached only the rank of lieutenant colonel in the SS and that it had not been his fault that he was not promoted."[6]

To do this kind of "unthinkable" acts, that is, you want people who are able and consistently willing to close what they do day after day out of the reflective consciousness almost all of us do have, the thoughtful consciousness from which consciences arise. And you want them surrounded at work by colleagues similarly caught up not so much in narratives of *what* they are doing (narratives make sense of things, and sense is precisely what engineers of extensive evil do not want the many who do the real work to be seeking), nor in the *how* of it (except as cast in terms of professional proficiency in techniques, with gadgets), but in mindless sayings, slogans, that by their very familiarity flow off the tongue without thought and are readily recognized by others, reassuringly so. You want, that is, to keep minds turned off on the meta-level: no questions about, no looking back at and wondering, no reaching for connections to beliefs, to other meanings. Techniques: sure. Gossip: sure. Insider knowledge and language: yes. Strategy and tactics: yes. How to get promoted: absolutely. Not, *What is the relation of what we are actually doing to people, to the earth?*

JOBHOLDERS: THINKING WHAT WE ARE DOING

"Providing jobs" is not an adequate answer to, *What are we really doing?* although it is used often as a claim of social merit by companies. The Janjaweed had jobs; executioners have jobs; laborers in salt mines have jobs. So did all those employed by Enron, and by Bernie Madoff, and Boeing doing its rendition flights. More broadly, what matters is that, increasingly, people now live as jobholders. Jobs are not peripheral to who and how we are: they are needed to feed ourselves even as they are also increasingly key to defining ourselves. There is no point whatsoever in pretending otherwise, and I do not think we have come anywhere near thinking through what this change in the human condition really means. But no matter what, it is essential to remember particularly among people definable as jobholders that *What kind of jobs?* is always a relevant question.

For extensive evil, you want many job-focused workers surrounded on site and at home by people who do not question, do not push toward reflection. That is, what you want is massive, active collusion in being out of touch with the realities of one's own and others' actions. You want people who see their lives in terms comparable to the guys who experienced the realities of combat as if they were a video game; enjoy their ambition as if it were the motivation of a hero overcoming dragons; take pride in achievement within the bounds set as if nothing existed except that playing field, that chess board, that organization's competitive hype, bonding, game plan, and "skill set" required to succeed. You want people who can be proud of their pay, their status, their success no matter how it is gained.

Social life is part of it: "The company recreation room was decorated with racist slogans, and a Star of David hung above the bar. A mark was made on the bar door for each Jew shot, and 'victory celebrations' were reportedly held on days when high scores were recorded."[7] This is monstrous, and, in the ways competitive careerism often hypes itself, not really unusual, is it? "Get some," say the "spearhead" troops in Iraq, and this sexualized, misogynist game-playing at killing even when it is entirely real is encouraged like locker room competitive-spirit raising, like corporate ladder-climbing. And so we practice being "team players" while dreaming of being "winners," and so we remain vulnerable to going with them when systems go bad. Even very bad.

Except when we do not, and it is also the case that not everyone does. Alone, in our groups, even in our numbers, sometimes we do stop and think, and simply say, at the right moment, the *No* that is actually a profound *Yes* to what we will not violate because *that* is something we just cannot do and still live with ourselves. It happens that many of us can also come together to say just that if we have practiced something as ordinary as paying attention, reflecting- thinking, as Arendt put it, what we are doing.[8]

Afterword

Teaching Thinking

WHAT MAY WE HOPE?

There is no neat ending to this inquiry. People have thought about questions of good and evil, about moral responsibility, across all times, in all cultures and all disciplines secular and of faith. And way down on the personal level, I am sure it is all too evident to you that I could go on thinking about the evils of banality, the simple directness of good. Every day, I encounter fresh instances, glimpse further illumination, experiencing each time, yet again, how stirring, agitating, inspiring and, above all, thought-provoking such awakenings are.

When I turn to reflections on *what ought we to do*, preceded by its companion, *Is there hope that is not in vain?* I realize that the distinction between *intensive* and *extensive evil* leads eventually also to this observation: *We may not be able to stop intensive evils from erupting among us any more than we can guarantee there will always be a few super-heroic, saintly individuals, but we, the people, could limit or even stop extensive evils.*

It is obvious, is it not? Unlike brief if monstrous harm-doing, extensive evils cannot take over or sustain themselves if many of us do not reliably do their work. Facing and integrating that realization can indeed be deeply troubling. It can suggest that *never again* for any horrific, lasting harm-doing is entirely hopeless because, to tell the truth, so very many people actually have become so very complicit. But in that is also the realization that we have a great deal of power as well as responsibility. I say it again: *They*, whoever they are, *could not do it without us.*

That applies also to extensive good. Remembering that, I think: *We will never know how many extensive evils have in fact been stopped* just because enough decent people said, individually, and sooner rather than later also

215

in concert, *I can't do* that. *That's not who I am. That's not who we are, my community, my country, my faith. I will not do it:* That *is not my job.* I cannot prove this, either; you cannot prove a negative, but I am for now convinced that it is the case. We have found it where there is extensive good, and when we look, we see it quietly around us all the time. To this, perhaps most of all, we need to pay attention: goodness is also seeded in the ordinary. There is mercy as there may be hope on the other side of realizing that neither monsters nor saints are needed to shape our worlds. We in our numbers do that.

WHAT OUGHT WE TO DO?

I am keenly aware of a realistic sense of urgency, that the time to be startled back into thought and action, alone and crucially also with others, is always now. The consequences of our not-thinking are great. What then are we to do? That is also an unending question. For one thing, it cannot remain abstract if we are serious about it and it comes and settles on our particular shoulders, in our time, place, situation. *What then am I to do?* with its corollary *What am I best able to do?* in my case are questions asked of an educator, and most of all, a teacher for whom philosophy has always been concerned with comprehending what is going on, a practice of thinking in and with the world and others. I realize now just how this, my chosen work in the world, is related to my quest to comprehend the greatest evils and goods. If *People who are not thinking are capable of anything*, then surely education must be among the significant human endeavors to which we turn.

Nonetheless, through many years as an educator in differing roles, I have had to realize that highly educated people have not notably stopped extensive evils in time, nor refrained from benefiting from them, nor from doing their work. Nor, I fear, have the highly educated been often enough involved with extensive goodness to allow us to rest our faith in them. It is not that educators are worse than others, or especially prone to do the work of extensive evil, I hasten to add. It just breaks my heart that I cannot here, of all places, say, *Quite the contrary.*

It is past time to ask, *Are we—in schools, but also anywhere at all— teaching thinking that is an antidote for the evil of banality?* Are we learning, and teaching, responsive attentiveness, agile and patient reflection, reaching for comprehension and better questions? Or are we aiming only for mastery, offering preset ways of processing experiences of the world, of the self, of others? Are we making it more or less likely that those who learn with us can be startled back into thought, stop and think what they are doing?

So many questions, both so familiar and elusive to me. Through all these years, I have been teaching. Without my often realizing it, that calling—which is what teaching is to me, and an art never mastered—has been on my mind, in touch with my research. No surprise there, but I do not mean with regard to content. I have not taught, although I have often talked, about extensive evil and good. Perhaps by now it will sound less utterly peculiar to say that my teaching has related to those subjects by way of reflection on *how* not *what* I, and others, teach. Increasingly, it has seemed necessary to me to pay attention to that *how*. I have little doubt that it has very significant effects, and that those effects last longer and may well do more good or harm than any content learned. People remember their teachers, whatever they taught and even when the subject has long since faded.

When I was in Eastern Europe a while ago doing some work with educators there, someone said to me, *If we cannot change the way we teach, we will never become democratic.* I take that very seriously indeed. It, too, raises many questions, threading through which is this very large and basic one: *How can we teach an ability, a practice, an art that is the very wellspring of human freedom? How do we make the restless, troublemaking activity of thinking the heart of all education? How might we enliven, engage consciously with all learners such that conscience can arise, and thinking what we are doing become a second nature? How do we teach thinking so that those who are educated—as many of us as humanly possible—are simply disinclined to take seriously, let alone to give their minds, their consciences, their work, their power, to anyone or anything that requires them* not *to think?*

In my next book, the one that has kept trying to write itself as I worked on this one, I will try to think through an education that can free us not only from the weight of ignorance, but from the deadening, deadly hold of banality.

Notes

INTRODUCTION: WHAT WERE THEY THINKING?

1. Jewan Hatzfeld, *Machete Season: The Killers in Rwanda Speak*. Farrar, Straus and Giroux, New York: 2003, p. 22.

2. Pumla Gobodo-Madikezela, *A Human Being Died That Night: A South African Story of Forgiveness*. Houghton Mifflin Co., New York: 2003, p. 20.

3. Jeff Guin, *Manson: The Life and Times of Charles Manson*. Simon & Schuster, New York: 2013.

4. iim.edu.org website, International Institute of Management.

5. David Cesarani, *Becoming Eichmann: Rethinking the Life, Crimes, and Trial of a "Desk Murderer."* Da Capo Press/Perseus Book Group, New York: 2004, pp. 16–17.

6. Ibid.

7. Ibid.

8. Pumla Gobodo-Madikezela, *A Human Being Died That Night: A South African Story of Forgiveness*. Houghton Mifflin Co., New York: 2003, p. 38.

9. Ibid., p. 34.

10. Elizabeth Kamarck Minnich, "Why Not Lie?" *Soundings: An Interdisciplinary Journal*, Vol. LXVIII. No. 4: Winter 1985, pp. 403–507.

11. Hannah Arendt, *Men in Dark Times*. Harvest/HBJ Book, Harcourt Brace Jovanovich, New York: 1968, p. 8.

12. George Packer, "Betrayed: The Iraqis Who Trusted Americans the Most." *The New Yorker*, March 26, 2007, p. 64.

1. TRUTH AND FICTION: CAMUS' *THE PLAGUE*

1. Albert Camus, *The Plague*. Translated by Stuart Gilbert, Random House/ Vintage Books, New York: 1991, p. 128.

2. Ibid., p. 308.

3. Ibid., p. 4.
4. Ibid., p. 3.
5. Ibid., p. 4.
6. Ibid., p. 6.
7. Ibid., p. 134.
8. Hannah Arendt, "'A Daughter of Our People': A Response to Gershom Scholem," in *The Portable Hannah Arendt*. Edited by Peter Baehr. Penguin Books, New York: 2000, p. 392.

2. THINKING ABOUT NOT-THINKING

1. Karl Jaspers, *The Question of German Guilt*. Translated by E. B. Ashton. Capricorn Books, New York: 1961 (Fourth Impression), p. 29.
2. James Waller, *Becoming Evil: How Ordinary People Commit Genocide and Mass Killing*. Oxford University Press, New York: 2002, p. 238.
3. Russ Shafer-Landau, *The Ethical Life: Fundamental Readings in Ethics and Moral Problems*. Oxford University Press, New York: 2012, p. 258.
4. There were five extermination camps, so called because that was their sole purpose: no pretenses, virtually no survivors.
5. Gitta Sereny, *Into That Darkness: An Examination of Conscience*. Vintage Books/Random House, New York: 1983, p. 111.
6. Ibid., p. 114.
7. *Hannah Arendt, Karl Jaspers Correspondence 1926–1969*. Edited by Lotte Kohler and Hans Saner, translated by Robert Kimber and Rita Kimber. Harcourt Brace Jovanovich, New York: 1992. Letters 46, p. 62, and 50, p. 69: 1946.
8. Hannah Arendt "Thinking and Moral Considerations: A Lecture," *Social Research*, Vol. 38. No. 3: Fall, 1971.
9. See Hannah Arendt, *The Human Condition*, 2nd edition. The University of Chicago Press, Chicago and London: 1958.
10. Among Arendt's books, *The Human Condition* concerns the *vita activa*, the life of action; her last book is a two-volume reflection on *The Life of the Mind*. By then, the phrase "the life of the mind" had taken on profoundly worldly meanings, implications, responsibilities.
11. Cf. Thomas Pegelow Kaplan, *The Language of Nazi Genocide: Linguistic Violence and The Struggle of Germans of Jewish Ancestry*. Cambridge University Press, New York: 2009; and Victor Klemperer's invaluable works. Klemperer, a German Jewish linguist, noticed and recorded changing language, concepts, categories. See Victor Klemperer, *The Language of The Third Reich: A Philologist's Notebook*. Translated by Martin Brady. Continuum, New York: 2000.
12. Arendt "Thinking and Moral Considerations," p. 417.
13. Perhaps the most lasting anger was raised by her discussion of the role of the leaders of the Jewish Councils.
14. "New York Daily News," August 26, 2014; on website, under "News" tab.

15. In the first seminar I took with her, "Political Experiences of the 20th Century," at the Graduate Faculty of Political and Social Science, The New School, New York: Spring, 1968.

16. Hannah Arendt, *Eichmann in Jerusalem: A Report on the Banality of Evil.* The Penguin Group, New York: 1994, p. 5.

17. Arendt, "Thinking and Moral Considerations," p. 417.

18. Ibid., p. 418.

19. John Burns, "Judgment Days: From Banality to Audacity." *New York Times.* December 11, 2005, p. 1, section 4.

20. Peter Z. Malkin and Harry Stein, *Eichmann in My Hands.* Warner Books, New York: 1990, p. 216.

21. The sublime, observed Kant in his *Critique of Judgment*, is a feeling awakened in us by "the starry heavens above, and the moral law within"—a feeling that can be very uncomfortable, making us feel small, inadequate, unimportant. A merely pretty picture rarely has that effect; on the contrary.

22. Arendt, *Eichmann in Jerusalem*, p. 288.

3. CHANGING MINDS

1. Gitta Sereny, *Into that Darkness: An Examination of Conscience.* Vintage Books/Random House, New York: 1983, p. 134.

2. Jean Hatzfeld, *Machete Season: The Killers in Rwanda Speak.* Farrar, Straus and Giroux, New York: 2003, p. 178.

3. Claudia Koonz, *The Nazi Conscience.* The Belknap Press of Harvard University Press, Cambridge, MA: 2003, p. 75 (quoting from Klemperer).

4. Ibid., p. 5.

4. ESCAPING EXPLANATIONS, EXCUSES

1. Hannah Arendt, *The Life of the Mind: Thinking.* Harcourt Brace Jovanovich, New York and London: 1971, p. 88.

2. I believe that Mary McCarthy and, later, Claudia Card also came upon this flaw in the familiar explanation used as excuse, *They made me do it.*

3. Christopher Browning, *Police Battalion 101 and The Final Solution in Poland.* Harper Perennial/Harper Collins, New York: 1993, pp. 65–66.

4. Lorraine Hansberry, "Preface" to *Raisin in the Sun. I have not been able to find my source. Available editions of Hansberry's classic play appear to have erased her preface in favor of introductions by other people.*

5. Claudia Koonz, *The Nazi Conscience.* The Belknap Press of Harvard University Press, Cambridge, MA: 2003, p. 246.

6. Hannah Arendt, quoted in *Responsibility and Judgment.* Edited and with an introduction by Jerome Kohn. Schocken Books, New York: 2003, p. vii.

7. Jean Hatzfeld, *Machete Season: The Killers in Rwanda Speak*. Farrar, Straus and Giroux, New York: 2003, p. 178.

5. MEANING, TRUTH, RATIONALITY, KNOWLEDGE, THINKING

1. Hannah Arendt, *The Life of the Mind: Thinking*. Harcourt Brace Jovanovich, New York and London: 1978, p. 5.

2. Claudia Koonz, *The Nazi Conscience*. The Belknap Press of Harvard University Press, Cambridge, MA: 2003, p. 91.

3. Michael Foucault, *The Foucault Reader*. Edited by P. Rabinow. Pantheon Books, New York: 1984, p. 388.

4. Although I am not here drawing directly on her (although I am throughout thinking with her in mind), it is interesting to note that Arendt reflected on Augustine, and in particular the *questio*, in many of her writings. She was still doing so in her late work, *The Life of the Mind.* In Volume II, *Willing*, she used this quotation as the title of the second section.

5. An undisputed source for this quotation remains elusive.

6. David Cesarani, *Becoming Eichmann: Rethinking The Life, Crimes, and Trial of a "Desk Murderer."* Da Capo Press/Perseus Book Group. New York: 2004, p. 46.

7. Koonz, *The Nazi Conscience*, p. 1.

8. Ibid., p. 3.

9. Delef Muhlberger, *The Social Bases of Nazism, 1919–1933*. Cambridge University Press, Cambridge: 2003, pp. 51–52.

10. Ibid.

11. For a thorough analysis of the consequences of defining "kinds" of people out of the supposedly inclusive category of *people* (or, *man*), see Elizabeth Kamarck Minnich, *Transforming Knowledge* 2nd Edition. Temple University Press, Philadelphia, PA: 2005.

12. Cesarani, *Becoming Eichmann*, p. 47.

13. Koonz, *The Nazi Conscience*, p. 11.

14. Azadeh Moaven, "For ISIS Women, Fraught Choices." *New York Times*, Sunday, November 22, 2015: p. 1.

15. Dagmar Herzog, "Handouts from Hitler," review of *Hitler's Beneficiaries: Plunder, Racial War, and the Nazi Welfare State, by Gotz Aly. NYT Sunday Book Review*, February 18, 2007, p. 20.

16. Wislawa Szymborska, "The Nobel Lecture," in *Poems New and Collected 1957–1997*. Translated from the Polish by Stanislaw Baranczak and Clare Cavanagh. A Harvest Book/Harcourt, Inc., San Diego, New York, London: 2000, p. xviii. The Nobel Lecture is © 1996.

17. Ibid.

18. Ibid. p. xvi.

19. *The Origins of Totalitarianism*. Harcourt, Inc: Harvest Book, New York; new edition with added prefaces; 1968, p. 464.

20. For a thorough, nuanced discussion along related lines, see Corey Robin, *Fear: The History of A Political Idea*. Oxford University Press, New York: 2004.

21. Evan Wright, *Generation Kill*. Berkley Caliber, New York: 2004, p. 7.

22. Ibid., p. 5.

23. Nicholas Schmidle, "Bringing up the Bones: Kosovo's Leaders Have Been Accused of Grotesque War Crimes. But Can Anyone Prove It?" *The New Yorker*, May 6, 2013, p. 49.

6. ROMANTICIZING EVIL

1. Albert Camus, *The Plague*. Translated by Stuart Gilbert. Random House/Vintage Books, New York: 1991, p. 308.

2. Jane Mayer, "Whatever It Takes: *Torture on '24'.*" *The New Yorker*, February 19 and 26, 2007: pp. 66–82, 72.

3. Hannah Arendt, "Thinking and Moral Considerations," in *Responsibility and Judgment*. Edited and with an introduction by Jerome Kohn. Schocken Books, New York: 2003, p. 188.

7. INTENSIVE EVIL, EXTENSIVE EVIL

1. Albert Camus, *The Plague*. Translated by Stuart Gilbert. Random House/Vintage Books, New York: 1991, p. 179.

2. Charles Simic, *That Little Something: Poems*. Quoted by Katha Politt in *New York Times* Sunday Book Review, May 18, 2008, p. 22.

3. Hannah Arendt, *Eichmann in Jerusalem: A Report on The Banality of Evil*. The Penguin Group, New York: 1994, pp. 26–27.

4. Joan V. Bondurant, *Conquest of Violence: The Gandhian Philosophy of Conflict*, revised edition. University of California Press, Berkeley: 1965, p. 7.

5. borgenproject.org.

6. Cf. William Finnegan, "The Countertraffickers: Rescuing the Victims of the Global Sex Trade." *The New Yorker*, May 5, 2008, pp. 44–59.

7. Raymond Bonner, "The Dogs of War: Philip Gourevitch and Errol Morris Collaborate to Tell the Story of the Abu Ghraib Prisoner Abuse." A review of *Standard Operating Procedure*, The Penguin Press, in *New York Times* Sunday Book Review, May 25, 2008: p. 10.

8. Dagmar Herzog, "Handouts from Hitler." Review of *Hitler's Beneficiaries: Plunder, Racial War, and the Nazi Welfare State, by Gotz Aly*. *New York Times* Sunday Book Review, February 18, 2007, p. 20.

9. Ibid.

10. Dan McMillan, *How Could This Happen: Explaining the Holocaust*. Basic Books, New York: 2014, pp. 6–7.

11. Irmgard A. Hunt, *On Hitler's Mountain: Overcoming the Legacy of a Nazi Childhood*. Harper Perennial, New York: 2006, p. 83.

8. THE ORDINARY FOR GOOD AND ILL

1. Withoutsanctuary.org.

9. PHILIP HALLIE: IT TAKES A VILLAGE

1. Philip Hallie, *Lest Innocent Blood Be Shed: The Story of the Village of Le Chambon and How Goodness Happened There*. Harper & Row, New York: 1979, p. 129.
2. Hallie uses this rather odd phrase throughout his book, starting with his title.
3. Hannah Arendt, "Thinking and Moral Considerations," in *Responsibility and Judgment*. Edited and with an introduction by Jerome Kohn. Schocken Books, New York: 2003, p. 167.
4. Hallie, *Lest Innocent Blood Be Shed*, p. 7.
5. Ibid.
6. I think over the years I have received some of the most angry notes from professors about this point, even though it really is Socrates/Plato, not me, who credits Diotima, and no one has disagreed with that.
7. Hallie, *Lest Innocent Blood Be Shed*, p. 176–177.
8. Ibid., p. 175.
9. Philip Hallie, *Tales of Good and Evil, Help and Harm*. Harper Perennial/Harper Collins, New York: 1998, p. 43.
10. Hallie, *Lest Innocent Blood Be Shed*, p. 30.
11. Hallie, *ibid.*, p. 89.
12. Caroline Moorehead, *A Train in Winter: An Extraordinary Story of Women, Friendship, and Resistance in Occupied France*. Harper Perennial/Harper Collins Publisher, New York: 2012, p. 13.
13. John Dewey, *Democracy and Education: An Introduction to the Philosophy of Education*. The Free Press, New York: 1944, p. 88.
14. Moorehead, *A Train in Winter*, pp. 33–34.
15. Ibid., p. 24.

10. PREPARING FOR EXTENSIVE GOODNESS

1. Philip Hallie, *Lest Innocent Blood Be Shed: The Story of the Village of Le Chambon and How Goodness Happened There*. Harper & Row, New York: 1979, p. 148.
2. Ibid., p. 86 (quoting Alexander Werth on the early days of the French Resistance).
3. Ibid., pp. 92 and 93.

4. Ibid., p. 35.

5. Ibid., p. 93.

6. Ibid., p. 85.

7. Ibid., p. 26.

8. Hannah Arendt, *The Origins of Totalitarianism*. Harcourt, Inc.: Harvest Book, New York; new edition with added prefaces; 1968, p. 67. Arendt works with these terms, drawn from her reading of Bernard Lazarre, in a number of her writings.

9. Caroline Moorehead, *A Train in Winter: An Extraordinary Story of Women, Friendship, and Resistance in Occupied France*. Harper Perennial/Harper Collins Publisher, New York: 2012, p. 25 ff.

10. Hallie, *Lest Innocent Blood Be Shed*, p. 55.

11. Ibid., p. 56.

12. Ibid., pp. 172–173.

13. Ibid.

14. Ibid., p. 127.

15. Ibid., p. 10.

16. Ibid., p. 37.

17. Ibid., p. 38.

18. J. Glenn Gray, *The Warriors: Reflections on Men in Battle*. University of Nebraska Press, Lincoln & London: 1998.

19. Hallie, *Lest Innocent Blood Be Shed*, p. 58.

11. LOOKING FOR GOOD BEYOND THE VILLAGE

1. George Packer, "Betrayed: The Iraqis Who Trusted Americans The Most." *The New Yorker*, March 26, 2007, pp. 62–63.

2. Eyal Press, *Beautiful Souls*. Farrar, Straus and Giroux, New York: 2012, p. 59.

3. J. Glenn Gray, *The Warriors: Reflections on Men in Battle*. University of Nebraska Press, Lincoln & London: 1998, p. xvii.

4. "Librarians Vs. The Patriot Act." *WNYC*, June 5, 2015 (WNYC website).

5. Markus Zusak, *The Book Thief*. Alfred A. Knopf, New York: 2005, p. 394.

6. Jeff McMillan, "The Rosenstrasse Protest: A Moment of Courage in Hitler's Berlin." *The Chronicle of Higher Education*, October 18, 1996, p. A9.

7. Eyal Press, *Beautiful Souls*. Farrar, Straus and Giroux, New York: 2012, p. 28.

8. Philip Hallie, *Lest Innocent Blood Be Shed: The Story of the Village of Le Chambon and How Goodness Happened There*. Harper & Row, New York: 1979, pp. 20–21.

12. THE BANALITY OF GOODNESS?

1. Hannah Arendt, *The Life of the Mind: Thinking*. Harcourt Brace Jovanovich, New York and London: 1978, p. 4.

2. John Dewey, *Democracy and Education: An Introduction to the Philosophy of Education*. The Free Press, New York: 1944, p. 360.

3. Albert Camus, *The Plague*. Translated by Stuart Gilbert. Random House/ Vintage Books, New York: 1991, p. 253.

4. Tracy Kidder, *Mountains Beyond Mountains: The Quest of Dr. Paul Farmer, a Man Who Would Cure the World*. Random House Trade Paperback, New York: 2004, p. 17.

5. Ibid., pp. 16–17.

6. No, Aristotle did not include the majority of humankind in his politics; we can correct that conceptual, moral, political error.

7. Paul Eluard, quoted in "'I Hate to Leave This Beautiful Place'," by Howard Norman. *The New York Times*. Sunday July 28, 2013, p. 12.

PART III

1. Bernhard Schlink, *The Reader*. Translated from the German by Carol Brown Janeway. Vintage Books/Random House, New York: 1997, pp. 149–151; esp. p. 151.

13. SEEDING PREPARED GROUND

1. Hannah Arendt, *Eichmann in Jerusalem: A Report on the Banality of Evil*. The Penguin Group, New York: 1994, p. 287.

2. Christopher R. Browning, *Ordinary Men: Reserve Police Battalion 101 and the Final Solution in Poland*. Harper Perennial/Harper Collins, New York: 1992, p. 75.

3. Ibid.

4. Ibid.

5. Claudia Koonz, *The Nazi Conscience*. The Belknap Press of Harvard University Press, Cambridge, MA: 2003, p. 75.

6. Ibid., p. 74.

7. Ibid., p. 11.

8. *Machete Season: The Killers in Rwanda Speak*: A Report by Jean Hatzfeld, translated from the French by Linda Coverdal. Farrar, Straus and Giroux, New York: 2003, pp. 177–178.

9. Koonz, *The Nazi Conscience*, p. 5.

10. See Elisabeth Young-Bruehl's *Anatomy of Prejudices* for a useful study of how differing prejudices work with differing psychiatric conditions in differing historical/ political situations, for example.

11. Koonz, *The Nazi Conscience*, p. 13.

12. Quoted in Jonathan Bennett, "The Conscience of Huckleberry Finn," p. 258 in Russ Shafer-Landau, *The Ethical Life: Fundamental Readings in Ethics and Moral Problems*. Oxford University Press, New York: 2012.

13. Ibid.

14. LARGE-SCALE ENCLOSURES: MEANING SYSTEMS

1. Russ Shafer-Landau, *The Ethical Life: Fundamental Readings in Ethics and Moral Problems*. Oxford University Press, New York: 2012, p. 257.

2. Claudia Koonz, *The Nazi Conscience*. The Belknap Press of Harvard University Press, Cambridge, MA: 2003, p. 105.

3. Andrew M. Kamarck, *Economics as a Social Science: An Approach to Nonautistic Theory*. The University of Michigan Press, Ann Arbor, MI: 2002, p. 14. (Full disclosure: Dr. Kamarck is my father.)

4. Raul Hilberg, *Perpetrators, Victims, Bystanders: The Jewish Catastrophe 1933–1945*. Aaron Asher Books/Harper Collins, New York: 1992, pp. 82–83.

5. Omer Bartov and Phyllis Mack, *In God's Name: Genocide and Religion in the Twentieth Century*. Berghahn Books, New York: 1991, p. 28.

6. Gary J. Bass, "The Prague (Berlin, Paris, Milan) Spring: An Overview of the Pan-European revolutions of 1848." Review of *1848: Year of Revolution*, by Mike Rapport. Basic Books. *New York Times* Book Review, March 15, 2009, p. 15.

7. Benedict Anderson, *Imagined Communities: Reflections on the Origin and Spread of Nationalism*. Verson, Longdon: 2006.

8. For more analysis along these lines, cf. Elizabeth Minnich, *Transforming Knowledge*, 2nd edition. Temple University Press, Philadelphia, PA: 2005.

9. Evan Wright, *Generation Kill*. Berkley Caliber, New York: 2004, p. 2 (and throughout).

10. Cf. Cynthia Enloe, *Globalization and Militarism: Feminists Make the Link*. Rowman & Littlefield, Lanham, MD: 2007. There is a larger body of significant feminist literature to be consulted here.

11. Alexis Okeowo, quoting Bruce Hall; "Freedom Fighter: A Slaving Society and an Abolitionist's Crusade." *The New Yorker*, September 8, 2014, pp. 38–40.

15. PHYSICAL ENCLOSURES OF BODIES, MINDS

1. Mark Dow, *American Gulag: Inside U.S. Immigration Prisons*. University of California Press, Berkeley: 2004, pp. 1–2.

2. Ibid., p. 3.

3. Ibid., p. 52.

4. Ibid., p. 3.

5. Ibid., pp.57–58.

6. Ibid., pp. 58–59.

7. Ibid., p. 261.

8. Ibid.

9. David Cesarani, *Becoming Eichmann: Rethinking the Life, Crimes, and Trial of a "Desk Murderer."* Da Capo Press/Perseus Book Group, New York: 2004, p. 46.

10. Dow, *American Gulag*, p. 261.

11. Ibid., p. 78.

12. Ibid.

13. Ibid., p. 79.

14. Eyal Press, *Beautiful Souls*. Farrar, Straus and Giroux, New York: 2012, p. 69.

15. Jane Mayer, "The CIA's Travel Agent," *The New Yorker*, October 30, 2006, pp. 34–37.

16. Ibid.

16. LAYING OUT THE STRANDS

1. Nicholas D. Kristof, "Genocide in Slow Motion," *The New York Review of Books*, February 9, 2006, pp. 14–17. The two books under review are *Darfur: A Short History of a Long War*, by Julie Flint and Alex de Waal, and *Darfur: The Ambiguous Genocide*, by Gérard Prunier.

2. Ibid. Unless otherwise indicated, this and subsequent quotes in this chapter come from Kristof's review article. Search by author and title; page numbers not given.

3. Jane Mayer, "The CIA's Travel Agent," *The New Yorker*, October 30, 2006, pp. 34–37. Unless otherwise indicated, this and subsequent quotes in this chapter are from Mayer's article. Searched by author and title; page numbers not given.

4. Jean Hatzfeld, *Machete Season: The Killers in Rwanda Speak*. Farrar, Straus and Giroux, New York: 2003, p. 86.

5. Ibid., p. 87.

6. Hannah Arendt, *Eichmann in Jerusalem: A Report on The Banality of Evil*. The Penguin Group, New York: 1994, p. 287.

7. Christopher R. Browning, *Ordinary Men: Reserve Police Battalion 101 and the Final Solution in Poland*. Harper Perennial/Harper Collins, New York: 1992, p. 41.

8. Hannah Arendt, *The Human Condition*, 2nd edition. The University of Chicago Press, Chicago and London: 1958, p. 5.

Bibliography

Sources and Resources

Anderson, Benedict, *Imagined Communities: Reflections on the Origin and Spread of Nationalism.* Verso, London: 2006.

Arditti, Rita, *Searching for Life: The Grandmothers of the Plaza de Mayo and the Disappeared Children of Argentina.* University of California Press, Berkeley: 1999.

Arendt, Hannah, *Eichmann in Jerusalem: A Report on the Banality of Evil.* The Penguin Group, New York:1994.

———, *Essays in Understanding 1930–1954: Formation, Exile, and Totalitarianism.* Edited and with an introduction by Jerome Kohn. Schocken Books, New York: 2005.

———, *Hannah Arendt, Karl Jaspers Correspondence 1926–1969.* Edited by Lotte Kohler and Hans Saner; translated by Robert Kimber and Rita Kimber. Harcourt Brace Jovanovich, New York: 1992.

———, *The Human Condition*, 2nd edition. The University of Chicago Press, Chicago and London: 1958.

———, *The Life of the Mind: Thinking.* Harcourt Brace Jovanovich, New York and London: 1978. *The Life of the Mind: Willing.* 1978.

———, *Men in Dark Times. Harvest/HBJ Book.* Harcourt Brace Jovanovich; New York: 1968.

———, *The Origins of Totalitarianism.* Harcourt: Harvest Book, New York; new edition with added prefaces; 1968.

———, *The Portable Hannah Arendt.* Edited by Peter Baehr. Penguin Books, New York: 2000.

———, *Responsibility and Judgment.* Edited and with an introduction by Jerome Kohn. Schocken Books, New York: 2003.

———, "Thinking and Moral Considerations: A Lecture," *Social Research*, Vol. 38. No. 3 (Fall), 1971.

Aristotle, *Nicomachean Ethics*, 2nd edition. Translated, with Introduction, Notes, and Glossary by Terence Irwin. Hackett Publishing, Indianapolis: 1999.

Bartov, Omer, and Phyllis Mack, *In God's Name: Genocide and Religion in the Twentieth Century.* Berghahn Books, New York: 1991.

Bass, Gary J., "The Prague (Berlin, Paris, Milan) Spring: An Overview of the Pan-European Revolutions of 1848." *Review of 1848: Year of Revolution, by Mike Rapport. Basic Books. The New York Times, Book Review*, March 15, 2009: p. 15.

Black, Edwin, *War against the Weak: Eugenics and America's Campaign to Create a Master Race.* Four Walls Eight Windows, New York: 2003.

Bondurant, Joan V., *Conquest of Violence: The Gandhian Philosophy of Conflict,* revised edition. University of California Press, Berkeley: 1965.

Bonner, Raymond, "The Dogs of War: Philip Gourevitch and Errol Morris Collaborate to Tell the Story of the Abu Ghraib Prisoner Abuse." *A review of Standard Operating Procedure. The Penguin Press, in The New York Times Book Review*, Sunday, May 25, 2008, p. 10.

Borgenproject.org (International/slavery).

Browning, Christopher R., *Ordinary Men: Reserve Police Battalion 101 and the Final Solution in Poland.* Harper Perennial/Harper Collins, New York: 1992.

Burns, John, "Judgment Days: From Banality to Audacity," in *The New York Times.* December 11, 2005, p. 1, section 4.

Camus, Albert, *The Plague.* Translated by Stuart Gilbert. Random House/Vintage Books, New York: 1991.

Cesarani, David, *Becoming Eichmann: Rethinking The Life, Crimes, and Trial of A "Desk Murderer."* Da Capo Press/Perseus Book Group, New York: 2004.

Cohn, Carol, "Sex and Death in the Rational World of Defense Intellectuals," *Signs,* Vol. 12, No. 4, University of Chicago Press: 1987.

Conroy, John, *Unspeakable Acts, Ordinary People: The Dynamics of Torture, an Examination of the Practice of Torture in Three Democracies.* University of California Press, Berkeley: 2000.

Dewey, John, *Democracy And Education: An Introduction to the Philosophy of Education.* The Free Press, New York: 1944.

Dow, Mark, *American Gulag: Inside U.S. Immigration Prisons.* University of California Press, Berkeley: 2004.

Films Drafthouse, *The Act of Killing.* Documentary (mass murder by policy, Indonesia) directed by Joshua Oppenheimer: 2012.

Enloe, Cynthia, *Globalization and Militarism: Feminists Make The Link.* Rowman & Littlefield, Lanham, MD: 2007.

Finnegan, William, "The Countertraffickers: Rescuing the Victims of the Global Sex Trade," *The New Yorker*, May 5, 2008, pp 45–59.

Foucault, Michel, *The Foucault Reader.* Edited by P. Rabinow. Pantheon Books, New York: 1984

Friedlander, Henry, *The Origins of Nazi Genocide: From Euthanasia to the Final Solution.* University of North Carolina Press, Chapel Hill: 1995.

Gerwarth, Robert, *Hitler's Hangman: The Life of Heydrich.* Yale University Press, New Haven, CT: 2011.

Giddings, Paula J., *Ida: A Sword Among Lions – Ida B. Wells and the Campaign against Lynchings.* Harper Collins, New York: 2008.

Gobodo-Madikezela, Pumla, *A Human Being Died That Night: A South African Story of Forgiveness.* Houghton Mifflin, New York: 2003.

Goldhagen, Daniel Jonah, *Hitler's Willing Executioners: Ordinary Germans and the Holocaust*. Vintage Books/Random House, New York: 1997.

Glenn, Gray J., *The Warriors: Reflections on Men in Battle*. University of Nebraska Press, Lincoln and London: 1998.

Guin, Jeff, *Manson: The Life and Times of Charles Manson*. Simon & Schuster, New York: 2013.

Hallie, Philip, *Lest Innocent Blood Be Shed: The Story of the Village of Le Chambon and How Goodness Happened There*. Harper & Row, New York: 1979.

———, *Tales of Good and Evil, Help and Harm*, Harper Perennial/Harper Collins, New York: 1998.

Hamill, Dennis, "School Resumes in Sandy Hook, but People of Newtown, Connecticut, Struggle with Memories of Horrific Shooting," *The New York Daily News*, Tuesday, August 26, 2014. The Daily News Website, "News" tab.

Hansberry, Lorraine, *A Raisin in The Sun*. Vintage Books/Random House, New York: 1994.

———, *To Be Young, Gifted and Black*. Signet Classics, New York: 2011.

Hatzfeld, Jean, *Machete Season: The Killers in Rwanda Speak*. Farrar, Straus and Giroux, New York: 2003.

Hedges, Chris, *War Is a Force That Gives Us Meaning*. Anchor Books/Random House, Public Affairs, New York: 2002.

Herzog, Dagmar, "Handouts from Hitler," *review of Hitler's Beneficiaries: Plunder, Racial War, and the Nazi Welfare State*, by Gotz Aly. *The New York Times* Sunday Book Review, February 18, 2007: p. 20.

Hilberg, Raul, *Perpetrators, Victims, Bystanders: The Jewish Catastrophe 1933–45*. Aaron Asher Books/Harper Collins, New York: 1992.

Huggins, Martha K., Mika Haritos-Fatouros, and Philip G. Zimbardo, *Violence Workers: Police Torturers and Murderers Reconstruct Brazilian Atrocities*. University of California Press, Berkeley: 2002.

Hunt, Irmgard A., *On Hitler's Mountain: Overcoming the Legacy of a Nazi Childhood*. Harper Perennial, New York: 2006.

International Institute of Management website: iim.edu.org.

Jaspers, Karl, *The Question of German Guilt*. Translated by E. B. Ashton. Capricorn Books, New York: 1961 (Fourth Impression).

Jonas, Hans, *The Imperative of Responsibility: In Search of an Ethics for the Technological Age*. University of Chicago Press, Chicago: 1984.

———, *The Phenomenon of Life: Toward a Philosophical Biology*. Northwestern University Press, Evanston: 2001.

Kamarck, Andrew M., *Economics as a Social Science: An Approach to Nonautistic Theory*. The University of Michigan Press, Ann Arbor, MI: 2002.

Kaplan, Thomas Pegelow, *The Language of Nazi Genocide: Linguistic Violence and the Struggle of Germans of Jewish Ancestry*. Cambridge University Press, New York: 2009.

Keith, LeeAnna, *The Colfax Massacre: The Untold Story of Black Power, White Terror, and the Death of Reconstruction*. Oxford University Press, New York: 2008.

Kidder, Tracy, *Mountains Beyond Mountains: The Quest of Dr. Paul Farmer, a Man Who Would Cure the World*. Random House Trade Paperback, New York: 2004.

Klemperer, Victor, *The Language of The Third Reich: A Philologist's Notebook.* Translated by Martin Brady. Continuum, New York: 2000.

I Will Bear Witness 1933–41: A Diary of the Nazi Years. Translated by Martin Chalmers. The Modern Library, New York: 1999.

Knausgaard, Karl Ove, "The Inexplicable," *The New Yorker*, May 25, 2015, pp. 28–32.

Koonz, Claudia, *The Nazi Conscience.* The Belknap Press of Harvard University Press, Cambridge, MA: 2003.

Kracauer, Siegfried, *The Salaried Masses: Duty and Distraction in Weimar Germany.* Translated by Quintin Hoare. Verso, London: 1998.

Kristof, Nicholas D., "Genocide in Slow Motion," *The New York Review of Books*, February 9, 2006. pp. 14–17. The two books under review are *Darfur: A Short History of a Long War*, by Julie Flint and Alex de Waal; and *Darfur: The Ambiguous Genocide*, by Gérard Prunier.

Lanzmann, Claude, *The Last of the Unjust.* Documentary, interview: 2013.

"Librarians Vs. The Patriot Act," *WNYC*, June 5, 2015 (WNYC website).

Lifton, Robert Jay, *The Nazi Doctors: Medical Killing and the Psychology of Genocide.* Basic Books, New York: 1986.

———, *Witness to an Extreme Century: A Memoir.* Free Press, New York: 2011.

Lopez, Ian F. Haney, *White by Law: The Legal Construction of Race.* New York University Press, NY: 1996.

Malkin, Peter Z., and Harry Stein, *Eichmann in My Hands.* Warner Books, New York: 1990.

Mathewes, Charles T., *Evil and the Augustinian Tradition.* Cambridge University Press, Cambridge: 2001.

May, Larry, and Stacey Hoffman, Editors, *Collective Responsibility: Five Decades of Debate in Theoretical and Applied Ethics.* In the series, *Studies in Social and Political Philosophy*, General Editor, James P. Sterba. Rowman & Littlefield, Lanham, MD: 1991.

Mayer, Jane, "Whatever It Takes: Torture on '24'," *The New Yorker*, February 19 and 26, 2007: pp. 66–82.

———, "The CIA's Travel Agent," *The New Yorker*, October 30, 2006, pp. 34–37.

McMillan, Dan, *How Could This Happen: Explaining the Holocaust.* Basic Books, New York: 2014.

McMillan, Jeff, "The Rosenstrasse Protest: A Moment of Courage in Hitler's Berlin," *The Chronicle of Higher Education*, October 18, 1996: p. A9. Review of *Resistance of the Heart: Intermarriage and the Rosenstrasse Protest in Nazi Germany*, by Nathan Stoltzus, W.W. Norton & Co., 1996.

Milgram, Stanley, *Obedience to Authority.* Harper Perennial, New York: 1983.

Millard, Candice, "Amazon Ambassador," *The New York Times* Sunday Book Review, June 1, 2008. Review of *Tree of Rivers: The Story of the Amazon*, by John Hemming, Thames & Hudson.

Miller, Arthur G., Editor, *The Social Psychology of Good and Evil.* The Guilford Press, New York: 2005.

Minnich, Elizabeth Kamarck, "Arendt, Heidegger, Eichmann: Thinking in and for the World," *Soundings*, Vol. 86, No. 1–2 (Spring/Summer), 2003.

————, *Transforming Knowledge*, 2nd edition. Temples University Press, Philadelphia, PA: 2005.

————, "Why Not Lie?" *Soundings*: 76, 1–2 (Spring/Summer), 2003.

Moaven, Azadeh, "For ISIS Women, Fraught Choices," *The New York Times*, Sunday, November 22, 2015. Front page story.

Moorehead, Caroline, *A Train in Winter: An extraordinary Story of Women, Friendship, and Resistance in Occupied France*. Harper Perennial/Harper Collins, New York: 2012.

Moyers, Bill, *Bill Moyers Interviews Filmmaker Pierre Sauvage about "Weapons of the Spirit," his documentary on the villagers of Le Chambon*. http://www.chambon.org/weapons_moyers_interview_en.htm.

Muhlberger, Delef, *The Social Bases of Nazism, 1919–1933*. Cambridge University Press, Cambridge: 2003.

Nash, Henry T., "The Bureaucratization of Homicide," *Bulletin of the Atomic Scientists*, April, 1980.

Neiman, Susan, *Evil in Modern Thought: An Alternative History of Philosophy*. Princeton University Press, Princeton: 2004.

Okeowo, Alexis, quoting Bruce Hall, "Freedom Fighter: A Slaving Society and an Abolitionist's Crusade," *The New Yorker*, September 8, 2014.

The News Hour with Jim Lehrer, March 23, 2007. Paul Solman and Vandana Shiva, interview in series on "Globalization." Transcript titled, "Environmental Activist Questions the Goals of Globalization."

Orizio, Ricardo, *Talk of the Devil: Encounters with Seven Dictators*. Translated from the Italian by Avril Bardoni. Walker & Company, New York: 2002.

Packer, George, "Betrayed: The Iraqis Who Trusted Americans the Most," The New Yorker March 206, 2007, pp. 54–73.

Pagden, Anthony, *Lords of All the World: Ideologies of Empire in Spain, Britain and France c. 1500–c. 1800*. Yale University Press, New Haven, CT & London: 1995.

Phillips, Arthur, "Dangerous Games: A Sandor Marai Novel about Adolescence in a Time of War," *The New Yorker*, p. 82.

Power, Samantha, "A Problem from Hell": *America and the Age of Genocide*. Basic Books/A New Republic Book, New York: 2002.

Press, Eyal, *Beautiful Souls*. Farrar, Straus and Giroux, New York: 2012.

Riding, Alan, "Britain's Slave Empire, As the Sun Set," *New York Times*, Sunday, February 18, 2007, p. 18.

Robin, Corey, *Fear: The History of A Political Idea*. Oxford University Press, New York: 2004.

Robinson, Marilynne, interview: "Saying Grace: The Revelations of Marilynne Robinson," by Wyatt Mason. *The New York Times Magazine*, October 5, 2014: pp. 24–47.

Rosen, Fred, *Contract Warriors: How Mercenaries Changed History and the War on Terrorism*. Alpha/Penguin Group, New York: 2005.

Schlink, Bernhard, *The Reader*. Translated from the German by Carol Brown Janeway. Vintage Books/Random House, New York: 1997.

Schmidle, Nicholas, "Bringing Up the Bones: Kosovo's Leaders Have Been Accused of Grotesque War Crimes. But Can Anyone Prove It?," *The New Yorker*, May 6, 2013, p. 49.

Sereny, Gitta, *Into That Darkness: An Examination of Conscience*. Vintage Books/ Random House, New York: 1983.

Shafer-Landau, Russ, *The Ethical Life: Fundamental Readings in Ethics and Moral Problems*. Oxford University Press, New York: 2012.

Simic, Charles, *That Little Something: Poems*. Quoted by Katha Politt in *The New York Times Sunday Book Review*, Sunday, May 18, 2008, p. 22.

Solzhenitsyn, Aleksandr, 1993; public address in Vaduz, Liechtenstein; quoted in "Boundary Issues," by David Remnick, *The New Yorker*, August 25, 2008, p. 21.

Szymborska, Wislawa, *View with a Grain of Sand: Selected Poems*. Translated by Stanislaw Baranczak, Clare Cavanagh. and Harcourt Brace. San Diego, NY, London: 1995.

———, "The Nobel Lecture," in *Poems New and Collected 1957–1997*. Translated from the Polish by Stanislaw Baranczak and Clare Cavanagh. A Harvest Book/ Harcourt, San Diego, New York, London: 2000, pp. xi–xvi. The Nobel Lecture is © 1996.

Takaki, Ronald T., *Iron Cages: Race and Culture in 19th Century America*. University of Washington Press, Seattle: 1979.

Waller, James, *Becoming Evil: How Ordinary People Commit Genocide and Mass Killing*. Oxford University Press, New York: 2002.

Withoutsanctuary.org website.

Wright, Evan, *Generation Kill*. Berkley Caliber, New York: 2004.

www:yadvashem.org/yv/en/holocaust/Eichmann_trial.

Zimbardo, Philip G., *The Lucifer Effect: Understanding How Good People Turn Evil*. Random House, USA: 2007.

———, "The Psychology of Power and Evil: All Power to the Person? To the Situation? To the System?" Zimbardo says, "This chapter is a modified version of my PowerPoint presentation for the DHS course, The Psychology of Terrorism." Cf. also Zimbardo chapter in *The Social Psychology of Good and Evil*. Edited by Arthur Miller. New York: Guilford: pp. 21–50.

Zusak, Markus, The Book Thief. Alfred A. Knopf, New York: 2005.

Index

Author Biography

Elizabeth K. Minnich is senior scholar for the Association of American Colleges and Universities and a professor of moral philosophy at Queens University. She holds a PhD in philosophy from the Graduate Faculty of Political and Social Science of the New School for Social Research, New York, where she was teaching assistant for Hannah Arendt. She wrote her dissertation on John Dewey and has continued to work on issues of justice, equality, democracy, and education, with particular focus on inclusive and engaged scholarship, curricula, teaching, and institutional practices. Her books include *Transforming Knowledge* (winner of the national Ness Award) and *The Fox in The Henhouse: How Privatization Threatens Democracy*, with coauthor Si Kahn.

CPSIA information can be obtained
at www.ICGtesting.com
Printed in the USA
BVOW08*1239291116

469114BV00003B/10/P